"This book is an absolutely urgent warning sent from America's heartland. Sonja Trom Eayrs has spent years fighting the corporate takeover of the rural community where she grew up, and the story she tells here is riveting. This is a real-life David and Goliath story that matters to everyone who eats and everyone who cares about the future of farming and small-town America. While the pollution, animal cruelty, and exploitation of Big Ag can be dismaying, the fighting spirit of Trom Eayrs and her neighbors is truly inspiring."

—**CHRISTOPHER LEONARD**, *New York Times* best-selling author of *The Meat Racket: The Secret Takeover of America's Food Business*

"Sonja Trom Eayrs rings the alarm in *Dodge County, Incorporated*, speaking poignantly from her personal experience about how the American dream in southern Minnesota has been taken away from so many. It also reminds us that the people have the power to fight back and reclaim our broken food system for farmers, rural communities, and all Americans."

—**CORY BOOKER**, U.S. senator (New Jersey) and member of the Committee on Agriculture, Nutrition, and Forestry

"For more than a generation, the relentless—and reckless—profiteering of Big Ag corporations has decimated the rural economy, hollowed out tightly knit communities, and turned once-proud independent farmers into modern incarnations of the sharecropper and the serf. . . . Sonja Trom Eayrs brings this Kafkaesque upheaval to life in a narrative as personal as it is essential. Hers is the story of one farm family's stand against a multibillion-dollar global juggernaut, a searing indictment of Big Ag's rapacity and greed, and an inspiring vision—still a ways off but attainable—of a food system and a rural landscape redeemed from the oppressor's hand."

—**CORBAN ADDISON**, author of *Wastelands: The True Story of Farm Country on Trial*

"A riveting tour of one family's journey fighting the barons that control our food system."

—**AUSTIN FRERICK**, author of *Barons: Money, Power, and the Corruption of America's Food Industry*

T0326870

"*Dodge County, Incorporated* is the wrenching saga of how the rise of industrialized hog farming upended the work and the quality of life of a multigenerational Norwegian farm family in rural Minnesota. But as Sonja Trom Eayrs relates to us in her gripping account, the Trom family is just one of many rural families thrust into crisis in recent decades by dangerous changes in agriculture. These mega-farms do indeed produce more pork, much of it bound for Mexico and Japan and China, but they leave a trail of victims in America's backyards. Communities hollow out, with the holdouts unable to fill the pews, not able to keep the hardware stores open, and too scattered to help raise a barn. This book is a first-hand account of an unfolding crisis and a wake-up call to policymakers that the industrialized model of agriculture is a cancer in rural America."

—**WAYNE PACELLE**, president of Animal Wellness Action and the Center for a Humane Economy and *New York Times* best-selling author

"Sonja Trom Eayrs has written a fast-paced legal thriller, filled with a few good guys and too many villains. I wish it was fiction, but it isn't. *Dodge County, Incorporated* exposes the connection between lax regulation of a dangerous type of farming and the disastrous consequences to human health and the environment. . . . Buy it; read it; this is an important book for urban and rural people."

—**SARAH VOGEL**, author of *The Farmer's Lawyer: The North Dakota Nine and the Fight to Save the Family Farm*

"Written with passion, meticulously researched, and vibrantly told, Sonja Trom Eayrs's *Dodge County, Incorporated* gives a riveting insider's account of how major food corporations infiltrated rural communities, hollowing out their economic vitality and leaving behind environmental ruin. The story of the Trom family farm and its intergenerational legacy draws us in, showing how individual lives have been harmed by the food monopolies. This is a must-read for anyone wanting a behind-the-curtain understanding of why rural farm communities are struggling—and a blueprint for reclaiming rights and equitable opportunities for family farmers."

—**JOE MAXWELL**, cofounder of Farm Action

"Sonja Trom Eayrs's *Dodge County, Incorporated* is a rare firsthand, blow-by-blow account of the battles of a farm family and their neighbors defending themselves against the environmental and public health threats of large-scale, corporate-controlled concentrated animal feeding operations, or CAFOS. The book also reveals the global context within which these local battles are fought . . . [and] the inhumanity, if not outright evil, that seems an inseparable aspect of industrial animal agriculture. Trom Eayrs's book is particularly compelling because hers is a story of a conventional farming family that, when surrounded by CAFOS, decided to take legal action and discovered the corporate takeover of their county."

—JOHN IKERD, professor emeritus of agricultural economics at the University of Missouri–Columbia

"Sonja Trom Eayrs is a CAFO-fighting whirlwind; she has the heart of a farmer's daughter, the mind of an experienced attorney, and the will of someone who knows in their bones they are right. And she is right. Her *Dodge County, Incorporated* exposes Big Ag's do-anything, community-destroying fight to impose its cruel industrial meat and poultry systems on America. Her vivid writing, detailed reporting, and deep honesty brighten every page of this important untold story."

—ALAN GUEBERT, columnist and author of *The Land of Milk and Honey*

"The heartache caused by industrial agriculture's plunder of the rural American Midwest has rarely been captured more movingly than in the lines and pages of *Dodge County, Incorporated*. Orwell famously said, 'Those who control the present control the past, and those who control the past control the future.' *Dodge County, Incorporated* is an effort to wrest control of the present from the forces of Big Ag and place it in the hands of rural Americans, so they can take the reins of our heartland's destiny."

—CHRIS JONES, author of *The Swine Republic: Struggles with the Truth about Agriculture and Water Quality*

"*Dodge County, Incorporated* tells the story of the unrelenting conversion of the traditional family farm system composed of many diversified farms to a bleak landscape of industrial animal operations and the cropping system required to support it. It is a story, expertly told by Sonja Trom Eayrs, of the intimidation, ostracism, and even threats her family faced as it sought to protect traditional farming and to minimize damage to the environment and local communities caused by the spread of industrial animal agriculture. [The book] is a must-read for anyone who cares about the future of agriculture in the United States."

—BOB MARTIN, former director of the Pew Commission on Industrial Farm Animal Production and retired senior advisor to the Johns Hopkins Center for a Livable Future

"Children used to wait by the mailbox for the school bus along the back roads of southern Minnesota, Sonja Trom Eayrs among them. They wait no longer, squeezed out by decades of corporate consolidation. The family farm was supplanted by hog confinements. Trom Eayrs came home to find that the independent yeoman is gone. So is a sense of community, such that you don't really know those neighbors anymore, along with the idea that free people can practice self-governance when money controls the system. Trom Eayrs tried to confront it, to unravel it, but it is so big, so entrenched, right down to the county courthouse. She believes you can construct home again. It makes you wonder."

—ART CULLEN, Pulitzer Prize–winning editor and publisher of the *Storm Lake (IA) Times Pilot*

publication supported by a grant from
The Community Foundation for Greater New Haven
as part of the Urban Haven Project

DODGE COUNTY, INCORPORATED

Big Ag and the Undoing of Rural America

SONJA TROM EAYRS | *With assistance by Katherine Don*

University of Nebraska Press | Lincoln

The University of Nebraska Press is part of a land-grant institution
with campuses and programs on the past, present, and future
homelands of the Pawnee, Ponca, Otoe-Missouria, Omaha,
Dakota, Lakota, Kaw, Cheyenne, and Arapaho Peoples, as well as
those of the relocated Ho-Chunk, Sac and Fox, and Iowa Peoples.

Library of Congress Control Number: 2024005603

Set in Minion Pro by A. Shahan.

OPPOSITE: My parents, Evelyn and Lowell Trom, lifelong Dodge
County residents, initiated three separate legal actions during their
twilight years against county officials and area swine factory farm
operators in opposition to the eleventh and twelfth swine factory
farms in a three-mile radius of our family farm. Photo by Alex Kolyer.

To my parents, Lowell and Evelyn Trom, who taught me the ethic of care, compassion, and community. Thank you for staying true to your core values and, in turn, for inspiring me to do the same.

CONTENTS

ILLUSTRATIONS

TABLES

ACKNOWLEDGMENTS

It has been a privilege to write this book. For those who have been willing to share your stories, even anonymously, know that you are appreciated. It is my hope that your courage will enable others to step forward.

First and foremost, I wish to acknowledge my father, Lowell, for his tireless efforts to fight for the land, for the environment, and, most of all, for our family and other farm families to stay on the land. I always admired his courage and tenacity. Even as he struggled with advanced age, he didn't give up and say, "To hell with it," as many would have. He stayed true to his core beliefs of stewardship of the land, care of others, and unwavering support of our democracy.

Special thanks to the University of Nebraska Press and my editor, W. Clark Whitehorn, for his commitment to this work and his ongoing support of my vision. I have truly appreciated the press's willingness to challenge corporate power in agriculture through its publication of other important works on similar topics.

I am thankful for the many organizations that not only provided moral and legal support during my family's litigation with Big Ag interests but also influenced my writing. Many thanks to the numerous individuals who offered me their feedback and expertise at the following organizations: Land Stewardship Project, Socially Responsible Agriculture Project, the Humane Society of the United States, Johns Hopkins Center for a Livable Future, Animal Legal Defense Fund, Minnesota Center for Environmental Advocacy, Environment America, Environmental Working Group, Izaak Walton League, Earth Justice, Food & Water Watch, and Farm Action, as well as the many other organizations that I have communicated with, in ways big and small, during the time I worked on this book.

Sincere gratitude to Viki Morris for encouraging this work and to Michael Metivier for getting me off on the right foot and helping me visualize the book. I also wish to thank Bob and Kristi Rosenquist for their assistance in analyzing hydrogen sulfide test results, and Danielle Diamond for insights concerning land use rules and the critical role that land use plays in the expansion, promotion, and control of the corporate empire.

Thank you to Chris Petersen, Scott Dye, Karen Hudson, Randy Coon, Lynn Henning, Dr. John Ikerd, Theresa Benda, Lisa Doerr, Diane Rosenberg, Lynn and Nancy Utesch, and other frontline warriors fighting concentrated animal feeding operations. You took away the sting of isolation and helped my family understand that we were not alone in this fight. Heartfelt thanks to contract grower Tom Butler for sharing his valuable insider's view of the swine industry.

Many thanks to my family for their steadfast love and support: my siblings Randy, Shelley, Brad, Peggy, and Jim; my amazing daughters, Rebekah and Katie; and the many other extended family members who have cheered me on along the way.

And thanks to my husband, Douglas, who jumped in with both feet and accompanied me to countless township and county board meetings, the Minnesota legislature, and numerous speaking engagements. If I have made a difference, it is because of your enduring love, support, and keen humor.

I also wish to acknowledge my editor and cowriter, Katherine Don. With a talent for storytelling and sharp attention to detail, she was an invaluable partner in this work. She pressed me to dig deeper and, in the process, found herself immersed in the story too. While Katherine may be a Chicago girl, she helped capture the heart and soul of rural America.

Finally, this story would not be complete without special thanks to my mother, Evelyn. During my parents' legal actions against local officials and neighboring factory farm operators, my mother left the nursing home to participate in an interview with Minnesota Public Radio. Suffering from the debilitating effects of advanced Parkinson's disease, she found it difficult to speak. She sat patiently for nearly two hours without uttering a word. Finally, at the end of the interview, the reporter turned to my mother and asked what she hoped to achieve. Evelyn whispered a single word: "Justice."

AUTHOR'S NOTE

This book includes information about events that occurred in Dodge County, Minnesota, as well as in other rural farming communities, over the course of three decades. I tell these stories from my unique perspective as both participant and chronicler. Some accounts are informed by my own recollections or those of close family and friends. My memories are corroborated by legal documents, public documents, press reports, and interviews with others who were present.

Many interviewees preferred anonymity, which I note in the text or end notes. In four cases, I have used a pseudonym, which I also note in the corresponding text or end note.

In telling the story of my family's legal proceedings with public officials in Dodge County, I hope to illuminate larger truths about Big Ag's influence in rural farm country across the United States. My intent isn't to single out specific residents or public officials. Wherever practical, I reference the role, title, or occupation rather than the name of the person. For people that are central to the story, real names are used, as required to establish a factual baseline and to enable readers to search publicly available information about these events.

ABBREVIATIONS

AFBF	American Farm Bureau Federation
AFO	animal feedlot operation
AMS	Agricultural Marketing Service
APHA	American Public Health Association
AU(s)	animal unit(s)
AVMA	American Veterinary Medical Association
CAA	Clean Air Act
CAFO	concentrated animal feeding operation
CCCCA	Cass County Concerned Citizens Alliance
CERCLA	Comprehensive Environmental Response, Compensation, and Liability Act
CFS	Central Farm Service
CUP	conditional use permit
CWA	Clean Water Act
DNR	Department of Natural Resources
EAW	environmental assessment worksheet
EIS	environmental impact statement
EPA	Environmental Protection Agency
EPCRA	Emergency Planning and Community Right-to-Know Act
EWG	Environmental Working Group
FCS	Farm Credit System
GIPSA	Grain Inspection, Packers, and Stockyards Administration
H_2S	hydrogen sulfide
LSP	Land Stewardship Project
MCEA	Minnesota Center for Environmental Advocacy
MDA	Minnesota Department of Agriculture
MPCA	Minnesota Pollution Control Agency

MPPA	Minnesota Pork Producers Association
NAITC	National Agriculture in the Classroom
NFO	National Farmers Organization
NPDES	National Pollutant Discharge Elimination System
NPPC	National Pork Producers Council
NRA	National Rifle Association
NRDC	Natural Resources Defense Council
OSHA	Occupational Health and Safety Administration
PAC	political action committee
PM 2.5	particulate matter of less than or equal to 2.5 microns
PSA	Packers and Stockyards Administration
USDA	U.S. Department of Agriculture
USFRA	U.S. Farmers & Ranchers Alliance
WHO	World Health Organization

Introduction

A Readiness for Responsibility

My father, Lowell, died in 2019 after living a long, full life. He appears often in this book; in a way, he was my motivation and my muse. During Lowell's lifetime, particularly in his twilight years, he witnessed dramatic changes in Dodge County, Minnesota, where his grandfather settled in 1892 upon emigrating from Norway. A palpable emptiness had overtaken farm country, marked by the absence of grazing animals that once peppered the landscape, the consolidation of local schools as the population declined and town centers eroded, and the shuttering of small-town businesses. The county and township roads were crumbling, laden with potholes and frost boils thanks to the large semis carrying hogs, manure, and feed between the nearby factory farms and the corporate delivery points.

In my youth, families put us children on bus number 2, which wound its way through the countryside and dropped us off in our hometown of Blooming Prairie on the southwestern edge of Dodge County. During a conversation with my father several years before his death, he described the specter of a new driver operating school buses in Dodge. It was a corporate driver, and the name of our transformed home was painted in bold, black lettering against the school-bus yellow: Dodge County, Incorporated. The corporate driver was not afraid to leave farm families and rural neighbors behind as it drove its empty bus. The children of farmers no longer stood waiting at the ends of long driveways. The main street in Blooming Prairie was lined with empty stores, and a sea of gray hair filled area church pews on Sunday mornings. A generation of farmers was ominously absent—and we knew the source of this sorrow.

Dodge County, Incorporated tells the story of industrial-scale factory farming: the pollution, the waste, the metamorphosis of the thriving, verdant countryside into bleak commercial zones. It is the story of my hometown, echoing with the story playing out in rural farm communities across the United States—one that is fueling a cultural and political shift in rural America. This is also the story of my family. We watched as our 760-acre farm was encroached upon in all directions by the look, feel, and overwhelming stench of "Big Agriculture." We witnessed firsthand the effects of Big Ag that are rarely discussed in mainstream food and farm media: the hollowing-out of rural communities, the steady unraveling of the fabric that once stitched neighborhoods together, and the erosion of democratic values in service to the corporate bottom line.

What big box stores have famously done to shutter Main Streets across the United States, Big Ag has been doing, with the same ruthless efficiency, to rural farm communities such as ours. My family's fight to preserve our farm, and our community's reaction to it, laid bare the growing societal tensions and even violence shaped by the rural populism that has been on display across the nation. We were ostracized, harassed, and subjected to false police reports, threatening phone calls, and garbage dumped in the roadside ditches bordering our farm—all for asserting our right to live free of the air and water pollution that comes from cramming thirty thousand hogs cheek by jowl within a three-mile radius of our home.

For me, this journey of heartache and sadness has turned to hope and determination to fight for Big Ag reform. When I left Dodge County decades ago to forge my path as a mother and attorney, I never would have guessed that my frequent visits home would lead to where I am today.

In the fall of 1977, my parents put me on a plane bound for New York City with my bright red electric typewriter in tow. I was a farm girl through and through, having spent my childhood weekends and afternoons sitting on the fender of my father's John Deere 4020. During fall harvest, I had darted straight to the fields after school, enjoying many peaceful hours on the combine as we combined soybeans or picked corn. Now I was hundreds of miles away, at Vassar College in

Poughkeepsie, New York. I suffered terribly from homesickness during my freshman year.

The Hudson River Valley was admittedly beautiful. I relished the history tucked into every corner and visiting the lavish mansions of the Roosevelts and the Vanderbilts. It was an aesthetic, dignified backdrop as I ran around with new friends and danced with handsome men in uniform at the nearby U.S. Military Academy at West Point. But none of it compared with the beauty of waving grain. I longed for fall harvest. During my sophomore year, I transferred to Carleton College and the familiar, pastoral setting of Northfield, Minnesota. There, I graduated with a degree in political science and an appreciation for the democratic process.

I returned to the family farm often. I still loved working the fields. Though I had wanted to attend law school for many years, I postponed that dream as my husband, Douglas, and I did things backward and had our children first. In the fall of 1986, now a mother to two young daughters, I entered law school. After I graduated from Marquette University Law School in Milwaukee, Wisconsin, we moved to the Twin Cities metro area, where I work as a family law attorney. Our family returned to southern Minnesota almost every weekend so our daughters could see their two sets of grandparents. Like me, Douglas was raised on a family farm in Dodge County.

During those drives home, we realized rural America was changing. The changes were slow at first; then they happened fast—very fast—as multinational corporations such as Hormel Foods, JBS Foods, Tyson Foods, and Smithfield Foods asserted control over rural areas, including Dodge County, during the late nineties and the aughts. Small, independent livestock farmers left farming altogether or signed Big Ag contracts, allured by terms that supposedly offered financial stability but ensnared many of them in debt. This period, as well as those contracts, are explored in chapter 3, "The Big Pig Pyramid"; chapter 4, "The Meeting at Lansing Corners"; and chapter 5, "Get Big or Get Out."

We observed the transforming landscape. Fences disappeared. Cows, hogs, and other animals no longer grazed in the fields. I recall saying to my husband, as I looked out the window with a creeping feeling of bewildered sadness, "Where are the animals?"

That was the beginning of a long journey. My family became involved in local efforts to halt the advance of factory farms and the air pollution, water contamination, and emerging cancer clusters that came with them. As I recount in chapter 6 ("The Battle in Ripley Township"), members of my family were involved in two citizen's efforts: one, to prevent the installation of a large gestation sow facility near the Swiss community of Berne in northern Dodge; the other, to challenge the installation of Ripley Dairy, which would have been the largest dairy operation in the state of Minnesota at the time.

Douglas and I watched these battles—one successful, the other not—from somewhat of a distance, and our feeling of responsibility grew.

Then, in 2014, a young farmer sought a permit for yet another factory farm, this one right next door to my parents' farm. This industrialized swine feedlot would have no family living on it—no farmhouse with people who cared for the land, only corporate interests hoping to squeeze every dollar out of the 2,400 hogs that would stand, every day, stuffed into a crude, dark building. The proposed project would produce manure equivalent to a town of nearly seven thousand people and spew hydrogen sulfide, methane, ammonia, and other dangerous gases into the air encircling my parents' home.

That is when I jumped in with both feet. My mother, Evelyn, had just entered the local nursing home, and my father, at eighty-five years old, was tasked with becoming her caretaker while continuing to farm the land. In chapter 9, "Getting to Know Your Neighbors," I begin the story of how my family banded together to prevent the county's approval of the permit for that factory farm. When our initial efforts failed, my parents filed a lawsuit against Dodge County officials and local swine operators. Chapters 10, "Industry Watchdogs"; 13, "The Corporate Bully"; and 14, "In the Trenches," recount the harassment and intimidation that frontline families such as ours face in our own communities when we become involved in the national movements to fight back against the excesses of Big Ag.

The book's final chapters tell the larger story of Big Ag's negative impacts on rural communities across the country and of the hyper-local citizens' efforts that have arisen to protect communities from the environmental and health consequences. Though sparsely covered in the national press, disagreements over agricultural issues in rural communities deeply impact our national politics, coloring everything from agricultural policy to antitrust legal scholarship to the trajectory of environmental policies and regulations.

I was first driven to write Dodge County, Incorporated after experiencing how my family was—and continues to be—treated in the years following our initial lawsuit. But as the book unfolded, I homed in on something bigger—namely, the corporate model itself. It perverts people's best impulses and amplifies our worst, as local economies are highjacked and as communities increasingly serve not themselves but the interests of multinational conglomerates, many of them based overseas.

For me, the questions raised by factory farming aren't only about the economy, the environment, and the well-being of rural residents—though these issues are certainly important—but also about the nature of community. Are we, as people, beholden to one another? And if not, to whom, or what, are we beholden?

In these pages, I hope to show that despite what the industry wants us to believe, most farm communities are not united in their acceptance of the corporate-driven farming model. We don't need to organize our economy, our communities, and our agricultural practices around the profiteering of Hormel, Cargill, Smithfield, Tyson, and other multi-national giants. We must instead reclaim and celebrate what many generations of farmers embraced: nurturing the land and the animals, maintaining a sustainable food supply, promoting public health, valuing clean air and the opportunity to swim and fish in healthy local streams and lakes, and cherishing nearby neighbors and friends. In failing to align with these values, large corporate interests continue to create conflicts in rural areas, conflicts that then reverberate in America's cities and towns.

The German theologian Dietrich Bonhoeffer once wrote, "Action springs not from thought, but from a readiness for responsibility." We must wrestle the steering wheel back from the hands of the corporate driver. In rural America today, we must support the steady, growing resistance of people who are committed, not to restoring an imperfect past that led to our current predicament, but to building a future in which we are no longer dependent on the corporate trough.

PART 1
The Takeover

To sin by silence, when we should protest,
makes cowards out of men.
—ELLA WHEELER WILCOX

1

Moving to the Country

"Living in the country can be a wonderful way of life for your family. The experience will be more rewarding and enjoyable if you recognize the challenges of rural living and plan accordingly."—MINNESOTA FARM BUREAU FOUNDATION, "Moving to the Country"

It was fall harvest in Dodge County. As I had done hundreds of times before, I drove up the long driveway leading to the farmhouse on my family's 760-acre farm, our slice of heaven in the once-idyllic rural countryside of southeastern Minnesota. After I parked, I spotted my father, Lowell Trom, in the field just south of the house. I made a beeline for the field and joined him on the combine. At the ripe age of eighty-nine, my father's hands were rough and weathered, yet he still found such joy in fall harvest.

For farmers, fall harvest is the emotional equivalent of bringing in the herd for cattle ranchers. We watched the yield monitor and smiled when it jumped to over two hundred bushels per acre. Technology had changed considerably during my father's lifetime, but Lowell expertly traversed the field in his beloved John Deere combine equipped with an autosteer system. The yellow corn, like liquid gold, poured out of the hopper and into the grain wagons waiting at the end of the field. From there, my brother Jim pulled the wagon to the farm site, where the grain was dried to just the right moisture content, then stored in towering steel grain bins.

This harvest would be the last with my father, who passed away the following year, in October 2019, at the age of ninety. His twilight years were consumed by a series of legal battles that he and my mother initiated in 2014 to protect our family farm from the encroachment of industrial factory farms that had scarred the rural landscape, polluted the air and water, harmed the economy, and affected human health in Dodge County. Despite the lasting emotional costs of these lawsuits,

I wouldn't hesitate to help them all over again. As my father once said of the corporate takeover of Dodge, "Enough is enough."

The Trom family farm is the heart of this story, and it's where we begin. The land was originally acquired in 1925 by my grandfather Elmer, who was raised by my great-grandparents on a neighboring farm in Dodge. Our operation is unusual for its meticulous layout, the result of decades of careful planning. If you look at an aerial photo of the farm, its core buildings—the farmhouse, the grain leg, the equipment sheds, the grain bins—are surrounded on four sides by a towering perimeter of more than five hundred arborvitae trees, which my father and uncle had planted in straight rows going north and south or east and west to provide a protective barrier from the high winds crossing the prairie.

For many years my mother, Evelyn, planted pink petunias each spring all around the farmhouse. As her Parkinson's advanced, she no longer planted fresh flowers, instead opting for perennials. To this day, her gardens and flowering crab trees burst with color each spring. The greenery and flowers are joined by wildlife making their appearances in seasonal turn: tundra and trumpeter swans in early spring; great blue herons and egrets in late spring; foxes, rabbits, and bald eagles in the summer; and, in the winter, the elusive snowy owl.

In my childhood memories of growing up on the farm, nothing was ever out of place. You didn't just drive along the field; you walked the field and picked up rocks. You didn't just mow the lawn; you carefully trimmed around each tree and building. You didn't just plant the fields; you pulled weeds and cut "volunteer" corn out of the bean fields. If there wasn't work, I think my parents created work to keep us six kids busy.

Today, the Trom farm looks much as it did during my childhood, notwithstanding the painstaking improvements in layout and technology made over the years, a reflection of my father's commitment to the operation, his pride and joy. But when you leave our land and turn onto the rural township road, it's a different universe. You are abruptly confronted with the realities of modern agriculture and industrial-scale hog production, and they aren't pretty.

The Large Footprint of Factory Farming

Though no generation has been exempt from witnessing change, often dramatic change, in U.S. agriculture, the rapid metamorphosis of the past thirty years has been unique in character, with the near extinction of independent farmers and the corresponding rise of corporate agriculture. I've witnessed this in Dodge County over the course of my life, to the point that the once-pastoral countryside that nurtured me as a child is hardly recognizable. Where most farms were once family run and diversified, many are now held within corporate entities and devoted monoculturally to a single crop or animal. (While the focus of this book is livestock agriculture, the macro trend lines of corporatization and consolidation are true for most agricultural commodities, from seed and grain to chemicals and other inputs.)

The uptick of industrialized livestock farms in rural America began in earnest in the early 1990s and accelerated during the first years of the new century.[1] Farms became larger as the industry consolidated and the corporate meat-packers contracted with livestock growers to raise more animals on fewer farms. Small farmers were methodically run off the land and squeezed out of the market. In 1992 the average pig farm held 945 animals; by 2004 that number had grown to 4,646. As of 2015, the average pig farm held 8,721 hogs.[2] Key counties within a handful of states became the commercial epicenters for the "Big Pig" meat-packers—zones of mass industrialization in patches of rural Iowa, Minnesota, Missouri, Illinois, North Carolina, and Nebraska.

Today's industrialized livestock facilities are called concentrated animal feeding operations (CAFOs). They're easy to spot, once you know what you're looking for: their long rectangular structures are typically white and built with bare-bones, cost-cutting simplicity. They hold thousands of animals, crammed in body to body, that stand suspended on slatted flooring eight feet above concrete manure pits. In rural areas now dominated by these feeding operations, it looks as though a nuclear bomb hit. Everything is barren—no trees, as even marginal land is put into production. No farm houses. Just bare land punctuated by the occasional white, rectangular CAFO structure.

Modern U.S. hog agriculture is widely considered to have begun in North Carolina in the late 1980s thanks to the designs of Wendell H. Murphy, a local farmer-turned-politician who converted his family's hog operation into a vertically integrated production machine that wedded area feed mills with massive, CAFO-style farrowing and finishing barns.[3] By 1997 industrialized hog facilities had created such pollution and nuisance in the Tar Heel State that the legislature passed a moratorium on new swine CAFOs. Then "Big Pork" turned its eyes to the Midwest, stepping up its existing development of new industrial-scale feedlots in Iowa, Minnesota, Illinois, and Missouri.

In Minnesota, the highest concentration of CAFOs can be found in the southern part of the state along the Interstate 90 (I-90) corridor, an area bursting with swine factory farms that line the freeway for hundreds of miles.[4] Dodge County is part of this corridor, where withering hometowns dot the countryside.[5] The loudest remaining activity is the constant roar of livestock trucks carrying animals on I-90, or "Hog Highway to Heaven," destined for nearby meatpacking plants owned by international conglomerates. The interstate connects several major slaughterhouses: Hormel Foods with its flagship in Austin, Minnesota; JBS Foods in Worthington, Minnesota; and Smithfield just across the border in Sioux Falls, South Dakota.

The industry uses various benchmarks to determine the size of a given CAFO facility. Animal units (AUs) are one way to quantify the anticipated manure output, dietary needs, and environmental impact of a given animal feedlot operation. The unit is based on weight ranges, with one AU corresponding to one standard weight–range cow. The Environmental Protection Agency (EPA) and state agencies use these units, along with weight ranges and the numbers of animals per facility, to classify feedlots based on their capacity as small, medium, and large CAFOs. These distinctions are important for regulatory reasons, with the vast majority of federal environmental permitting and reporting requirements only applying to so-called large CAFOs.

In Minnesota, the number of these large CAFOs has tripled since 1991, and among these new mega-size operations, 86 percent are swine feedlots.[6] For hog farms, a feedlot reaches the "large" threshold when it contains a thousand AUs, or more than 2,500 grown hogs.

Importantly, a significant proportion of today's hog feedlot operations clock in just below this large-feedlot threshold. It's an easy way to evade EPA regulation. In Dodge County, as well as in other hog-producing rural counties, a standard swine feedlot holds 2,400 hogs, conveniently only a hundred hogs short of qualifying as "large." Often you'll see two or three of these 2,400-head barns sitting side by side on the same small patch of land. Depending on the state in which they reside, these operations are classified either as "medium" CAFOS or simply as animal feedlot operations (AFOS). In reality though, large and medium CAFOS are functionally indistinct, with both characterized by their particular method of livestock production—to put it crudely, cramming lots of animals into small confinements.

As of 2020, 23,725 livestock feedlots in the state of Minnesota housed up to 10.9 million hogs, 1.2 million dairy cows, 1.6 million beef cows, and 66 million turkeys and chickens.[7] These feedlots produced 49 million tons of manure annually—the equivalent of the waste from 95 million people, or seventeen times Minnesota's human population.[8]

A recent Food & Water Watch report analyzed the economic impacts of hog feedlots in neighboring Iowa, which raises one-third of the nation's pigs. The rural counties with the most hogs had the highest rates of human population decline, and the counties with the highest concentration of CAFO operations were more likely to experience decreases in both wages and total household income. These relationships held true across all parts of the state.[9] The report's author, Amanda Starbuck, said the results pushed back on the narrative that factory farms "are good for rural communities and that they create jobs and economic opportunities, because we've seen the exact opposite. Counties in Iowa that had the most growth in factory farms are doing far worse among a number of different [economic] indicators."[10]

The number of hog farmers in Iowa plummeted by 90 percent since 1982, while the number of hogs sold *per farm* skyrocketed by a factor of twenty.[11] In other words, small, independent farmers have exited the industry, with livestock now concentrated inside a small number of large-scale operations. These trends in Iowa are true for the livestock industry writ large.

The market control and consolidation that the meat-packers have achieved over the past forty years has corresponded to lower prices for livestock farmers and wage decreases for meatpacking factory workers. In today's dollars, hog farmers now earn $2 less on every pound of meat than they did 1982, yet the price of pork is only a dollar cheaper.[12] To understand where much of the remaining dollar per pound ended up, look no further than the $14 billion in annual revenue of Smithfield Foods, the world's largest pork processor, or the $37.5 million compensation package its chief executive officer (CEO) received in 2015.[13]

The environmental consequences of this model of capital extraction from consolidated livestock operations are profound. When you're raising, say, 2,400 hogs in a factory-size facility situated on a tiny slice of land, that is quite a bit different from raising a hundred hogs each on twenty-four small farms spread out across a large area. With the former, you have geographically concentrated manure, which emits ammonia, methane, and hydrogen sulfide into the air and dumps phosphorous, nitrate, and antibiotics into the groundwater and area rivers and streams. For many livestock producers, animal agriculture has become decoupled from crop production, so the symbiotic relationship between the manure and the surrounding land has been altered. Gone are the days when hogs were fed with grain grown on the same farm, and their manure was spread on that same farm. While some CAFO operators still spread manure on immediately adjacent farmland, many others are dealing with millions of gallons of excess manure and are placing pressure on neighboring farmers to allow access to their land.

Today's CAFO manure is often spread on insufficient acreage, resulting in runoff and groundwater contamination. Agricultural pollution is the single biggest contaminator of U.S. rivers and streams, yet most industrialized feedlots—the sources of much of this contamination— are exempt from EPA oversight.[14] A 2020 analysis of air and water pollution in Minnesota, appropriately titled "Manure Overload," found that 56 percent of surface waters in the state failed to meet basic water quality standards, and 63 percent of public water utilities in the state had elevated levels of nitrate.[15]

The bit of propaganda repeated most often by "Big Ag" (big agricultural) lobbyists is that corporate agriculture "feeds the world." This lofty mission supposedly necessitates dead zones in the Gulf of Mexico from manure runoff and the economic decimation of rural small towns. But consider this: the U.S. Department of Agriculture (USDA) released numbers in 2018 that indicated the United States produced approximately seventy-three million hogs that year—the same number of hogs it produced in 1943.[16] This finding puts the lie to the claim that our current model for livestock agriculture is inevitable or necessary. (We further examine the "feed the world" myth in chapter 18.) What's unique about the corporate model isn't its enhanced success at feeding the world but its efficiency at running independent farmers off the land, erasing intergenerational farms, and creating a vertically integrated, top-heavy profit model where the majority of capital is siphoned away from farmers and rural communities.

In Dodge County, it doesn't take working papers and statistics to know this is true. Just turn left as you exit my family's farm and turn onto the township road straddling Westfield Township to the south and Ripley Township to the north.

The first thing you'll notice are the frost boils, defective patches of gravel road heaped over a foot high from frost that has escaped through the surface each spring—collateral damage from semitrucks brimming with pigs and feed that constantly traverse a township road never intended for this level of commercial activity. Breathe in the countryside air, and you're hit with the stench of ammonia, methane, and hydrogen sulfide rolling across the countryside from the many nearby factory farms. Soon enough you'll pass the stark rectangular CAFOs, many situated on just four or five acres of land and operated within limited liability companies (LLCs) that dropped in, seemingly overnight, from above. Hog, dairy, and turkey factory farms crowd the landscape, with 305 registered feedlots in Dodge County alone.[17] As of this writing, twelve factory farms and nearly thirty thousand hogs are housed within a three-mile radius of the Trom family farm; these large industrial operations spread across the rural landscape like sprawling urban shopping malls.

As the sizes of the operations grow and the land is owned or leased by anonymous faces, the care of the land diminishes. Invasive weeds such as water hemp tower above the corn, threatening neighboring fields. As you continue down the township road, farther from our family farm, you'll notice the vapor plume on the horizon from Al-Corn Clean Fuel, LLC, an ethanol plant that now dominates the town of Claremont to the north. The large plume is the result of converting corn to ethanol, which is then transferred into dozens of black rail tankers and shipped elsewhere for further processing. The residue, distiller's dried grains, is used as an ingredient in the feed given to animals confined in area factory farms.

Ethanol, nitrate, coliform bacteria—all lead to the "greening" of rural America. As large corporate agribusinesses line their pockets with greenbacks, area lakes and streams turn green with algae blooms caused by the sludge of corporate runoff.

The Dream of Countryside Living

Despite some of the unpleasant realities of today's rural farm communities, the dream of the countryside remains alluring to some urban Minnesotans, those who perhaps desire a bigger yard for their children, lower costs on their rent or mortgage, or simply the benefits of breathing the clean, fresh country air. Dodge County might seem to be the perfect fit: a quiet, bucolic place that is remote but not too remote, only an hour and a half south of Minneapolis and Saint Paul, and a short drive to Rochester and its world-famous Mayo Clinic medical center.

But before packing their bags and renting a truck, these urbanites might want to pick up a copy of "Moving to the Country: What You Should Know about Agriculture in Rural Minnesota," a brochure developed by the Minnesota Farm Bureau Foundation in cooperation with a host of Big Ag interests and the Minnesota Realtors Association. Country living, the brochure states, "can be a wonderful way of life for your family. The experience will be more rewarding and enjoyable if you recognize the challenges of rural living and plan accordingly."[18]

This ominous message is consistent with the remainder of the brochure, which pairs perky platitudes with forbidding rejoinders. At first glance, it seems to offer sensible advice along the lines of "look before you leap." The countryside is full of deer that can bolt across roads, the brochure warns, so you'll have to accept some amount of risk when driving. Fair enough. But other, rather specific expectations draw attention to the agenda of the industry trade associations responsible for the publication of "Moving to the Country": "Typical farm work . . . may . . . involve the use of large farm equipment. These activities are essential to Minnesota farmers as they work to produce food and fiber for the world. Minnesota residents have recognized the importance of these activities through 'Right to Farm' laws that help protect family farms from nuisance lawsuits when using generally accepted farming practices."[19]

The message is clear: you're welcome to move to the country, but there is big fat *if* attached—that is, *if* you resign yourself to how Big Ag is practiced, as determined by the Minnesota Pork Producers Association, other industry trade associations, and lobbyist groups. And don't get any ideas about speaking out against those practices, let alone challenging the industry-backed right-to-farm laws that insulate factory farm operators from "nuisance" lawsuits initiated by neighbors who suffer from dangerous air emissions and the other consequences of living near a factory farm.

The brochure's cover features an image of a cheerful red barn, the hallmark of the Norwegian ancestral farms that once dominated rural Minnesota. The Minnesota Farm Bureau is unwilling to show what industrialized feedlots really look like, even in its own publication. And despite carefully cataloging the dangers of country living—the wildlife that can "cause damage to your property," for example—the brochure fails to mention arguably more acute dangers, such as the coliform bacteria that makes its way into the groundwater of rural areas with large numbers of CAFOs. Dodge County resident Eugene Nilsen found it in his well at *fifteen times* the recommended safe level. (Eugene's story appears in chapter 12.)

And while "Moving to the Country" encourages readers to "patronize local businesses," it fails to mention that they are more likely to be

Walmart or Dollar General than family-owned stores or restaurants. Dodge County is home to several small towns, including Kasson, the largest in the county; Dodge Center; West Concord; Claremont; and Hayfield. As recently as the 1990s, they were vibrant towns, but as small farmers and business owners were forced to stop operating, they became less prosperous. Nowhere is this more evident than my hometown, Blooming Prairie. Many businesses have closed, and the few remaining storefronts haven't been updated in years.

Despite the numerous economic and public health degradations associated with the rise of CAFOs in rural farming communities, those responsible for them have asserted the opposite: that these regions remain healthy and pure; that the economy is thriving; that the farming regulations are strict, enforced, and dutifully followed; and that the smell of manure is the smell of money, even freedom. But whose?

My husband and I were married in Blooming Prairie during the summer of 1979. We scheduled the ceremony at four in the afternoon, yet no sooner had our invitations arrived in mailboxes than we received several calls from local dairy farmers, asking why we hadn't scheduled it for two o'clock, as per local custom. We immediately understood our error. Scheduling events at two allowed farmers to go home and milk their cows—which once grazed on pastureland and were given names, not numbers—before the reception. Douglas and I were both children of dairy farmers, yet somehow we had neglected this detail. We felt terribly. These types of social customs used to really matter.

Most of the small dairy farmers who attended our wedding have since been wiped out, victims of factory-size corporate operations and consolidation. In tandem, the social pressures that once nudged neighbors to look out for one another have been inverted. Today, the message is "don't complain" when nearby hog farms, many of them without resident farmers, become so plentiful that you can't hold your wedding, picnic, or birthday party outside due to the stench. As I explore throughout this book, Big Ag interests have bolstered an insider/outsider mentality characterized by suspicion, fear, and ostracization, making it difficult for community members to speak up.

Dodge County is the kind of place that touts itself as the Real America, free of the crime, greed, and pollution that supposedly plague larger population centers. Yet many of its residents turn a blind eye to the harms that CAFOs cause, and they refuse to ask themselves glaring questions about community accountability—that is, who benefits and who suffers as a result of these operations, who uses their own freedom to limit the freedoms of others, and why it matters. A belief system has emerged in rural America that undermines our ability to care for one another, that encourages people to ignore or deny the impacts of Big Ag and even to stop believing that our actions have consequences that we can, or should, control.

How did such sweeping change take root in a single generation, forging a fundamental shift in rural farming communities toward dependence on a corporate business model? As the following chapters describe, the factory farm explosion in rural America has been one of the many factors leading to a cultural shift characterized by rural populism and deepened partisan divides driven by the politics of animosity and aggrievement. The corporate model disconnected not only the animals from the land but also the neighbors from one another.

I believe that any version of a thriving future for farm country will include a reclamation of individual and community rights over the corporate power grab. But the Big Ag corporations, which dictate the methods and activities of their contract farmers, won't give an inch of their economic dominance without a fight. To understand why, and how we got to where we are today, let's travel back to the turn of the twentieth century, when farm country was undergoing an entirely different kind of metamorphosis.

2

Fertile Soil

"From the flat, rich soils of the Red River Valley to the rolling hills of the Mississippi River Valley, Minnesota's early settlers carved out a way of life on fertile soil. Their perseverance and hard work laid the foundation for what has made Minnesota a national leader in food production and one of the most prominent food producing and processing centers in the world."
—MINNESOTA FARM BUREAU FOUNDATION, "Moving to the Country"

The year: 1892. The place: the interior municipality of Hemsedal, a mountainous region in central Norway, where small farming towns are tucked into the valleys and scattered upon the mountains. A young man by the name of Odd (Ed) Troim prepared to travel across the Atlantic with two of his cousins, young men like himself.

As a second-born son, twenty-one-year-old Ed saw little opportunity for himself in Norway. The country's population was experiencing a historic boom, and younger siblings faced a choice between migration or an uncertain future at home. According to long-standing Norwegian tradition and law, farmland passed from eldest son to eldest son, a method of land transfer ensuring strong, multigenerational family ties. Land records indicate Ed's ancestors had held land in Hemsedal since the early 1600s, though Troim stories, retold through the centuries, suggest the family lived in Hemsedal since at least the 1300s.

The farm where Ed grew up was situated in a scenic valley along the Trøymsåne River, where verdant, rolling hills stretch out for miles against the grand backdrop of the Scandinavian Alps, known locally as the Skarvheimen mountain region. Among my family's treasured heirlooms are Ed's paintings of Norway, created during the course of his adult life in America and based on tender childhood memories of fjord-side villages, farmhouses, and his hometown of Trøym, known for its traditional Norwegian-style church made of wood and painted a bright white.

Imagine the mixed emotions Ed must have felt as he left Hemsedal, generations deep with family history, to embark upon a new continent. He boarded the *Thingvalla*, a passenger ship with a direct line from Scandinavia to Ellis Island, where he arrived on April 21, 1892. A sepia-tinted photograph shows a clean-shaven Ed dressed in a heavy wool coat, standing beside his mustachioed cousins donning impressive, heavy furs. In America, probably at Ellis Island, Ed assumed the name of Trom rather than Troim, and the trio embarked west: Ed to Dodge County in Minnesota, his cousins to the Red River Valley in North Dakota.

At the time, Dodge County was a welcoming place for the boom of young farmers from northern Europe. The borders of Dodge form a perfect rectangle, twenty-four by eighteen miles. The northeastern portion is hilly; the southern reaches, including the area around Blooming Prairie where many Norwegians settled, are flat—the typical landscape one imagines when thinking of the Midwest. At the time of Ed's arrival, Europeans—Norwegian, Swiss, Scottish, English, German—had been farming in Dodge for seventy years, and Minnesota had been a state for about thirty-four years. These immigrant farmers turned native sod with crude plows drawn by oxen, their necks put into the yoke, and transformed the prairie and woodlands into some of the finest farmland in Minnesota.

They were able to do this work only because of recent treaties negotiated with Native American communities. The key treaties were signed on July 23 and August 5, 1851, when the Wahpeton, Sisseton, Mdewakanton, and Wahpekute bands of the Dakota people ceded lands encompassing much of the southeast and central portions of present-day Minnesota, as well as portions of Iowa and South Dakota.[1] The United States agreed to pay $3,075,000 in cash and securities over a fifty-year period for this land.[2] Ultimately, only 80 percent of the promised funds were paid.[3] During the mid-1800s, Native Americans were cornered into such treaties, having been left with few options after a century's worth of war, violence, forced displacement, disease, population decline, and environmental destruction. Following the treaties of 1851, many Sioux bands were displaced to two reservations the U.S. government established along the Minnesota River.

The underlying soils throughout Dodge, regardless of topography, are prairie and savanna soils, their fertility the result not only of ancient geological processes but also of human history. The Native Americans were stewards of the prairie lands for thousands of years. Across the Great Plains, tribes farmed the land, growing crops known as the three sisters: maize, climbing beans, and squash. These crops were typically planted close together on human-made mounds of soil, with areas of production frequently rotated; such practices enhanced the fertility and sustainability of the soils. While the Dakota people were primarily a nomadic hunting and gathering tribe, some groups practiced three sisters agriculture or traded with neighboring farming tribes.

Within a generation, European settlers converted the same lands to suit the purposes of European-style commodity agriculture, characterized by plowing the land, growing one type of crop on a field (monoculture), and relying on draught animals. This conversion was particularly rapid in southeastern Minnesota. According to local historian Kenneth Carley, this portion of Minnesota "mov[ed] through its frontier phase and into a commercial wheat monoculture sooner than most of the rest of the state."[4]

I thought about this when rereading the Minnesota Farm Bureau Foundation's "Moving to the Country" brochure, which opens with the statement that "Minnesota's early settlers carved out a way of life on fertile soil." While the brochure is by no means a history book, its version of Minnesota history promotes industrial agriculture, as if that were the only plausible reality for the countryside. To believe this, certain truths must be elided or ignored.

Today's corporate takeover of agricultural land echoes, in some ways, with that of the late 1800s, when Minnesotan land was converted with dispatch. The European settlers imposed upon the land a way of life they had practiced for millennia in their home countries, yet to do so, they wrested it, often violently, from the peoples already there.

The attitude of entitlement intrinsic to the settler-colonialist mindset has been passed on through the generations. In Minnesota today, many have turned a blind eye to the corporate takeover of farmland and the corresponding environmental degradation and loss of community and economic vitality. An age-old cultural attitude supports the belief that capitalistic expansion at all costs is smiled upon from above, a manifest destiny reserved for those few who benefit.

Life on the Homeplace

My great-grandfather Ed was part of a mass wave of Scandinavian immigrants forging a new life in a foreign land. The arrivals were quick to establish close-knit towns and communities, enclaves serving as cultural anchors to attract and welcome more friends and family members to the region.

Ed wasted no time in creating a life for himself that closely reflected his dearly missed community in Hemsedal. He soon met Mary Knutson, my great-grandmother, whose parents had likewise immigrated from Hemsedal years prior. Mary's parents carved a traditional Norwegian sod-roofed hut into a hillside just a mile northeast of Blooming Prairie in Westfield Township, Dodge County. After marrying, Ed and Mary settled five miles northeast of Blooming Prairie, along the banks of the Cedar River, building a home that is reminiscent of Ed's childhood farm on the Trøymsåne River in Hemsedal.

Ed was an industrious man with a love for design and architecture. He constructed several homes, barns, and other structures through-out the Blooming Prairie area, many of which still stand today. His legacy remains Westfield Lutheran Church, for which he served as the chief architect. Westfield is made of wood, and both the aisle and the chancel are A-framed, similar to the barrel-arched aisle and chancel of Ed's home church in Hemsedal.

In 2005 I traveled to Norway with my mother and other family members, eventually making our way to the bell-towered Hemsedal church near the ancestral Troim farm. Entering the building was a moment I'll never forget, as I realized that Westfield Lutheran Church was more or less a replica of the building I was standing in. It was adorned with stained-glass windows, featured an altar at the front encompassed by a circular railing for communion, and was topped with a bell tower—just like the one in Westfield! In the chancel area I found one window in particular quite moving; it depicts the Good Shepherd with a citation from John 10:11 that reads (in Norwegian, of course): "I am the good shepherd. The good shepherd lays down his life for the sheep."

That evening I called my father in Minnesota and shared my revelation. I finally understood the deep connection to Hemsedal that my great-grandfather had brought with him to Blooming Prairie. My father said nothing in response; I only heard him crying.

Ed and Mary had seven children, including my grandfather Elmer. Extremely pleased with his growing brood, Ed wrote to his family in Norway that he had "as many descendants as the stars in the sky." The busy family's daily chores included attending to cattle, pigs, and other farm animals in addition to tending the production fields straddling the Cedar River. Yet Ed longed for Norway, as demonstrated in his frequent letters, penned in Norwegian, back home. In a writing called *A Spring River*, Ed fondly recalled the landscape of his childhood:

> Right next to my home runs a river called Tvaeraaen. It runs down from the mountains through a very narrow passage between two high and steep mountains. There are many magnificent waterfalls along it which make a loud and deep sound. During summer, the river is home to many dipper (a type of bird, fossekall), which either sit on the rocks surrounding it or wash themselves in its crystal clear and cold water. I remember when I was a child, I used to lie in the grass next to the river and listen to the sound it would make, occasionally drifting off to sleep and dreaming about all the warm countries far, far away that I had been told about, where there were palm trees as tall as church towers and tigers and snakes looking for prey and crocodiles on the rivers.[5]

Of course, Ed did end up traveling, in his waking life, to a faraway land. He ended up over four thousand miles away, in fact, though it wasn't warm and didn't have any palm trees. Nor did it have any of the dramatic mountaintops or waterfalls of Hemsedal. But it did have the Cedar River, and soon enough, it became home.

My grandfather Elmer, born in 1903, married my grandmother Marie Wilson, another Westfield Township farm kid, in 1924. They settled just two miles north of Ed and Mary's farm in an area known for its soggy topography at the headwaters of the Cedar River. As with many other neighboring farm families, my grandparents initially rented the land and eventually purchased the eighty-acre farm site in 1937.

This became my family's farm—the one I grew up on—and today my siblings and I operate it jointly.

Elmer and Marie—"Ma," as my dad and his siblings lovingly called her—raised ten children, nearly all of them born in the farmhouse. They tended the land, alternating crops such as corn, soybeans, barley, oats, and flax. They pastured and milked their small herd of dairy cows and traded their meat and dairy products at the local store for whatever they couldn't produce themselves. Twice a day they milked the cows, and neighbors took turns transporting fresh cream to the local creamery, where it was churned into butter.

The pigs on the farm occupied a grove of Norway poplar trees west of the driveway. As fall approached, they built nests in the wooded area and gave birth to fat baby pigs—"cute little devils," as my dad called them. When winter approached, the family moved them into the small hog barn, where the pigs were housed on deep straw bedding. Unlike most of today's pigs, which are raised in cramped, windowless facilities and rarely see the light of day, Elmer and Marie's pigs delighted in their deep straw bedding, which was routinely refreshed. Aside from fulfilling the pig's natural instincts to dig, chew, burrow, and roll around, straw bedding is a simple, convenient form of manure management. Manure mixed in the bedding makes a good fertilizer because the deep pack composts while it is in the barn, with the pigs' feet mixing it in. The deep straw also cuts odors and dangerous emissions, improving life for both farmers and neighbors.

Like the pigs, the chickens on the farm had access to soil, grass, and sunlight, and some even enjoyed perching in the trees. Each day, Marie and the children gathered eggs and carefully transported them across bumpy country roads to Blooming Prairie for sale. Local grocer Martin Nelson bought eggs, chickens, and geese from local families; to facilitate commerce, he stamped out metal coins that were only redeemable in his store. Local farmers used the small denominations to purchase flour and sugar, work clothes, dress clothes, and other basic items in exchange for fresh homegrown items produced on the farm.

Marie tended two or three gardens each year, typically consisting of lettuce, carrots, radishes, string beans, peas, cucumbers, and other vegetables, as well as a strawberry and rhubarb patch. On a high spot near the northwest corner of the farm, she grew potatoes, popcorn, and pumpkins. A third garden northeast of the farm produced citron melons, but the Trom children preferred the tasty watermelons across the road in Mrs. Rabe's garden. Between the animals, the crops, the gardens, and the bartering at Martin Nelson's store, the family never went hungry but had to work hard.

As my father grew into adulthood, he and his siblings assisted my grandparents with modernizing the farm. Electricity arrived in 1938 thanks to a sixty-foot wind charger. Several years later, large utility poles carried electrical lines to the farm that were installed by half a dozen German prisoners of war. During the summers of 1944 and 1945, hand-dug water lines transformed the Trom farming operation. And on a summer day in 1947, one year following my father's graduation from high school, he convinced his father to attend a nearby land auction, where he purchased the 160-acre farm across the road.

Back on the homeplace, during the fall of 1948 my father began working the permanent pasture just east of the building site that was full of bogs. From God's hands to Lowell's, he worked the virgin land with a single disk, carefully slicing the edge of each bog and taming the land. The disk lifted the ground and pushed it aside. He then plowed the area with a two-bottom plow and turned the soil, adding approximately thirty-five acres of tillable land to the farming operation that fall.

The following year, in 1949, my grandfather purchased an additional eighty-acre parcel just northwest of the homeplace. That same year, the family began the decades-long process of tiling the land and installing a drainage ditch. The extensive field tiling system removed water from the damp ground, allowing otherwise unusable land to be put into production.

I vividly recall that for years when I was growing up, my father caught hell from the neighbors over the extensive tiling of our farm. "There you go, burying your money again," they said. Eventually, they realized that Lowell was putting soggy land into production, and they began to tile their land too. Today our family's project is known as the Ripley–Westfield drainage ditch, connecting farmers in Ripley Township and Westfield Township to the Cedar River just a few miles to the south.

No wonder my father would often look lovingly out on our land when I was a child and state, "This whole farm is handmade."

The Bicycle Days

A sudden death brought the Trom family closer together. In 1959 my grandmother passed on unexpectedly, leaving behind her husband, Elmer; their ten children; and several grandchildren. My father and my mother, Evelyn, moved back to the farm with their young children. My older brother Randy, just five years old at the time, shared a bed with our grandfather. Poor Elmer, so heartbroken, cried himself to sleep each night. His grandchildren became the recipients of his tremendous love following Marie's passing.

Almost every Sunday during my childhood, one or two of my aunts and uncles, along with my cousins, returned to the homeplace. Eventually, it became home to my parents and their six children (in order of birth): Randy, Shelley, Brad, me, Peggy, and Jim. We played softball, hide-and-seek, or "Annie, Annie Over"; rode bicycles; splashed water in the drainage ditch; and, if we felt adventurous, got out Grandpa's old buggy. Strawberries, rhubarb, and other spring pleasures were ours for the taking. Later we enjoyed fresh tomatoes, sweet corn, green beans, and other savory items from a summer garden; an apple pie made from the fruit of a backyard apple tree; fresh butter and cream; chicken, beef, and pork from local farmers; and other delights.

My sister Peggy and I, less than two years apart in age, were collectively called "the little girls." We frequently walked along the buffer strips, chased monarch butterflies, picked wild roses or wild tiger lilies for our mother, and enjoyed a picnic lunch along the ditch bank. Our mother carefully packed our snacks, usually consisting of crackers and fresh creamery butter, as well as a mason jar of ice-cold water. Of course, no trip was complete until we gathered a few cattails and stomped in the trickling water, splashing and trying to get the other one wet.

The simple life continued during my youth in the 1960s. Milking cows was the highlight of the day. I called them from the pasture by yelling, "Come, Boss! Come, Boss!" We listened to KDHL AM 920 out of Faribault, Minnesota, on the aqua-colored radio tucked in the barn's rafters. The cows happily swished their tales as the "Checkerboard" song routinely aired during milking time:

> The checkerboard, the checkerboard,
> Look for the store with the checkerboard.
> With America's most, from coast to coast,
> Look for the store with the checkerboard.

Like many dairy farmers, during the 1960s my father joined the National Farmers Organization (NFO), a populist organization dedicated to the economic well-being of family farmers. The NFO believed that small farmers could "care for their land, for each other, and for their nation." Large agribusiness interests that supported economies of scale and price controls by processors challenged the NFO's goals. Early signs of the coming corporate war on rural America emerged during this time, as NFO members frequently discovered their yard signs peppered with bullet holes.

My father later recalled the prediction of fellow NFO member Emmit Filley during this time. Emmit said, "The goddamn corporations will wait until we get the land tiled, the tree stumps and rocks removed, and then they'll take it over."

Lowell carefully studied not only the art and science of farming but also its politics. Growing up on a farm with many brothers and sisters, from a young age he showed the most interest among his siblings in the farming operation. He learned from his father the nuances of tillage and harvest, as well as business practices and bookkeeping.

My father embodied the perfect combination of head, heart, and hands—the key ingredients of a successful farmer. He possessed the intellect to understand and foresee the painful corporatization of rural areas, and he had the heart and soul of a true farmer who shared an intimate relationship with the land. I often called the farm "Lowell's Garden," as he lovingly turned each square inch of the ground every spring, preparing it for another fruitful harvest. And of course he had strong hands—Viking hands—that hitched large machinery to the tractor, lifted heavy rocks out of the field, and milked cows daily.

Lowell had a sharp memory and recalled almost every day of his life, including, as he often claimed, the day he was born. While others watched TV shows, he watched the weather station; with his deep knowledge of weather patterns, he oftentimes lifted the planter or another piece of farm equipment out of the ground just minutes before a rain shower.

My parents were complementary life partners, each with different passions that filled the other's gaps. My mother was the consummate home keeper who enjoyed the craft and attention to detail required for baking, tending to the children's schedules and social lives, mending the family's clothing, and designing the home and gardens. She also maintained the books of the farming operation, meticulously entering each expense into the record book, while my father carefully watched the grain markets and timed the sale of corn and soybeans.

Always a daddy's girl, I loved the farming operation. Each spring I put graphite in the seed boxes to assist with seed flow. I loved the way the black substance covered the soybeans, with a small portion drifting away toward the sky. I hitched and unhitched equipment from the tractors, shouting, "Ho!" to my father and signaling the hitch was in just the right spot. My brothers Randy and Brad baled hay and performed other outside chores. Once the hay was stacked neatly in the haymow, they set aside a few bales and created a maze of tunnels, which we crawled through from one end to the other.

The 1970s, for me, were the bicycle days. We enjoyed the freedom of riding in the neighborhood, stopping at Great-aunt Borghild's or Mrs. Ebenhoh's to enjoy an ice-cold popsicle on a hot summer day. Blooming Prairie was a bustling place, with three grocery stores (Betlach Foods, SuperValu, and Oswald's Grocery); local banks (Farmers & Merchants

Bank and First National Bank); two drug stores (Reichert's Drug Store and Shaw Drug); a Ben Franklin store; several restaurants and barber shops; farm equipment and car dealerships; and an assortment of other businesses, such as clothing stores, doctors' offices, a pool hall, an accounting firm, and, of course, a bakery.

The children of farmers attended school activities together and shared rides home. We celebrated milestones and grieved losses and read all about both in one of the many local newspapers. The majority of farms were small, with farmers tending 80- to 160-acre farms. Nearly every farmer had a fenced pasture filled with grazing cattle and perhaps a secondary pasture for hogs. It was absolutely the norm for farmers and farm families to live on the land. One of the underappreciated, corrosive aspects of corporate farming is that when farmers don't live on the land, their absence has ripple effects and consequences for the well-being of the larger community.

In our teenage years, we danced to polka, country *and* western, and the latest rock 'n' roll on the sticky floor covered in three-two beer at Zeiner's Ballroom in nearby Bixby. As midnight struck and closing time arrived, we followed one another home across snow-filled gravel roads, ensuring everyone arrived safely. During summer months, we rode our bikes to the neighboring Bass farm, where they hosted horse camps for "city" boys and girls. The city kids showcased their riding skills at the Friday night horse shows. We straddled the fence, hoping to pet a horse and recognizing that was the closest we would get to attending horse camp, an extravagance not within the family budget.

Extravagant or not, horse camp—along with just about any other outdoor community activity you can think of—could not happen today. What child is going to spend a week at a horse camp in Dodge County and endure the constant stench? This is but one small example of how corporate factory farms have changed the economy and the community into something unrecognizable from what it was during my youth.

The transformation of farm country is often explained by larger market forces and sociopolitical realities: globalization, trade wars, integrated supply chains. Too often these explanations overlook how old-fashioned corporate greed harnessed these larger trends to achieve the simple goal of greater profits. To capture these profits, meatpacking corporations use a system of contracts between farmers and so-called integrators, converting small farmers into "contract growers" who no longer own their own livestock but rather temporarily board others' animals for a set price. Big Ag carefully guards the details of these contracts, but they find their way into public view nevertheless. Let's take a look.

3

The Big Pig Pyramid

"Livestock farmers are very concerned about the welfare of their animals. Farmers provide their livestock with a balanced diet, shelter from extreme weather, routine veterinary inspection, assistance with birthing, sanitation, protection from predators, and a stress-free environment."—MINNESOTA FARM BUREAU FOUNDATION, "Moving to the Country"

While delivering a load of grain to the local elevator, a young farmer was approached by a Big Ag peddler about an opportunity to own a state-of-the-art hog barn. The peddler spouted the corporate tagline: "This is how you get started in farming." The barn would house thousands of hogs; the details, from delivery to veterinary services, would be prearranged. The young farmer had no credit? No problem, the financing was all but ensured. He wouldn't see much income during the ten-year contract term, but once the loan was paid off, the building would be his.

This simple contract, innocuous on its face, has enabled the long arm of multinational corporations to reach deep into rural areas. In Dodge County, the period of rigorous recruitment began in the mid-nineties. Once the industry anchored the initial wave of factory farms, it achieved a foothold that quickly became a vise grip. Often using insiders' tips from the expansive network of Farm Bureau members, the industry identified young farmers who might be amenable to signing contracts. The business of the day was forcing the remaining independent farmers to "get big or get out," a phrase coined by Earl Butz, secretary of agriculture during Richard Nixon's administration.

One after another, independents either left farming or signed a contract, becoming trapped like animals on their own land, no longer owning the hogs, and depending on the whims of Hormel, JBS, Tyson, and Smithfield. When Big Ag began to ensnare the Dodge County countryside in this way, local farmers didn't grasp what was happening for several years. An air of secrecy surrounded the endeavor. We could plainly see the facilities known as CAFOs appearing in the area, but what happened inside them was, initially, a mystery. Today these mass feedlots dominate life in Dodge County, and we know all too much about the pyramid scheme that has transformed rural America.

The Meat-packers, the Integrators, the Growers: A Pyramid Model Emerges

The emergence of what I call the "Big Pig Pyramid"—a three-tiered, vertical integration model—can be traced back to the farm crisis of the 1980s, when land values plummeted, farm debt for land and equipment purchases soared, and banks imposed predatory interest rates. Unable to keep up with debt payments, farm families were forced into foreclosure and bankruptcy. In this context, corporate meat-packers looking to consolidate and expand their empires capitalized on those down-and-out farmers who had managed to survive the crisis yet were still struggling to stay on their family farms.

With so many uncontrollable variables in the life of a farmer (weather, for one), entering into a contract removes one major factor—price. The monthly contract payments, even if barely enough to cover costs, at least promise a predictable cash flow. The problem, of course, is that the industry offering a lifeline in one hand holds a metaphorical butcher's knife in the other.

Versions of this scheme have been employed for several commodity groups, including chickens, turkeys, and beef and dairy cows, but for purposes of illustration, my focus is hogs. At the top of the Big Pig Pyramid are the large, multinational *meatpacking conglomerates*, which today include Hormel Foods; JBS Foods USA (a subsidiary of Brazilian-based JBS S.A.); Smithfield Foods, the largest pork company in the world (and a wholly owned subsidiary of Hong Kong–based WH Group Limited, formerly the Chinese corporation Shuanghui Group); and Tyson Foods, the second-largest processor of beef, pork, and chicken worldwide.

The middle tier of the pyramid comprises the *integrators* who own the hogs at all stages of the process and provide feed, veterinary services,

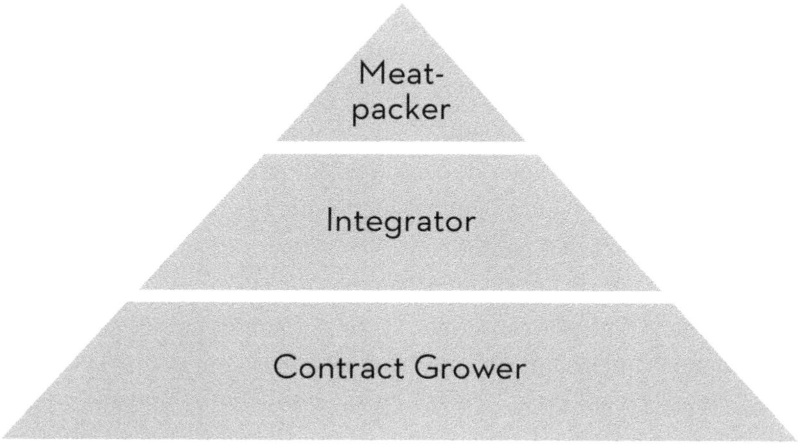

CHART 1. Basic "Big Pig" pyramid scheme. Created by the author.

and professional supervision to their contract growers. Forming the bottom of the pyramid are the *contract growers*—farmers—who enter into long-term contracts with the integrators.

The farmers (contract growers) no longer own the pigs, yet typically they provide the labor, utilities, and significant up-front investment capital to build and manage the feedlot operations. The integrator typically owns the hogs from gestation to slaughter. The sows are housed at massive gestational facilities; once weaned, the piglets are transferred to nearby nurseries that are managed by those growers who have contracted with the integrator. Then the pigs are moved along to finishing barns, or feeder operations, where they are fed to maturity. Again, these CAFOs are run by contract growers. Upon achieving a certain age and market weight, the integrators—not the farmers—sell and transport the hogs to slaughterhouses, which are usually operated by the meat-packers at the top of the pyramid.

Integrators often refer to themselves as "farmers" and to their CAFOs as "farms." In reality, integrators are corporate go-betweens facilitating the swine supply chain. Strategically headquartered in key geographic locations, they not only help recruit the contract growers but also provide feed and other services to them. In Minnesota and northern Iowa, major integrators include Holden Farms, Inc., which contracts with nearly 200 growers throughout southern Minnesota and northern Iowa; Christensen Farms, one of the largest pork producers in the United States with nearly 1,500 contractors; and Iowa Select Farms.

As aptly summarized by the meat-packer Hormel Foods in its 2018 filing with the U.S. Securities and Exchange Commission, "The live hog industry has evolved to large, vertically-integrated operations using long-term supply agreements."[1]

This way of livestock farming is so widespread that as of 2019, an Open Markets Institute analysis found that a small handful of meat-packing conglomerates, rather than independent farmers, owned more than 80 percent of the hogs in the United States.[2] Measured by the number of sows in the year 2020, the top ten U.S. "pork powerhouses" had between them nearly 2.8 million sows.[3] These sows are the key to the industry's control.

Ultimately, the contract system is designed to remove potential competitors from the marketplace, allowing the meat-packers at the top of the pyramid to enrich themselves on the backs of farmers, meatpacking workers, and immigrant laborers. The integrator-grower contract typically includes a multiyear payment plan in which the integrator pays a fixed monthly amount to the grower; it is arranged in parallel with a loan covering the construction of the CAFO and other startup costs. The industry, presumably embarrassed by the details and the threat of regulation, has always been vague about the nature of these contracts. They are kept carefully under a secretive cloak.

As a litigator, I know from experience that skeletons tend to be uncovered during discovery and trial. Sure enough, I found what I was looking for in a 2013 lawsuit brought by contract growers against Minnesota integrator Holden Farms, Inc. that proceeded to six days of trial in 2016 and 2017.[4] The thousand-plus-page trial transcript includes the testimony of several witnesses and references to more than a hundred trial exhibits that contained, to my delight, details about contract terms, cash flow projections, and financing arrangements.

The transcript shows that the Langdon family—the contract growers—sought to construct a three-thousand-head swine feedlot one mile north of our farm in Dodge County in 2008, requiring a $730,000 loan.[5] (As examined in chapter 8, loans to construct the CAFOS are backed by a variety of Big Ag interests and are easy to qualify for and obtain.) The Langdons entered into a contract with the integrator, Holden Farms, which would provide the hogs and feed, as well as veterinary and transportation services. Holden would pay the growers $108,000 annually for a period of twelve years, or $9,000 per month.[6]

In exchange, the growers assumed responsibility for remaining out-of-pocket costs for growing hogs to market weight, including providing the growing facility (i.e., the CAFO barn); maintaining and cleaning the facility; and paying the mortgage principal and interest on the loan to construct the CAFO, which in this case amounted to $6,391 per month. The growers would provide "labor and supervision as may be necessary to grow swine," which was budgeted as "$5 a pig space, give or take," according to expert testimony.[7] For a three-thousand-head swine operation, this estimate adds $15,000 per year, or $1,250 per month.

When you add up the typical expenses associated with running a CAFO, the estimated profits come in at $41 per month (see table 1). Not exactly a living wage.

Table 1. Monthly income and expenses

Income and expenses per month	Amount per month (estimated)
Contract payment	$9,000
Mortgage (principal and interest)	($6,391)
Labor	($1,250)
Utilities	($900)
Real estate taxes	($183)
Insurance	($75)
Pork checkoff fee	($160)
Net profit per month	**$41**

These razor-thin margins explain the growers' common reliance on cheap immigrant labor in factory farms to squeeze out as much profit as possible. As discussed in subsequent chapters, the management of manure, dead pig disposal, and undergrown or overgrown pigs, as well as obligations to the federal pork checkoff program (see chapter 17) and to industry associations, creates a financially precarious situation. Contract growers and factory farm laborers take all the manure and assume all the risk.

One can't help but admire the thoroughness of the contract; every eventuality is accounted for. One contract I came across stipulates that in the event manure is not removed from the CAFO before reaching twelve inches from the bottom of the support beams, the integrator may, at its option, arrange for the removal of the manure and deduct those costs from payments to the grower.[8] Another contract specified that growers are required to indemnify and hold the integrator harmless if any claim, cause of action, demand, or regulatory proceeding is commenced or if there is any loss to the integrator on account of manure storage, manure application, dead pig disposal, public or private nuisance, pit pumping and/or cleaning of the facility, operation of the facility, or acts or omissions related thereto.[9]

By signing a contract, young farmers essentially become low-wage corporate employees. Most growers do not receive a pay increase, not even a cost-of-living adjustment, during the contract term. Likewise, they do not get a pension contribution, profit sharing, or health insurance. Many economists and ag scholars deem the grower-integrator relationship today's version of sharecropping.

On such a short leash and having already signed on the dotted line, growers must be careful not to jeopardize their contracts or speak out against the system, even when their experiences turn to manure. Many growers who manage to emerge still standing after the decade-long arrangement with their operations become industry loyalists. As corporate soldiers of the American Farm Bureau Federation's hierarchy, they turn a deaf ear to those who want to change this system or merely want to pass commonsense reforms, such as fair loan practices and legal protections for contract growers who face retaliatory or discriminatory revocations of their contracts.

The ascent of this contract-based system has contributed to the tearing apart of the social fabric in rural areas, as many contract growers don't live on, or anywhere near, their "farms." Authored by a cohort of food system scholars, a recent report on the rapid concentration of the ag industry focused on its downstream social consequences. The authors wrote, "An agriculture system without people has depopulated rural communities, causing a collapse in social relationships."[10]

For many contract growers, letting someone else own the hogs and dictate the terms solved a lot of problems and promised a steady, if inadequate, cash flow. But at what cost?

For the hogs that spend their short time on Earth confined indoors in deplorable conditions, life begins in a gestational facility, where they are born in farrowing barns housing thousands of sows and newborn piglets. These facilities are the largest, most technologically sophisticated, and labor-intensive stop along the pork supply chain. Several complex processes occur within the same buildings, including artificial insemination or timed breeding, gestation, birth, and nursing.

In the earliest gestational facilities, CAFO operators experimented with something that had never been done before—that is, housing hundreds or even thousands of sows in close quarters. These large animals were selectively bred and engineered to carry as many piglets as possible per pregnancy. Sows can be aggressive when pregnant and will fight if they're packed in tightly. Yet expanding the size of their facilities isn't an option when the goal is to efficiently produce as many piglets as possible.

The solution is sow gestation crates, where the animals gestate for several months in a space so small they can't walk or even turn around. In some facilities, reproductive-age female pigs that haven't been impregnated yet—or gilts—are "crate broken" for several weeks prior to breeding so they grow accustomed to being unable to move.[11] When the piglets are born, the sows are typically allotted a tad more space—a larger crate—to nurse for about three weeks before the babies are taken away. Then the sows are artificially inseminated or bred again, and the process begins anew.

In Dodge County, the first gestational facility appeared in the 1990s just south of our family farm along Claremont Road, a sleepy ten-mile county road between the city of Claremont to the north and Highway 30 to the south. The facility is a sprawling industrial complex. We didn't know it at the time, but the appearance of this operation signaled that Big Ag already had major designs on Dodge. Gestational units are hubs that support and ultimately drive distribution of pigs to the outwardly radiating geography of spokes—that is, the feeder operations where hogs are grown to market weight.

The typical factory farm sow, weighing on average between four hundred and five hundred pounds, produces twelve piglets per litter.[12] When the piglets are weaned from their mother, they're transferred to a separate facility, the nursery. In Dodge County, two factory-scale nurseries are located along Highway 30, two miles east of the gestational hub. At the nursery, piglets are contained indoors and fed a diet designed for rapid weight gain; they arrive weighing between fifteen and twenty pounds, and leave the nursery when they are about eight weeks old and weigh between forty to eighty pounds.[13] Next, they are transferred to the next spoke on the wheel for further processing—the finishing barn.

In the finishing barns, the pigs spend about four months confined in the dark CAFOs, eating until they reach about 280 pounds. They stand above concrete pits of their urine and manure, breathing in the condensed stench and noxious gases. The industry has needed to develop various tools for keeping the pigs from being poisoned by the toxic air or trampled, suffocated, or killed by another pig in this unnatural environment. To mitigate the toxic air emissions sweltering up from the pits, the industry employs a variety of exhaust fans; indeed, CAFO operators like to boast about the latest models as proof of their tech-savvy manure management. But they're an imperfect fix. "The fans function like the ventilators of terminal patients: if they break down for any length of time, pigs start dying," journalist Jeff Tietz wrote.[14]

To reduce the risk of biting, fighting, and unintentional injuries between pen mates, hog producers might castrate the piglets, dock their tails, or clip their teeth. These efforts, too, are imperfect solutions. In such cramped conditions, deaths by injury or illness are inevitable, and portions of remains from deceased pigs are sometimes found in the manure pits below.

In the majority of today's CAFOs, hogs consume antibiotics daily, whether they're sick or not. It's a defensive tactic deployed in recognition of the animals' filthy, cramped conditions, where the obese, distressed, genetically engineered, immunocompromised hogs easily succumb to disease, and minor lesions can evolve into fatal infections. As explored in chapter 12, this practice in industrialized animal agriculture is a major contributor to the global antibiotic resistance crisis.

In the next step in this industrial supply chain, the animals are transported from the feeder operations to the meatpacking facilities. These operations are typically lined along a major highway, heavily fortified, and surrounded by chain-link fences. In Dodge County, the nearest such meatpacking "castle" is the world headquarters of Hormel Foods in Austin, Minnesota, just miles from our family farm along I-90. There, low-wage laborers working elbow to elbow process an estimated twenty thousand hogs daily under conditions that have spawned many labor lawsuits. In 2015 an employee at Quality Pork Processors (the Hormel plant's slaughtering section) leaked a video that showed still-conscious hogs strapped to the conveyer belt for dismemberment, fecally contaminated body parts processed for food, and other flagrant violations of existing regulations.[15]

Once this hub-and-spoke network is established in a rural area, the pressure is on for the farming community to join it. Today's major meatpacking facilities only accept hog deliveries from factory farms. Denied access to the marketplace and finding themselves at the base of the Big Pig Pyramid, many small, independent farmers choose to sign the contract, believing it is their only remaining option to stay on the family farm, as corporate conglomerates hold the keys to the castle and access to the private marketplace. Yet as I hope to show, this servitude to corporate agriculture is not desirable, not inevitable, and not the pathway forward for rural America.

But what does "corporate agriculture" mean anyway? Terms such as "industrial ag," "Big Ag," and "corporate ag" are often used interchangeably to refer to the same system of consolidated, vertically integrated agricultural supply chains. It's important to understand what I see as the fundamental problem with today's model of corporation-driven agriculture. Other forms of farm ownership and operation, of course, have involved profound, epoch-defining abuses of land, animals, and people. With today's iteration of Big Ag, abuses are immanent in a particular way that is tied to corporate dominance. Corporations, by law and definition, are antithetical to the values that the best versions of agricultural practice and culture ideally embody.

"Corporation" isn't a synonym for "business" or even for "big business." The simplest definition of a *corporation* is *a company or group of individuals that is authorized by law to act as a single entity*. As author and environmentalist Ted Nace wrote in his history of U.S. corporations, *Gangs of America: The Rise of Corporate Power & the Disabling of Democracy*, "[People] assume that corporations have always been a natural part of the American system of 'democracy and free enterprise,'" but this is not the case.[16] A corporation is just one form, among many, that a company can take. Corporations have evolved over time, growing in prevalence and influence. Thomas Jefferson was not a fan of such organizations, writing in an 1816 letter to former senator George Logan that "I hope we shall . . . crush in it's [*sic*] birth the aristocracy of our monied corporations which dare already to challenge our government to a trial of strength, and to bid defiance to the laws of their country."[17]

Why would Jefferson take such a view? To answer that question fully would take its own book (Nace's is a good one), but one major reason is that because corporations are legally mandated to function as a "single entity," they are bound to prioritize the financial value of that entity above other considerations. When a food corporation's spokesperson claims that it is driven by a mission to "feed the world," that is simply untrue. Corporate agriculture has not, in fact, been uniquely successful at feeding the world. The true intent of corporate agriculture is to feed its own bottom line. All other issues—the welfare of workers, animals, land, water, and communities, for example—have no bearing from the perspective of the entity of the corporation. This finding is not cynical; it is the technical (and the legal) reality of the matter. As Nace writes:

> I've repeatedly been struck by the paradox that even the most destructive corporations are populated by friendly, caring people. Sure, there are exceptions to that—corrupt companies, companies with poisonous internal cultures, even companies that ought to be classified as instances of organized crime. But in general, far more harm is caused by corporations acting in ways that are utterly legal and that seem, from the perspective of those inside the corporation, to be perfectly appropriate. Quite obviously, if corporations do harm, it is not because the people inside them lack souls. Rather, it is because the company as a whole, like any organization, is a complex entity that acts according to its own autonomous set of motives and dynamics.[18]

If my father, grandfather, or great-grandfather had inflicted as much damage on the land and caused as much suffering to their communities as today's industrial operations do, they not only would have been violating our family's deeply rooted ethic of care, compassion, and community but also would have been sued or chased off the land by their neighbors. But the Big Ag corporations are getting away with these abuses while being lauded as the champions of modern agriculture. In attempting to restructure our communities themselves, the corporations' philosophy has worked its way into politics at every level, all in a shameless bid to make the corporate way the only way.

4

The Meeting at Lansing Corners

"When you have an organization as large as ours, you will have folks, who are good folks, who disagree on certain issues. There are folks who want to create a division between large farms and other farms, and at the end of the day, the Farm Bureau is a place for all."—SAM KIEFFER, American Farm Bureau Federation VP of public affairs, 2022

As corporate farming ensnared my hometown, I began an entirely different kind of life as an attorney in the Twin Cities and a busy mother of two. But being less than two hours away from the farm, I felt as if I'd never truly left. I visited often, and when I couldn't, my parents updated me on events at the farm during our frequent phone calls. News from the homeplace changed substantively over the years as my father's preoccupation with soaring interest rates gave way to concern about small, independent farmers getting shut out of the market.

A lifelong populist farmer, Lowell had always believed in pursuing justice for all and in serving his community—two ethical pillars that he carefully taught us children. He was an attentive father who recognized our differences and guided us in individualized ways, yet he challenged each of us alike to be fiercely independent. My siblings and I are quite different in temperament and personality, but we all became adults who value fairness and are unafraid to challenge others if it's in the service of what we believe is right.

Looking back now as a parent myself, I'm awestruck that my father successfully passed these values to all six of us. Then again, we hardly could have avoided his message. Growing up, we saw the pursuit of fairness in action.

Our father served on the Dodge County Board of Commissioners for eight years, from 1973 to 1981. Feisty as hell, he challenged corrupt power structures as outside interests with their own agendas had a way of sneaking into Dodge County time and again. Lowell kept an eye toward ensuring the rules and regulations in Dodge were fair to local independent farmers, business owners, and workers rather than biased in favor of the larger companies and banks that did business locally.

He was the custodian of fairness in other, smaller ways. One of Lowell's proudest achievements was advocating for a highway building to be located centrally rather than near the county seat; then road crews could expediently reach residents all over the county. And he got the old nursing home, a decrepit and depressing building, condemned. My parents took us there when we were kids to visit the residents, many of whom were on public assistance. Lowell then helped push through construction of the new building, which today serves as "God's waiting room" for Dodge County's elderly. Later, during the farm crisis of the 1980s, he spoke out publicly against the banks and their predatory lending practices, and he helped area farmers negotiate fairer terms.

The Trom siblings watched much of his efforts as spectators, rooting our father on. It wasn't until the 1990s that we found ourselves involved—unwittingly, at first—in our own battles against the corporate encroachment that slowly permeated Dodge County.

Bringing Hogs to Market

The story of my own family's exposure to the corporate consolidation of the hog industry begins with my sister Shelley and her husband, Dave Williamson. Their experience is similar to what independent hog farmers across the United States faced in the nineties; only in retrospect do we appreciate that they were the targets of a corporate recruitment scheme.

In the 1990s Shelley and Dave were in their early forties, living, farming, and raising their two young sons in a beautiful home in a wooded area outside Blooming Prairie and near Dave's family farm, which was operated by Dave's father, Frank. The 320-acre operation included corn and soybeans, as well as pigs. Dave always imagined he would continue farming with his father and eventually take over the operations. This plan was well on its way.

Initially they had a farrow-to-finish operation, raising pigs from birth to market weight. Later they shifted to feeder pigs only, finishing the hogs and delivering them to local meat processor Hormel Foods, just fifteen miles away. They had a few consistent sources for feeder hogs—all of them independent suppliers—including South St. Paul Stockyard and Zumbrota Livestock Exchange, both of which held weekly auctions. Several local farmers owned sows and sold their piglets to these exchanges as well.

(These independent markets, each and every one, are gone. Integrators now own the sows and the feeder hogs in bulk.)

Dave would order batches of 250 hogs often, his sources filling his orders from the independent hog farmers in the area. When a trailer full of pigs was delivered to the Williamson farm, they were placed in the nursery and later moved to the finishing barn.

In 1993 a local feed mill in the nearby town of Hayfield built a new, state-of-the-art mill to grind and mix feed. Unbeknownst to Dave, this new mill was a building block, a key component of the industrial infrastructure needed to support the forthcoming area swine factory farms. Dave and Shelley attended the mill's grand opening and sat with fellow farmers Roger and Rhonda Toquam, chatting over hot dogs and potato salad. Roger proudly shared that he was getting ready to break ground on a new building that would house approximately two thousand hogs.

This announcement raised eyebrows.

"Aren't you worried about finding a supply? Who has two thousand pigs ready to go?" Dave asked. Such a concentration of hogs in a single building was unheard of then.

Roger responded, "Well, they'll all come from a single source."

It didn't occur to Dave that Roger did not own the hogs, that he had a contract with the integrator company that owned them. While it's common now, the notion of a farmer not owning his hogs was inconceivable then.

We Trom siblings had grown up alongside the Toquam children, and I babysat for Roger when we were kids. In retrospect, it makes sense that Roger was one of the first in Dodge to adopt the corporate model; his father was a longtime member of the Minnesota Farm Bureau, which was integral to recruiting small farmers to enter into contracts.

Roger's first two-thousand-hog concentrated animal feeding operation went up in 1993 and still stands one mile north of our family farm. A second was constructed alongside it in 1998. Today, the twin CAFOS produce an estimated ten thousand hogs per year.[1]

Independent farmers didn't fully grasp the changes underway and the threat to their livelihoods, yet clearly something was afoot. Along with Roger's CAFOS, a few other factory farms appeared in Dodge. It was something new. Meanwhile, most hog farmers continued their independent operations, raising pigs in a dedicated hog barn and adjoining pasture. The animals were free to roam outside and roll around in the dirt or on the grass, their natural way of cooling themselves.

Local farmers regularly attended dinner events at Lansing Corners, typically hosted by seed, chemical, or other vendors selling products. The restaurant, located a few miles north of Austin, was famous for its barbecue ribs and had a banquet venue upstairs for private parties. Farmers were always willing to take the free meal and try a little bit of the showcased product, but they usually didn't go whole hog.

Everything changed one night in the mid-1990s during a Lansing Corners event hosted by new faces. The dinner was widely attended, and Dave and Shelley sat at a banquet table with neighbors and friends. Farm Credit System—a financial institution run by the Farm Credit Administration, a federal government institution—played a central role at the meeting. Farm Credit was fast becoming a major source of factory farm loans. The hosts opened a PowerPoint presentation and described an upcoming opportunity.

The meeting felt decidedly different than the others. It was more informational, or educational, with presenters outlining changes to the industry. They weren't making the typical product sale of buy a little and try it. "It was more abandon what you're doing and try something new," Dave said. "The pitch was you really didn't need much money going into it . . . a few thousand dollars to get the ball rolling, and the rest was financed."

The presenters were pushing factory farms—CAFOS—saying easy money was on the horizon if you signed the contract, built the building, and received regular hog shipments from an integrator such as Holden

Farms or Christensen Farms. Farm Credit would provide the financing. The captive audience was told there would be debt service over a ten-year period to pay for the building, but after that time, you'd be debt free and making $60,000 at a job that didn't require many hours of work per week. (Later, farmers discovered that financial backing and loan guarantees were also available from integrators and local feed mills.)

Afterward, everyone was abuzz with talk about the pitch. On the one hand, Dave was apprehensive, thinking that if it sounds too good to be true, then it usually is. On the other hand, he was worried about missing the boat.

A number of attendees were looking for an agricultural opportunity for their kids. With a little out-of-pocket expense and some land to erect the building, this was how to get their sons into farming, even those who had never raised a hog in their lives. The pitch was enticing. Business hadn't been good lately. The big meat-packers, including nearby Hormel, were skillfully cutting off marketplace access to independent hog farmers in the area.

Dave and his father always called ahead to the meat-packers when it was time to deliver hogs to market, asking, "What will you give us tomorrow for a load of pigs?" Hormel lately had been giving them the cold shoulder. They were advised to call again later in the week, maybe the next week. When Hormel finally agreed to a delivery, the Williamsons noticed the growing number of semis delivering hundreds of pigs at a time. Hormel no longer wanted your hogs if they didn't fill a semi; only CAFOs could provide that many in one delivery. Independents such as Dave now waited an hour at Hormel's delivery point while the semis' loads from area industrial operations were rushed through.

Around this time, Hormel CEO Joel W. Johnson was pushing to enroll its Austin, Minnesota "cut-and-kill" slaughterhouse operation (where Dave delivered hogs) into a U.S. Department of Agriculture (USDA) pilot program known as the Hazard Analysis and Critical Control Point Inspection Models Project (HIMP).[2] The program allowed for fewer meat safety inspectors and faster line production speeds; hence, processors needed significantly more hogs for daily delivery. In anticipation of HIMP (which, after surmounting various legal objections, was fully implemented in 2002), Hormel sped up its development of technologies that would allow more hogs to be slaughtered per minute. Disallowed by federal law from contracting directly with hog farmers, Hormel propped up the middle people—the integrators—in its endeavor to blanket CAFOS throughout the countryside.

While Hormel's adoption of HIMP made the process particularly fast in Dodge County, hog farmers everywhere were folded into the rapid industry consolidation. Open markets were disappearing. In 1998 a series of circumstances, including the closure of a few major meat-packing plants and a short-lived, alleged decreased demand for pork in Asia, led to a crash in hog prices. These declining prices accelerated consolidation of the already narrowing market.

Typically, a price crash would be a transitory situation, with con-sequential but ultimately survivable ripple effects.[3] Hog farmers once controlled how many pigs they brought to market, and besides, they had other crops or types of livestock to sell. But by 1998, the industry was already consolidated and specialized enough that the crash spelled economic disaster for independent hog farmers in particular. Those who had already signed the contract to become growers and to erect CAFOS continued to deliver high volumes of market-weight hogs to the major meat-packers. They were paid much less with prices low, but they still had a point of delivery. For farmers who'd remained independent, there was nowhere left to turn.

"Small independent farmers reaped only the losses [of the crash]," ag journalist Christopher Leonard wrote in *The Meat Racket*. "And it drove them out of business. . . . The hog market started to recover in 1999, and eventually it returned to profitability. The farms affiliated with the nation's biggest meatpackers were the survivors."[4]

Dave and his father watched as, one by one, friends and neighbors fell like dominoes and either sold their farms or signed contracts, agreeing to build CAFOS to industry specifications. In 1998 Dave and Shelley made the agonizing decision to abandon the operation. Soon after, Dave's father sold the family farm. Dave believes his dad sold the farm so quickly for fear that Dave would get out and then try to get back in, but the truth was, there was nothing to get back into. Selling the farm was an act of love, and father and son together mourned a version of their future that had abruptly evaporated.

Thankfully Shelley was just finishing her education in information technology and started a promising internship at IBM. Dave enrolled in nursing school. Their family moved to the Twin Cities, where they raised their sons and have had successful careers. When I asked Dave recently for his reflections on this turbulent time, over twenty-five years now in the rearview mirror, he said he still misses farming, but he's grateful to have made the change when he was young enough to start a new career. It was a happy ending for his family. Friends in the Twin Cities are surprised when they learn he used to be a farmer. Dave tells them he was among the lost generation of small farmers pushed out during the "Walmartization" of agriculture.

He ended our emotional conversation with one of my dad's oft-spoken lines, one that we remember well: "It's a bunch of shit, eh!"

The single most important organization in enabling the rapid take-over of hog country was undoubtedly the American Farm Bureau Federation (AFBF) and its state affiliates. The Farm Bureau has a chapter in every state and is active in 90 percent of all U.S. counties.[5] Many of the first and largest factory farms were spearheaded by longtime, devoted AFBF members, and the organization rallied around—and often even wrote—the state and federal laws allowing agribusinesses and feedlot developers to elude zoning regulations, oversight, and accountability.

If you tell the average American that the Farm Bureau is a collective of farmers working for the benefit of small farmers and their families, they will believe you without question. The Farm Bureau's expansive PR machine often claims it is the voice of America's small farmer, harnessing the twentieth-century agrarianism evoked by its very name to great effect. Certainly, an organization called the "Farm Bureau" must be harmless.

In reality, the AFBF is one of the most powerful lobbies in Washington DC and is comparable to the National Rifle Association (NRA) in terms of its influence and reach. But unlike the NRA, many people are unaware of the organization's partisanship and politics.

The AFBF has long been the alternative to the liberal-leaning, populist farmer's groups, but only recently did the bureau become as hyperpoliticized as it is today. A group of farmers in Missouri formed the first statewide Farm Bureau in 1915, and in 1919 farmers from thirty states met to form the national organization. The AFBF soon established a lobbying presence in Washington to push back against New Deal programs, while state organizations pooled resources to provide members access to insurance plans. As early as 1925, an article in *The Atlantic* characterized the American Farm Bureau Federation as "dominated by the larger farmers and, compared with certain other agricultural associations, is conservative."[6]

In more recent years, various writers and scholars have described the AFBF as among the most potent political forces in Washington, perhaps the most influential player in the American farm lobby, and the most powerful institution representing rural Americans.[7] That speaks to the AFBF's power. What the AFBF actually *is* is a bit more complicated. The organization has many branches and subsidiaries, all of which connect to the corporate bottom line. Two of its most important functions are lobbying on behalf of corporate agribusinesses and partnering with insurance companies. Many of the AFBF's state chapters work with for-profit insurance companies, some of which have been folded into the FBL Financial Group and its operating subsidiaries, including the Farm Bureau Life Insurance Company and Farm Bureau Financial Services. In 2018 Farm Bureau Financial Services had almost $10 billion in assets and brought in over $700 million in revenue, making it the third-largest insurance company in the United States.[8]

The Iowa Farm Bureau is the largest of the state chapters, with $100 million in annual revenue, an investment portfolio worth more than $1 billion, and $1.4 billion in assets as of 2021, much of this deriving from its for-profit insurance partner.[9] The AFBF's insurance companies create an epic conflict of interest for its non-profit state chapters and its lobbyists. While the non-profit and for-profit branches are technically separate entities, many of them share the same staff and office space, and the board members of a state's Farm Bureau insurance company often serve on that state's nonprofit Farm Bureau board.[10] In addition, many of the AFBF's top staff members rely on the success of the insurance affiliate for their salaries. The FBL Financial Group and the Farm Bureau Life Insurance Company also are heavily invested in Big Oil and Big Ag corporations, including Cargill, Dow Chemical, Monsanto, and DuPont.[11]

The AFBF has more than six million members, yet many of these dues-paying members are not farmers; they were automatically enrolled when they purchased Farm Bureau insurance. These non-farmer members nevertheless help finance the well-oiled AFBF advocacy machine, which lobbies aggressively against environmental regulations and in favor of corporate-friendly tax and trade policies at the state and federal levels. The AFBF is second only to agribusiness giant Monsanto in lobbying expenditures on ag issues.[12]

The AFBF likewise donates to political campaigns, often endorsing the Republican slate up and down the ticket to promote the corporate agenda. State-level Farm Bureaus have been known to initiate litigation against county officials, county boards of commissioners, or individual citizens who attempt to regulate the industry or pass local ordinances unfavorable to Big Ag's business interests.

When my dad was a young farmer, the Farm Bureau was one choice among many; other organizations such as the National Farmers Organization were still thriving. Now the small farmers, family farmers, and independent farmers who once filled the NFO's membership rolls are mostly gone. In some farming states, the farmer population has been reduced by as much as 90 percent since the 1980s. Missouri, for example, saw its number of pig farms decrease from sixty-two thousand in 1964 to three thousand in 2007.[13]

The influence of AFBF members within many of today's rural farming communities cannot be overstated. Bureau members tend to serve as local elected officials; from these positions of power they're able to influence local ag policy. In some communities, bureau members shun and ostracize those who speak out against Big Ag's abuses.

Some small farmers are still among the bureau's membership, but they tend to be contract growers who rely upon giant agribusinesses for their livelihoods. While the AFBF claims to work for the small farmer, it does the opposite. During the same period that the bureau became more monied and powerful, farming bankruptcies and foreclosures reached historical highs. "By every metric, they've failed their membership," said Austin Frerick, a leading Farm Bureau expert and ag policy adviser, in 2021.[14]

My father denied several requests over the years to join the bureau, following his grandfather's advice: "Never join an association. They will never do you any good." The first recruitment attempt came soon after his grandpa Ed passed away, and a farmer's wife came by the homeplace to speak with Lowell—almost as though bureau members knew the passing of a patriarch was a good time to "get in" with the new generation. My father politely declined. Years later, another neighbor invited Lowell to hop on the bureau's bandwagon. He again resisted.

Looking back on this, I see that my family's independence from the Farm Bureau plays a larger role in this story than I'd previously understood. We never "drank the Kool-Aid"; we never signed the contracts. This stance made us personae non gratae in farm country, but it also gifted us the freedom to make choices according to our own moral compass rather than beholden to interests that are not truly our own.

The Americanization of Odelsrett

Before he died in 1949, Great-grandfather Ed told my father in his broken Norwegian accent, "You'll get that farm someday." Though Lowell was one of ten children, Ed recognized his love and affinity for farming, and knew he was the right heir to care for the land. Over the years, when Lowell had the opportunity to acquire more land, he declined, saying that beyond a certain size, "you can't do a good job."

When Great-grandpa Ed arrived in Minnesota in 1892, he carried with him the Norwegian legal concept of *odelsrett*, meaning the right of an individual "to own agricultural land because they or their ancestors have owned it for a certain time period."[15] Odelsrett is a type of allodial right, meaning absolute ownership of land as opposed to tenancy, and its main purpose was to preserve land within a family. Interestingly, Article I of the Minnesota State Constitution holds that "all lands within the state are allodial and feudal tenures of every description with all their incidents are prohibited. Leases and grants of agricultural lands for a longer period than 21 years reserving rent or service of any kind shall be void."[16] However, whereas the Norwegian concept of odelsrett was connected to strengthening family ties, Minnesota's constitution makes no connection between allodial land and families. Land in the United States is a commodity that can be bought and sold and subdivided to whomever, and though it can be inherited and often is, that outcome is not a cultural expectation.

After arriving in the United States, many Norwegian families kept the spirit of odelsrett, or adjusted it, as they did with *åsetesrett*, the right of a living heir (traditionally the first-born male but the modernized version embraces any heir or relative) to assume the undivided ownership of landed property. To this day my family carries a level of pride both in nurturing our farmland and in keeping it in the family, and we meticulously maintain our farm with the certainty that no other owner would keep it to the same standard. No doubt this approach is deeply connected with the generational influence of odelsrett.

Decoupling land ownership from familial ties has been an important legal advancement in developed societies, giving women access to land ownership and property rights, allowing racial and ethnic minorities to become landowners, and creating more avenues for upward social and economic mobility. Yet this decoupling also allowed businesses and institutions rather than families to gobble up land, creating all sorts of downstream social and cultural impacts along with economic vulnerabilities. We see its effects reflected in today's affordable housing crisis, as investors and corporations bid against individuals and families for home ownership. We see it likewise in rural America, where farmland is owned by investors, LLCs, and faraway businesspeople.

A significant consideration that comes hand in hand with caring for the land is, and always has been, environmental protection and ecological sustainability. When a family expects to keep its land in the family for generations, its members have an incentive, if not an imperative, to take care of it and to ensure that the surrounding community thrives. When my family spearheaded the installation of the

Ripley–Westfield drainage ditch, tiling the land to put wet land into production, we did so with an eye to future generations. For years, the Dodge County conservation officer took area farmers to the Trom farm to teach them how to properly seed down and create wide buffer strips along waterways.

When contract farmers were recruited into the corporate model in Dodge, the cultural tradition and mindset of *odelsrett* were harnessed, redirected, and misused to serve the corporate agenda rather than the vitality and longevity of rural communities. Many of the first contract growers were young men from farm families with parents who, understandably, hoped to keep farming within the family. Yet by relinquishing ownership of their hogs, these contract growers played a role (if often an unwitting one) in handing the meatpacking conglomerates dominance over the marketplace and unrestrained access to the family farm, anchoring a form of animal agriculture that puts the community's health, economy, and environment at risk.

5

Get Big or Get Out

"Regardless of size, almost all farms in the state are family owned. Small
and large farms co-exist to maintain the infrastructure and economic fabric
of our rural communities."—MINNESOTA FARM BUREAU FOUNDATION,
"Moving to the Country"

During the first decade of the twenty-first century, the consolidation
of the hog industry pushed forward with astonishing momentum.
Commodities traders on Wall Street made fortunes while thousands of
farmers saw their livelihoods vanish. In North Carolina and throughout the Midwest, the four meatpacking giants Hormel, JBS, Tyson,
and Smithfield coordinated with integrators, feed suppliers, and local
lenders to methodically build a network of production contract growers, restructuring the sector from open markets to contract farming.[1]
They took control of the production line from squeal to meal, from
birth to bacon.[2] In 1995 the four meat-packers controlled 46 percent of
the market. By 2006 they controlled 67 percent, a number that's held
more or less steady since.[3]

And that's just the big four. When you add in the handful of other,
smaller corporate meat-packers, the open market for hogs has all but
evaporated. In the early 1990s, nearly 90 percent of hogs were still purchased on the open market, whether sold at an auction, through dealer
transactions, or directly to the meat-packers. But by 2010 production
contracts between growers and integrators, as well as marketing contracts between the integrators and the meat-packers, were so dominant
that the percentage of spot-market hogs had plummeted to between 5
and 7 percent. Today the number is less than 2 percent.[4]

Smithfield Foods in particular was responsible for this rapid integration. Under the leadership of Joseph W. Luter III, its ambitious CEO,
Smithfield gobbled up competitors and took control of each stage of the
production process with a monomaniacal intensity. In 1999 Smithfield

became the largest hog producer and processor in the world, a distinction it's held ever since.

In 2000 the Iowa attorney general launched a high-stakes antitrust lawsuit against Smithfield when it sought to acquire Murphy Family Farms, one of its main competitors. Murphy, based in North Carolina, was itself a formidable industry giant. Then owner Wendell Murphy arguably invented the modern hog CAFO and the industry standard of recruiting contract growers to raise and finish hogs. The U.S. Department of Agriculture deemed the Murphy acquisition "absurdly big" and asked the Justice Department to scrutinize the deal for antitrust violations. Amid bipartisan opposition in Congress, Senator Chuck Grassley issued a statement saying that "the aggressive pursuit of megacorporate agriculture that Smithfield is making will ruin the family farm."[5]

The litigation against Smithfield was unsuccessful, paving the way for further monopolization. In the coming years, lobbyists for the meat-packers effectively neutered the threat of antitrust enforcement.

For vertical integration to function at scale, the meat-packers required a broad base of contract growers. Recruitment was everything. Setting their baits at the local grain elevators, recruiters fished the next catch as another young farmer delivered a load of corn or soybeans. For many years, my father wondered how Holden Farms, one of our major local integrators, knew exactly whom to target—mainly, "young farmers without a pot to piss in," as Lowell delicately put it. Back then, we didn't know the answer. Now we do.

One of the feed suppliers for Dodge-area contract growers was Interstate Mills (which was later folded into a much larger entity, Central Farm Service). Interstate was a key partner in the rapid commercialization of the swine industry in Dodge. According to court testimony from a former Holden employee, a "good portion" of Holden's CAFO operations in Dodge originated with prospecting contract growers through one of Interstate's feed mills.[6] Interstate also partnered with banks and financiers to run cash flow projections, provided loan guarantees, and helped ensure financing to young farmers, many of whom were so inexperienced that they lacked a credit record.

By 2002 nearly everyone in Dodge County knew someone who had either built a CAFO or left farming. The impacts of CAFO-style manure mismanagement and air pollution were becoming noxiously apparent, and alarming reports of drinking water contamination were first reaching the public. In this context, two major legal battles were waged—one in southern Dodge, the other in the county's northern reaches near the community of Berne.

Let's begin in Berne, where a four-year battle divided the community and prompted local officials to pass new ordinances that cut off further resistance to the proliferation of industrialized feedlots in the countryside.

The Battle over Berne

The beautiful hills of Berne, an unincorporated community in northern Dodge, lend the area a different character than the rest of the county, which otherwise unfolds as a polite, monotonous carpet of Midwest-style flatness. Berne was settled in the 1850s by Swiss immigrants, including the ancestors of my husband, Douglas. While the area's hillsides don't approach the majesty of the Alps, its undulating vistas and limestone outcroppings are about as close as it gets in the Midwest to the mountainous city of Bern, Switzerland, for which Berne is named.

I developed a better appreciation of Berne's culture and history after I met Douglas. We were both Dodge County kids, but we'd been raised in our own little universes, ensconced by the closeness of our tiny communities. Douglas feels quite connected to his Swiss heritage, the same way I feel about my Norwegian heritage. My parents met Douglas first, when I was away at college in New York. I'll never forget that phone call from my mom, in the days when long-distance calling was expensive and often brought important news: "We met the nicest young man. You'll have to meet him," she said.

I rolled my eyes at my mother's matchmaking, but in fact I did meet Douglas when I returned home that summer. He had recently graduated from the University of Minnesota with a degree in political science and lived at his family's farm while working at a local accounting firm. His interest in local politics led him to attend a meeting of the Dodge County Board of Commissioners, on which my father served at the time. Lowell introduced us, and the rest is history. We got along immediately. We share an interest in reading, history, and politics yet have differences that make life interesting. He is the yin to my yang. He is more sentimental, firm yet gentle, while I'm more direct, with the will of a bull. We have learned a great deal from one another.

Douglas's childhood in Berne wasn't so different from mine in Blooming Prairie; we were both raised on a family farm where every schedule and activity revolved around the farming operation. Douglas's mother, Ruth Eayrs, ran the operation while his father, Stewart, traveled the Midwest as an engineer on the Great Lakes ore boats. Each morning, Ruth awakened her four children at six o'clock and enlisted them to milk the cows and prepare breakfast. After school, the family repeated the routine of milking the cows around 5:30 p.m. before enjoying their supper.

The Berne community was close-knit. Many residents are descended from the original Swiss settlers, and the Zwingli United Church of Christ serves as the community's religious anchor. During Berne's heyday in the mid-twentieth century, it had a cheese factory, a lumber mill, a general store, and a country school—signs of prosperity. Most of them closed decades ago, but the church remains a vibrant mainstay, drawing thousands each summer for wood-fired pizza and outdoor concerts overlooking the picturesque landscape.

Berne's countryside is populated by two dozen or so residences clustered unusually close together within a two-mile radius. By local standards, one might even call the area "densely populated." By comparison, the square mile where my family's farm is located has only two farms—ours and another farm owned by a Trom cousin. The square mile directly across the road from our farm does not contain a single home.

Not so long ago, Berne area residents were small dairy farmers milking twenty to forty cows, plus young cattle, on two-hundred-acre parcels. In the early nineties, a major dairy operation—the first industrialized facility in northern Dodge—forced several area farmers to abandon their dairies and switch solely to grain. The new dairy operation included a large open manure pit. Due to environmental concerns relating to this pit, residents became worried that another factory farm might appear in the immediate area.

In the fall of 2002, residents learned that, as feared, another factory farm was coming to town. The industrial-size hog operation, a sow gestation facility, would produce thousands of piglets and serve as a hub for further CAFO development in the region. The facility would include two confinement buildings with 2,400 pigs apiece in addition to the thirty-five head of cattle already existing on the 136-acre farm.[7]

The feedlot buildings would be situated on top of the sensitive karst topography—fractured limestone characterized by soluble rocks, sinkholes, and underground drainage—that was unique to the Berne area. The Minnesota Department of Natural Resources (DNR) describes the impact of karst on groundwater wells: "Water dissolves fractures and joints in the bedrock forming a network of interconnected underground conduits that can carry groundwater long distances at speeds up to miles per day."[8]

Surface pollution in karst areas can reach groundwater within hours; the area immediately surrounding the proposed CAFO was rated six out of seven on a sinkhole-risk probability scale.[9] Berne is therefore designated a "highly sensitive groundwater area," meaning its shallow depth to bedrock increases the risk of groundwater contamination.[10] The proposed CAFO would inject the untreated liquified manure from the 2,400 hogs, or the equivalent of the human waste of nine thousand people, directly onto this karst topography.

The community of Berne, population two hundred, give or take, objected. Given recent history with the dairy operation and its football field–size pool of liquid manure, residents knew they had to act quickly. Neighbors called one another, arranged a meeting in a neighbor's home, and developed a plan of action. Some worried about the drinking water; others about air pollution. Virtually everyone was concerned about property values, which are known to plummet when a CAFO goes up nearby.

The feedlot proposal was put forth by Mark Finstuen, a Berne resident and young farmer who once rode the school bus with my husband, his siblings, and other neighbor children. Given the size of the project, Dodge County officials, as per state and county law, asked him to obtain an environmental assessment worksheet (EAW) and to pursue his request with the Minnesota Pollution Control Agency (MPCA).[11] The MPCA request indicated that the bureaucratic machinations to rubber-stamp the factory farm had begun.

The citizens of Berne faced an uphill battle. The Dodge County Board of Commissioners was known to be friendly to Big Ag. No application for a new feedlot permit—also known as a conditional use permit (CUP) and often shortened to a feedlot CUP—had ever been denied on the board's watch. Still, the county's planning commission reviewed proposals and made recommendations to the board. Given the unique geological conditions in Berne, residents hoped that reason would prevail.

Neighbors formed a community group, the Berne Area Alliance for Quality Living; hired an attorney; and initiated a lawsuit asking for an injunction to prohibit the proposal from proceeding. In the complaint, the alliance's attorney wrote, "The nuisance impacts from the proposed hog feedlot would with reasonable certainty cause the citizens health problems, including asthma, would increase nitrate contamination of groundwater supplies, substantially impair their quality of life and would diminish and destroy their property values, thereby clearly constituting a nuisance under Minnesota law."[12]

As the lawsuit went forward, Berne Alliance members canvassed the area and collected signatures on a petition requesting an interim moratorium on the construction of CAFOs in the county. An estimated eight hundred residents signed the petition, which was presented to the Dodge County Board of Commissioners. The board's response? Radio silence.

Or so it seemed. The application for the conditional use permit would follow the standard procedure for feedlots in Minnesota farm country: the county's planning commission assesses the CUP application and oversees a public hearing; then based on these proceedings, it votes on whether to recommend the CUP. If the commission recommends the

CUP, it advances to the Dodge County Board of Commissioners for the deciding vote. Behind the scenes, board members went on the offensive.

At the time, the county board was dominated by pro-industry advocates, but the planning commission was not. So board members worked doggedly to ensure the commission would be as CAFO-friendly as the board was. At the time, planning commission openings were not publicly posted, and commission members were secretively vetted. In January 2003, the county board appointed three new members—all of whom were factory farm operators—to the seven-member planning commission.[13]

And so it happened that the planning commission was stacked with sympathetic factory farm operators before the vote to approve yet another factory farm. This tactic was, and is, used across the country to push factory farms into rural areas. What happened in Berne is an informative case study in how Big Ag gets its way, even when the majority of the community is dead set against it.

Democracy à la Dodge County

In March 2003, as expected, the feedlot developer received the results of the environmental assessment worksheet, formally applied for the CUP, and requested a public hearing.[14] During a special meeting to review the EAW, a professor in earth sciences at the University of Minnesota addressed the county board.[15] He had walked the area surrounding the proposed feedlot and discovered sinkholes in the karst topography, presenting a heightened danger of groundwater contamination. He advised the board to deny the CUP and encouraged Finstuen to scout a different location for the facility.

The following month, the planning commission held its regular meeting. Berne Area Alliance members asked the commission to require an environmental impact statement (EIS) as part of the assessment process for the CUP application. Under Minnesota law at the time, an EIS would be appropriate if the feedlot held over a thousand animal units or if the project posed a "potential for significant environmental effects."[16] Dodge County's planning and zoning administrator denied this request, claiming, without evidence, that the feedlot did not pose the potential to cause such effects.[17]

The commission passed a motion to vote on the CUP and destroy the ballots, citing the contentious public debate surrounding the proposal. The results were three ayes, presumably corresponding to the three new pro-industry appointees, and four nays. The commission did not recommend approval of the CUP, and the matter then advanced to the county board for final review.

The Berne Area Alliance members thought they had prevailed.

But during the planning commission's next meeting in May, commission members were advised that the county board was concerned about the voting process, specifically citing the destruction of the ballots during the prior meeting.[18] The board consulted with the county attorney, who recommended a new vote. Further, the attorney wished to remind the planning commission that its role was only to provide a recommendation regarding the CUP and that the county board was not required to follow that recommendation.

That evening, the commission conducted a revote on the proposed project. The tally was four ayes, two nays, and one abstention. The commission's three new members voted yes, along with a fourth who had apparently changed their vote.

The following month, the county board approved Finstuen's CUP.

The stage was now set for a protracted legal battle. While the county's board and its planning commission, both stacked with pro-industry members, sought to rubber-stamp the facility, the citizens' group was determined to secure an adequate environmental review. The Berne Area Alliance initiated a lawsuit challenging the CUP on grounds that further environmental analysis—namely, an environmental impact statement—was required.[19] The following year, in 2004, the Dodge County District Court affirmed that an EIS was not required.

The Berne Area Alliance appealed the decision to the Minnesota Court of Appeals. In April 2005 the appeals court overturned the lower court's ruling, nullifying the CUP granted by the Dodge County Board of Commissioners and requiring further environmental review.

At issue was a Minnesota law concerning the EIS threshold. As mentioned, proposals for enclosures housing more than 1,000 AUS necessitated an EIS. Cleverly, Finstuen's CUP application proposed 995 AUS, barely skirting the threshold for environmental review; yet the proposed barns had the capacity to hold 1,440 AUS. In other words, facilities designed to hold 1,440 AUS would allegedly be filled with only 995.

The appeals court justices asked pointed questions as to why the Dodge County Board of Commissioners didn't pursue this discrepancy. In a concurring opinion, one of the justices noted that the board "should have recognized the entire capacity in determining whether this project has a significant environmental effect . . . the [Dodge County] record is silent on why the buildings would not be used at maximum capacity and whether there are alternative uses for the buildings."[20] The justices also expressed concern about the karst topography and steep slopes surrounding the proposed feedlot, concluding that in the absence of the full environmental review, it was "unclear" whether the feedlot would create a significant environmental effect.[21]

At this point, Big Ag smelled trouble in Dodge. It brought in the big gun, industry attorney Jack Perry, who is known to appear in remote county courtrooms when rural citizens push back against industrial-size feedlots.

In July 2005, several months after the appeals court decision, the Dodge County Planning Commission held a public meeting to reconsider the project.[22] With Perry as his attorney, Finstuen circumvented the concerns raised by the appeals court by submitting an amended CUP with a reduced building size. In lieu of the more stringent EIS review, Finstuen's team presented a number of supposed solutions to mitigate environmental impacts, such as biofilters, a windbreak to reduce odors, and various assurances that a responsible manure management plan would be followed.

A number of Berne residents spoke before the commission, citing their continued concern regarding water quality, property devaluation, and public health. Theresa Benda, a Berne resident who works in health care market research, presented peer-reviewed studies showing an increased risk of respiratory disease in people living near hog CAFOS.

Prior to the meeting, Theresa and other members of the Berne Area Alliance also met with a hydrologist with the Minnesota Department of Natural Resources. The hydrologist affirmed that the operation posed a groundwater contamination risk due to its site on karst topography, corroborating the concerns that several other experts had already raised.

However, when invited to testify before the commission, he declined, saying, "The last guy who spoke against it no longer has a job."[23]

As expected, the commission voted to recommend the amended CUP. It was formally approved at the next county board meeting.

In January 2006 construction of the swine gestational facility was completed. Soon thereafter, Finstuen and his family moved several miles away, leaving their former neighbors to smell the stench and breathe the ammonia, methane, and hydrogen sulfide emitted from the operation, as well as to drink the nitrate-ridden water.

In the coming years, residents living near the facility tested their water and found nitrate levels significantly above state safety standards. When one family's doctor advised against bathing in the water, the family dug a new well at a cost of over $10,000. Another family made the painful decision to move away, selling the intergenerational family farm after two family members experienced asthma that worsened and became uncontrolled following installation of the CAFOs.[24] Other residents in the Berne area experienced a high incidence of cancers. While the area's small population makes research into causation virtually impossible, the correlation is certainly present. (The connections between CAFOs and human health are explored in chapter 12.)

Looking back on the legal battle that ensnared the tiny village of Berne, I'm overcome with sadness at the lasting impact on the community. A friendly wave from a passing neighbor was replaced with a wag of the middle finger. Farmer turned against farmer, neighbor against neighbor. In the small, multigenerational village, even family members were pitted against one another. Berne Area Alliance members involved in the lawsuit had garbage dumped in their ditches and manure spread near their homes. One resident recalls that an industry insider swerved his vehicle and nearly hit her as she walked along the county road. Another resident was pressured and advised not to testify at one of the public hearings concerning the CUP; it was made clear that her husband's job would be at risk if she testified.

I recently spoke with a Berne Area Alliance member who said the experience was exhausting. The disheartened resident concluded that it's "nearly impossible to beat Big Ag in Minnesota."[25]

Even all these years later, only one Berne Area Alliance member consented to my using her full name in this book. Residents in Dodge County continue to fear retaliation for speaking out against Big Ag's dominance in the community. The days of the Berne Area Alliance were ones of naivete; back then, residents didn't understand what they were up against.

It was a hard-learned lesson. The loss sustained in those days still cuts deep. The community fault lines became enduring rifts, divisions in Dodge County that sometimes feel irreparable—all over a hog barn. It seems preposterous. But when we widen the lens, we see that the drama in Berne was propelled not by a single farmer who desired to expand his operation and make some money but by an industry undergoing a profound metamorphosis.

6

The Battle in Ripley Township

"Rural communities in Minnesota and the rest of the nation are changing. This guidebook is designed to provide insight and assistance for local governments and communities in addressing controversies caused by rural economic development. It is particularly focused on the influence of activist groups who may have a much different view of what is in the best interest of each individual community."—MINNESOTA FARM BUREAU FOUNDATION, "When an Activist Group Comes to Town"

By the time the feedlot battles hit hard in Dodge County, it felt as if the industrial machine was intent on completely saturating Minnesotan farm country. In his book *The Meat Racket*, Christopher Leonard referred to this period in the hog industry as "the great chickenization," when genetic technologies and processing speeds enabled hog producers to adopt the vertical integration model that Tyson Foods had perfected decades earlier in the chicken industry.[1] In part because the pork meat-packers worked from an existing model, the change happened quickly, in about a decade.

Meat-packers became dependent on nonstop deliveries from CAFOS to feed the system—and their profits—without pause. Pressure to keep operations running at full capacity intensified. We saw during the early days of the COVID-19 pandemic in 2020 what happens when factories within this highly concentrated supply chain shut down, even for a day.

Leonard argued that by 2011, "meat companies like Tyson controlled the market for hogs," which now lived primarily in expensive confinement operations housing thousands of animals. "Modern hog barns had to be filled," he wrote, "almost regardless of the price hogs commanded on the open market. The scale of the industry demanded it . . . the industrial machine couldn't be slowed down."[2]

When rural residents, as in Berne, pushed back against the negative community impacts associated with rapid industrialization, the meat-packers immediately understood this as an existential threat. They mounted a counteroffensive, from engaging lobbyists in Washington DC to having industry-backed attorneys appear on demand in county courtrooms. This fight even made its way into little Ripley Township in southern Dodge County, where citizens discovered that the local mechanisms of democracy and governance were soft targets for the deep pockets of the meat-packers and other industry giants.

Creating a "Farm-Friendly" Environment in Your County and Township

In 2003, one year into the legal drama in Berne, the Minnesota Farm Bureau Foundation published a pamphlet titled "When an Activist Group Comes to Town: Protecting Your Community from Unwanted Division."[3] The surprisingly detailed guide purports to offer advice to "local governments and communities in addressing controversies caused by rural economic development." In reality, the publication addresses only one type of rural economic development—industrial-size animal feedlots. The guide's release was in response to the lawsuit in Berne and the other contemporaneous citizen's lawsuit unfolding in Ripley Township.

"When An Activist Group Comes to Town" encourages readers to "work to create a 'farm-friendly' environment in your county and township." More specifically, it instructs them to "vote for and support pro-agriculture candidates for county commissioner and township officer. Actively recruit farmers to serve as elected officials, and don't be afraid to take your turn serving as a township supervisor. Work with your farm groups to educate local elected officials about modern agriculture. Make sure farmers are represented in land use planning discussions in your county. . . . Be there to support other farmers in your community if they apply for a permit for a new or expanded facility."[4]

It appeared that Dodge County officials were astute pupils of these battle tactics encouraged by the Farm Bureau. They stacked the local planning commission, the feedlot advisory board, and other public offices with Big Ag advocates, as the guide suggested. This effort began conspicuously during the Berne lawsuit and has continued ever since.

A 2017 article in Minneapolis's *Star Tribune* about area hog wars characterized Dodge County as "an intensely agricultural county where many farmers and livestock operators also serve as elected officials."[5]

"When an Activist Group Comes to Town" characterized those who oppose factory farms as "activists" and "outside special interests." This wording was an unsubtle reference to the Land Stewardship Project (LSP), a Minnesota nonprofit that works with communities to promote sustainable agriculture. The group was founded in the early 1980s, and over the years it became increasingly involved with legal battles over CAFOS in Minnesota as residents in rural communities faced off against industry lobbyists and attorneys.

In 1997, when the CAFO wars were just getting started, the LSP published "When a Factory Farm Comes to Town: Protecting Your Township from Unwanted Development." This guide, which has been updated and still exists today, provides a number of resources and guidance to townships on how to use municipal land use laws to fight against factory farm development.[6]

The Minnesota Farm Bureau Foundation's 2003 counter-publication, "When an Activist Group Comes to Town," cast Minnesota-based, grassroots nonprofits such as the Land Stewardship Project as outside interests. That description was quite a stretch, not to mention ironic. The Minnesota Farm Bureau Foundation relies on donations from bona fide outside interests, including the multinational meatpacking conglomerate Hormel Foods, Compeer Financial, Farm Bureau Financial Services, Farm Credit System, and other multibillion-dollar entities with a direct financial stake in the "rural land use" matters that the guide discusses.

In Minnesota, county boards not only approve factory farm permits but also have the power to create land use and zoning ordinances that promote or, alternatively, limit other types of development. Another pro tip highlighted in "When an Activist Group Comes to Town" involved these zoning ordinances. The guide asks its readers to "sponsor or seek out training for elected officials and local leaders" on "feedlot rules, current research and technology related to manure and odor management, and zoning and land use policies."[7] Lo and behold, as the Berne Area Alliance's lawsuit made its way through the courts, Dodge

County officials proceeded to amend the county's zoning and feedlot ordinances to better accommodate industrial-size feedlots.

In late 2003, rather than respond to a citizen's petition for a moratorium on large feedlots, the county board did the opposite: it placed a moratorium on the construction of homes—"non-farm dwellings"—in Dodge County's agricultural district. During a planning commission meeting, the county's planning director referenced "manure acres" as "a new issue we hadn't dealt with in the past" and explained that "long term, we need to address compatibility of the farm community with impacts of non-farm dwellings."[8]

In this statement, the term "farm community" really referred to CAFO operators; it was the CAFO operators who were concerned about "non-farm" homes in the agricultural district, not the independent farmers, many of whom opposed unconstrained factory farm development. "Manure acres" referred to the large number of acres required to safely spread—or attempt to "safely" spread—the millions of gallons of manure produced within the CAFOs.

In other words, it was becoming evident that factory farms were rendering the ag district unlivable. Rather than explore Big Ag reforms and land use policies to better protect individuals and families living in the area, county officials amended existing ordinances and turned rural areas into a paradise for large corporate interests by seeking to limit residential development while stripping protections from those already living in the ag district.

During a December 2003 planning commission meeting, yet another factory farm operator serving on the commission advocated for changing the county's zoning ordinance, specifically as it applied to the acreage required for "farm dwellings" and "non-farm dwellings," and to manage the "proliferation of rural housing in the agricultural district." In April 2004, the commission called a special meeting to address these proposed amendments to the Dodge County Zoning Ordinance. At the contentious, four-hour meeting, residents debated the definition of "a farm" and the intended usages of agricultural land.[9]

Failing to hear the pleas of hundreds of residents, the planning commission ultimately recommended changing the requirements for a dwelling in the ag district from a minimum of thirty-five acres to one requiring fifty-three acres. While constructing a home or dwelling on fewer than fifty-three acres was still possible, the change created significant hurdles. Meanwhile, factory farms had no minimum acreage requirements. With the stroke of a pen, the county commissioners cleared the way for uncontrolled industrial-size feedlot development while limiting opportunities for nettlesome people to be living nearby. As for the folks already living in the ag district—many, including my family, having lived there for generations—the message was that we should deal with the air and water contamination without complaint.

Such amendments to county-level zoning ordinances were becoming a tool of choice for Big Ag advocates in farm country in the Midwest. These changes became an effective means to limit community resistance in the longer term.

In the fall of 2002, citizens in southern Dodge learned about Ripley Dairy, a limited liability partnership with a New York City–based developer seeking to construct a dairy operation housing 2,115 dairy cows and 195 calves, adding up to three thousand animal units. The proposed industrial complex was sited only a few miles north of the Trom farm. It was the largest feedlot size allowed by local ordinance and the largest proposed dairy operation in the state of Minnesota at the time. Ripley Dairy would include an earthen basin the size of seven football fields and eighteen feet deep to hold thirty-nine million gallons of liquid manure, which would pose major environmental threats to the surrounding community.[10]

Local citizens who were inattentive during the approval and installation of the initial wave of area factory farms now were determined to have their voices heard. As in Berne, a citizen's resistance group known as Citizens for a Healthy Dodge County sprung up quickly and held its initial meetings in a resident's home. The first order of business was to circulate to the residents of Ripley Township—the township in Dodge where the proposed dairy would be located—a petition that asked the township to adopt a temporary moratorium on new feedlot development, thus providing the township time to draft and vote on new local planning and zoning to limit the proliferation of CAFOs.

The vast majority of Ripley Township residents signed the petition in favor of a moratorium. But at the next township meeting, township officers—some of whom were known industry advocates—announced they had lost the petition. (My brother Brad, a Ripley Township resident at the time, maintains to this day that he knows where this petition landed when the township officers saw it: "In the garbage—file 13.") The citizens' group had to start over and obtain signatures. Again, the majority of township residents signed and supported the petition.

In Minnesota, townships can adopt their own local planning and zoning, including ordinances that are more restrictive concerning industrialized animal feedlots than the county's zoning ordinance. This remains one of the few remaining avenues under Minnesota law for resisting uncontrolled factory farm development. It also contrasts with neighboring Iowa and Illinois, where Big Ag advocates created a number of state-level permitting regulations and loopholes that effectively eliminated township and local control over factory farm development.

In the Hawkeye State, for example, cities can impose zoning restrictions as far as two miles outside their boundaries on virtually every type of development save for CAFO development. Gene Tinker, Iowa's former coordinator of state feedlot operations, said in 2020 that Big Ag groups have a "stranglehold" on the state legislature, making it impossible to pass commonsense CAFO regulations.[11]

In Illinois, the infamous Illinois Livestock Management Facilities Act, passed in 1996, placed almost total control of CAFO permitting with the state's Agriculture Department, while Illinois zoning laws prohibit local county boards from issuing agricultural zoning restrictions. A legal analysis of CAFO permitting in Illinois concluded that while county boards can make recommendations to the state, ultimately "the CAFO decision is completely removed from local counties."[12] County residents have little ability to control development in their own backyard. A 2016 *Chicago Tribune* investigation of Big Pork's abuses in Illinois characterized the Livestock Act's few provisions for CAFO oversight and environmental accountability as akin to "a frontier-era timber blockade in the path of a bullet train."[13]

Minnesotans in counties across the state have rallied together and used the privilege of local governance to create at least a baseline of oversight over CAFO development. Yet the dominance of Big Ag proponents in county-level politics, paired with state-level regulatory loopholes and noncompliance, makes the task feel Sisyphean. Interestingly, in states such as Minnesota with more local control over CAFO permitting, Big Ag has stacked local governance, while in states such as Iowa with more state control, Big Ag has stacked state governance. It's all very Machiavellian.

In Ripley Township, residents partnered with the aforementioned Land Stewardship Project, the Minnesota nonprofit that has been instrumental in organizing and assisting local communities across the state in resisting CAFO developments such as the Ripley Dairy. (While the Battle for Berne took place during the same period, Berne Area Alliance members worked independently, largely disconnected from the battle occurring on the south end of the county.) Dodge County officials were keenly aware of the resistance in Ripley, as residents staged protests, published editorials in local papers, and packed public hearings.[14]

One prominent community leader, whom I will call "Sarah," wrote an op-ed in a Minnesota newspaper opposing the dairy. She was taken aback and traumatized by the subsequent pushback from those who hoped to profit from the large operation. Even twenty years later, Sarah asked me to use a pseudonym for fear of industry retaliation.

Within days of the op-ed's publication, the dairy's New York–based project developer called Sarah and asked her to refrain from making public comments against the dairy.[15] It was a contentious conversation. The developer initially seemed to believe that Sarah had a financial stake in preventing the development. "What is your investment?" he asked. She replied that her investment was clean air, clean water, and a thriving community in Dodge County, where her family had lived for many generations. "Oh, so you don't have an investment," he responded. Sarah recalls that at this point, he became indignant and unbelieving.

"He was angry that citizens dared oppose what he wanted," she said. Soon after that call, a pro-industry group published a countering op-ed in the same newspaper, calling her out by name. Sarah feared for her safety and began to drive carefully through the county, vigilant for vehicles that might try to drive her off the road.

Her fears were real. As she looked out the window of her home one morning, Sarah noticed a pickup truck sitting outside and immediately recognized the vehicle. She had seen it parked outside several meetings regarding the proposed dairy CAFO. A large business logo on the doors confirmed her suspicions. For hours, the industry advocate sat outside Sarah's home. She interpreted this being watched as an intimidation tactic to signal that the offended parties knew where she lived.

The intensity of industry interest over Ripley Dairy became most evident during a township meeting on October 6, 2003, a notorious gathering that many attendees can recall clearly to this day.[16] The change in the meeting's location was the first red flag. Township meetings were typically held at Ripley Town Hall, a small venue originally serving as a one-room school for local children. The meeting's location changed multiple times and ultimately took place in the Claremont High School gymnasium.

When township residents walked into the gymnasium, they were shocked to discover that nearly two hundred factory farm proponents had descended from all over the county, the state, and even the country. In attendance were representatives from Land O'Lakes, Hormel, Cargill, and AgStar Financial Services (a factory farm lender). According to one person in attendance, also present were "no less than five Monsanto representatives, including one who came all the way from corporate headquarters in St Louis, MO."[17]

Factory farm proponents arrived from around the nation, all for a local meeting concerning a township with 109 registered voters, 75 percent of whom had already signed a petition in favor of adopting local planning and zoning, the subject of the meeting.[18] It should have been an easy township-level decision. But Ripley residents were discovering that their desire to prevent one of the largest manure cesspools in the United States from overtaking its backyard was a threat to the profit models of some very large companies. Adam Warthesen, then the policy organizer at the Land Stewardship Project, wrote at the time, "Factory farming's supporters feel that if they can slam dunk local control in Ripley Township, the door will be opened wide for CAFOS throughout the state."[19] (As of this writing, Warthesen is the director of government and industry affairs at Organic Valley.)

My brother Brad, who was in attendance, recalls that township residents were frightened and alarmed. They had to lean against the wall and sit on the floor of the gym as lenders, bankers, and representatives of major corporations had taken the available seats. What followed was a three-hour marathon of pressure tactics. An out-of-state commodity broker "facilitated" a choreographed question-and-answer session. Pro-industry visitors recited prepared presentations while the previously submitted written questions from township residents were ignored. After the meeting, a Dodge County resident was verbally accosted, and another person who had helped organize the citizen's petition for a feedlot moratorium was pushed from behind.[20]

That night it became abundantly clear that Big Ag proponents in Dodge County were networked with the national lobbying infrastructure and using the playbook from "When An Activist Group Comes to Town." Feedlot owners and industry advocates had quietly assumed key positions in local governance during the several years prior, and residents were not aware of their intentions until the consequences became known. The residents' only option was to beat the industry at its own game. Township residents just had to wait for election day.

In the 2004 and 2005 township elections, the residents voted out those officers who were known Big Ag patsies. The newly constituted town board approved an interim moratorium in March 2005 that temporarily halted construction of feedlots with more than a thousand animal units.[21] With Ripley Dairy on hold and the threat temporarily held at bay, the township began to work on a comprehensive land use ordinance.

In response, Ripley Dairy hired a top industry attorney and filed a lawsuit against the township, challenging the interim moratorium.[22]

(The dairy's attorney at that time, Gary Koch, serves as the vice president and general counsel at Christensen Farms, one of the largest hog integrators in the Midwest.) As that lawsuit advanced, Dodge County officials moved forward with the process to grant the CUP, ignoring the township's moratorium, which took legal precedence over the county's zoning laws. During a public hearing, a Dodge County citizen living near the proposed development testified that the developers had tried to buy him off, and he wasn't the only resident who testified about bribery and other forms of coercion.[23]

In a move that did not surprise anyone who was paying attention, the Dodge County Board of Commissioners approved the CUP for Ripley Dairy in open defiance of the township's moratorium.

In December 2005 township officials took another step toward independence from the county by adopting the Ripley Township Land Use Ordinance "for the purpose of promoting the health, safety and public welfare."[24] The new ordinance prohibited new or expanded feedlots with a capacity greater than 1,500 animal units and prohibited open lagoons or storage structures for liquid manure from more than 500 animal units.

Yet the Ripley Dairy project developers continued to press forward, filing a new lawsuit against the township to challenge its zoning ordinance. In a parallel effort—perhaps anticipating they would lose the lawsuit—the developers quietly worked with officials in the neighboring city of Claremont, located outside of Ripley Township a few miles north of the project site.[25] Using a questionable tactic, officials sought to annex the dairy site into the city and circumvent the township's zoning ordinance with a "string and balloon" maneuver, with a bordering county road being the string and the 120-acre project site being the balloon. "More like a herd of cows on a string," a local journalist wrote.[26]

The audacious scheme drew widespread criticism, even from the Minnesota Association of Townships, which was typically sympathetic to factory farm development. One member of the Claremont City Council said the annexation attempt "divided the town" and "turned neighbor against neighbor."[27] ("Neighbor against neighbor"—I hear this refrain so very often in reference to the local divisions that unwanted feedlot development causes.)

The following year, in 2006, the project developer's lawsuit failed. A county judge ruled in favor of the township and denied Ripley Dairy's attempt to override the local ordinance.[28] Facing that loss and continued public outrage over the shady annexation plot, the developers announced their withdrawal of the plan.[29] The citizens of Ripley Township had caused too much trouble for the developers; lawsuits are expensive. They decided to take their business elsewhere, no doubt causing problems for the unsuspecting residents of some other remote rural district.[30]

It was a dramatic win and a true David and Goliath story. Yet even as citizens rejoiced, Big Ag was taking notes, learning how to prevail over local efforts to hold the industry at bay.

During the four-year legal battle over Ripley Dairy, members of the Citizens for a Healthy Dodge County came to understand that a protracted war was taking place in American farm country, and rural residents were the reluctant conscripts. Those who rose up against the corporate takeover of rural farm country found themselves using analogies of war to describe what was taking place: "The battle was lost, but the war continues." And so on. Having read hundreds of articles in local papers about disputes over feedlots, I came upon this language time and again. It is no accident. Residents feel as if they're under siege, battling a relentless, well-financed corporate army.

It's a war of attrition. Most of the time, people give up after losing their county's feedlot battle. Who can blame them? These factory farm fights are exhausting. Most of the folks who were involved in the days of the Ripley and Berne fights are no longer active; instead, they've been replaced by new constituents protesting new developments. The fight sometimes feels akin to running on a treadmill—that is, going nowhere. Yet slowly but surely, rural America has seen a movement arise, one that advocates for sustainable agriculture and independent farming to overcome corporate greed and degradation. (Chapters 14, 19, and 20 review where this movement stands today.)

In southern Minnesota, the battle over Ripley Dairy gave many residents their first taste of this emerging rural activism. One of my fondest stories of this period took place on August 11, 2004, when the Land Stewardship Project joined with the Citizens for a Healthy Dodge County to organize a protest on the county road bordering the Trom family farm.[31] Local citizens learned that the Minnesota AgriGrowth Council, a pro-industry group, had planned a bus tour of the area. Its first stop was the Hormel Foods meatpacking plant in Austin, twenty-three miles south of our farm; the second stop was the proposed site of Ripley Dairy, three miles north of our farm.

This route would take the tour bus right past our farm. That morning, neighbors and friends assembled in the Trom barn and went to work at long tables piled with tagboard and magic markers. A large homemade sign declared "GET OUT OF DODGE!" And soon printed signs emblazoned with "NO FACTORY FARMS!" in bright yellow letters against a bold, black background were strategically placed every hundred feet or so along the Claremont Road. Local citizens then assembled on the Claremont Road, eagerly anticipating the arrival of the bus. My father drove one of his John Deere tractors along the drainage ditch and parked it near the bridge where citizens first expected to see the approaching Greyhound.

Eventually, the expected bus appeared, and residents watched in satisfaction as the riders silently took note of the handmade signs. One read "WE WANT CLEAN AIR, CLEAN WATER, STRONG COMMUNITY." Nearly twenty years after this early Dodge County protest, protecting these rights remains the movement's goal, and we have no intention of retreating.

Whose Land Is It Anyway?

In response to the dual lawsuits and citizen's protests in Berne and Ripley, Dodge County officials became part of a nationwide, industry-led effort to create CAFO-friendly zoning ordinances at the local level. As mentioned previously, Dodge County amended its zoning ordinance in 2004 and 2005 to hamper residential development in the countryside as part of a larger effort to redefine the purpose of agricultural land in Dodge County and to streamline the installation of industrial animal operations to the exclusion of other types of development and rural living.

The capstone of that endeavor was an amended agricultural covenant, titled "The Agricultural Use Covenant and Official Notice to Landowners in the Agricultural Zoning District," first placed within the zoning ordinance in 2005. The covenant effectively redefined who, or what, was entitled to possess land in the agricultural district. It is analogous to the covenants once widely used to keep certain ethnic groups out of specific neighborhoods.

It's worthwhile to take a close look at the agricultural use covenant. The covenant stipulates:

> The County will view the agricultural district as a zone in which land is used for commercial agricultural production. Owners, residents, and other users of property in this zone or neighboring properties may be subjected to inconvenience or discomfort arising from normal and accepted agricultural practices and operations, including but not limited to noise, odors, dust, operation of machinery of any kind including aircraft, flying debris, the storage and disposal of manure, and the application of fertilizers, soil amendments, herbicides, and pesticides. Owners, residents, and users of this property or neighboring property should be prepared to accept such inconveniences or discomfort from normal agricultural operations, and are hereby put on official notice that this declaration may prevent them from obtaining a legal judgment against such normal agricultural operations. When an owner of land in an agricultural district has received a permit for purposes of an agricultural use on his or her property . . . then such use is a part of *normal and accepted agricultural practices* [emphasis mine] and operations in Dodge County, Minnesota.[32]

The covenant's intent is clear: it redefines land in the agricultural district as intended for "commercial" production, implicitly excluding traditional farming practices and placing the industry in a power position.

The covenant essentially limits the ability of neighboring rural families to bring a nuisance action against the factory farms next door.

"Normal and accepted agricultural practices" is an Orwellian phrase that the industry often uses to normalize problematic industry practices. Its position is that unlivable odors, rampant waste, and unending pollution are the realities of modern agriculture, and rural residents must simply accept them. This wording worked successfully during earlier nuisance lawsuits, and the industry ran with it.

The updated zoning ordinance also formally redefined Dodge's agricultural district, stating the purpose of the agricultural district is to "retain, conserve, and enhance agricultural land in the County and *to protect this land from scattered residential development* [emphasis mine]."[33]

The corporate-friendly zoning ordinance squanders the dream of living in the country for future generations while limiting the county's ability to bring in other forms of economic development. The impact of the ordinance continues to be a live issue in Dodge County today. Some residents owning land in the ag district have been unable to develop their own property as desired. Dodge County native Darin Johnson, for example, sought to develop his family's wooded acreage for residential use and the opportunity for others to enjoy the peace and tranquility of the countryside. He views it as inevitable that this eastern portion of Dodge will need to support residential growth given its vicinity to Rochester and its Mayo Clinic facilities.

Johnson's township approved his proposal, yet he was told, "Good luck with the county." As feared, the proposal hit a blockade before it even reached the planning commission. A commission member, as well as the planning and zoning director, told Johnson not even to bother submitting his proposal. "I'm caught in the middle of it," Johnson recently said. "Land use rules designed to help corporate agriculture and a multi-billion-dollar initiative [referring to a new Mayo development] designed to encourage economic development."[34]

Johnson's dilemma is emblematic of the larger problem posed by factory farm–friendly and pro-corporate zoning rules in ag districts across rural America. When Big Ag proponents reserve land for their own purposes, they're cutting off other types of development and stifling social and economic growth, vitality, and heterogeneity in the very areas that need it the most.

Such changes to county-level zoning ordinances have worked in lockstep with state and federal policies to benefit corporate agriculture. Amendments to preexisting state-level right-to-farm laws, for example, are used as blunt tools to further protect industrial ag operations from nuisance lawsuits over odor, health impacts, pollution, and other matters. A 2006 article in the *Drake Journal of Agricultural Law* analyzed the expansion of legal protections to feedlot operators in several midwestern states. The author, law professor Terence J. Centner, explored the complex and competing interests between agricultural investments and other community interests, recognizing that right-to-farm laws can be reasonable avenues for balancing "competing rights." Yet Centner noted that the more recent exceptions "that offer protection for new nuisance activities are not so benign. Their favoritism of agriculture comes at the expense of neighboring property owners . . . and may infringe upon constitutional rights."[35]

In 2005, the year that Dodge amended its zoning ordinance, another matter came before the planning commission—a zoning amendment to permit "churches, chapels, temples and synagogues" to be built in the ag district under a conditional use permit, following a local family's request to hold weddings on their rural property. Then commission member Rhonda Toquam—owner of two CAFOs in Dodge—objected to the proposal and asked the commission "how that would affect the farmer's rights to spread manure and other common farming practices."[36] The commission put forth a motion to oppose the proposed ordinance change.

The motion passed unanimously.

PART 2
The Lawsuit

To begin by bluster, but afterwards
to take fright at the enemy's numbers,
shows a supreme lack of intelligence.
—SUN TZU, *The Art of War*

7

The Economics of the Great Pig Explosion

"It is critical that, as a livestock producer, you are able to clearly communicate how your livestock production facility will address the following legitimate concerns: offensive odor, air pollution, ground and surface water contamination, forcing small producers out of business, and decreasing value of neighboring properties. It might be wise to do some research on other livestock facilities in your area to find out what has happened to nearby property values."—MINNESOTA FARM BUREAU FOUNDATION, "When an Activist Group Comes to Town"

By 2006 the corporate campaign to saturate Dodge County with industrialized farms had overcome early hurdles. Lights that had flashed yellow for several years turned green. The gestational facility that citizens in Berne had resisted was up and running. The county's zoning ordinance favored industrialized operations and disfavored small farms and residential development. The newly amended agricultural covenant was a thrown gauntlet, a declaration from factory farmers holding public office in Dodge that the countryside belonged to Big Ag.

With the zoning ordinance now customized for industrialized hog barns, the proliferation of such barns was immediate. The pig explosion had begun. Like a fire upon the scorched earth, county officials approved factory farms with swift assiduity. Perhaps they feared their dominance within local politics was temporary (it wasn't). Approving new concentrated animal feeding operations (CAFOs) rapidly was one way to prevent townships from adopting local planning and zoning, as had been done successfully in Ripley Township.

Under Minnesota law, specified counties, known as delegated counties, possess the authority to implement animal feedlot programs and issue permits for feedlots of less than a thousand animal units, which are exempt from environmental review.[1] The delegated county program was created by the Minnesota Pollution Control Agency, which was originally intended to promote community involvement and oversight.[2] Each county's feedlot officer takes the lead on permitting and monitoring livestock facilities on behalf of the MPCA. Paved with good intentions and respect for local governance, the program handed foxes control of the hog house.

I believe that the Farm Bureau network in Minnesota saw delegated counties as another means to achieve an end. With the network's guidance, industry promoters and insiders joined township boards, planning commissions, and county seats. The MPCA has shown little interest in exercising more authority over the local feedlot permitting and inspection process despite the cronyism that has evolved in local governance.

Beginning in 2006, factory farmers and industry sympathizers serving on the Dodge County Planning Commission boldly abused Dodge's delegated county status (the county has since left the program) and recommended approval of several CAFOS with capacities a hair less than a thousand animal units. Then the Dodge County Board, cleverly sidestepping environmental review and other oversight, promptly rubber-stamped them.

> March 2006: The commission recommended approval of a conditional use permit for a hog feedlot, capacity 960 AUS (or 2,400 hogs).[3]
> April 2006: The commission recommended approval of a CUP for a hog feedlot, capacity 960 AUS.[4]
> May 2006, part 1: The commission recommended approval of a CUP to expand an existing confinement, increasing total capacity to 960 AUS.[5]
> May 2006, part 2: The commission recommended approval of a CUP to expand an existing feedlot by building a second barn, increasing capacity to—you guessed it—960 AUS.[6]
> May 2006, part 3: The commission recommended approval of two new hog barns, with a total capacity of 960 AUS.[7]

Three new 960-AU-capacity feedlots were all recommended at the same meeting in May 2006! And so it went for several years, as the industry-stacked planning commission took advantage of new rules and barebones regulations. Community members attempted to resist several of these new feedlots, but after the defeat in Berne, many in Dodge County were simply worn out, and many of the independent farmers who might have led a resistance had already left farming.

That the county didn't intend to fully adhere to the lax rules that *did* exist soon became clear. The commissioners began expeditiously approving substantial expansions to existing feedlots, converting many of the area's small CAFOs into large CAFOs. Apparently by expanding feedlots that previously came in under the thousand-AU threshold, some of these feedlots continued to be treated as smaller CAFOs, which were not required to seek more extensive review under the MPCA and the National Pollutant Discharge Elimination System (NPDES) permitting program.

Regulations regarding manure management and dead hog disposal were likewise often elided or glossed over, though officials sometimes made vague assurances. In April 2008, for example, the commission recommended approval to expand a feedlot to 3,750 head of finishing hogs, or 1,500 animal units.[8] One of the planning commission members—himself a swine factory farm operator—expressed concern about the existing incinerator's ability to handle the increased volume of pig mortalities. The issue, though raised, wasn't addressed, and there wasn't much discussion regarding manure disposal from the 3,750 hogs on the tiny five-acre site.

Dead hog disposal, incidentally, is no small matter. These operations create extremely localized concentrations of dead animals, not only because each CAFO contains so many animals in the first place but also because CAFO-raised hogs are more likely to kill each other or die of disease than animals raised outdoors. Feedlot operators are required to follow rules for dead animal disposal, but as with other factory farm regulations, inspections are minimal, and the rules aren't generally enforced. The so-called dead boxes containing dead pigs attract flies and vultures, and composted bodies, incinerated bodies, and buried bodies all pose additional environmental risks, including contamination of the groundwater with antibiotics and hormones.

In August 2008 a CUP application that looked all too familiar came before the planning commission. Derek Finstuen, the son of Mark Finstuen, proposed a 960-AU swine feeder facility on sensitive karst topography in Berne. As reported in chapter 5, Mark Finstuen built a 960-AU swine gestational facility in Berne despite the community's protracted efforts to stop it. Within a few years of this feedlot's completion, area residents, who were already suffering from health problems, detected nitrate levels beyond drinking standards in area wells.

During the public hearing over the proposed new facility, several former members of the Berne Area Alliance shared their concerns. In response, Dodge County zoning administrator Melissa DeVetter stated, "There is nothing in the county ordinance or state rules that would prohibit construction in karst area."[9] And she was exactly correct. Feedlot rules at the state and county levels are designed to facilitate the expansion and maintenance of corporate agriculture while providing insufficient protections for community health.

The pig explosion continued throughout the county, and by 2013 ten swine factory farms were located within a three-mile radius of my family's farm. My family fought back when the eleventh was proposed (see chapter 8).

Corporate Consolidation and the Decline of Rural America

The proliferation of industrialized livestock operations wasn't happening only in Dodge County. It hugely impacted rural farm communities in several states during the first decades of the twenty-first century. The raw data tells the story well.

The EPA estimates there were more than 17,000 large CAFOs (buildings holding more than a thousand AUs) in 2012 compared to 6,600 in 1995.[10] That's nearly a threefold increase in less than seventeen years. Looking at hogs specifically, the data coming from Iowa, the top hog-producing state, is alarming: CAFOs increased fivefold between 1990 and 2019, with 94 percent of this growth attributable to hog barns.[11]

The straight line between this corporate consolidation and the extinction of independent farmers is easy to follow. Since the mid-1990s, 70 percent of hog farmers have gone out of business.[12] The meatpacking conglomerates seized near-total market control, while their loyal contract farmers have captured an ever-dwindling proportion of profits. In the mid-1980s, thirty-seven cents of every dollar that Americans spent on food went back to farmers, but by 2019 that had decreased to fifteen cents of every dollar.[13] More than half of all farmers have lost money *every year* since 2013.[14]

Meanwhile, the corporate meat-packers enjoy profits of a previously unimagined scale. Smithfield Foods saw sales increase tenfold between 1990 and 2005 thanks largely to its corporate strategy of buying up competitors and then maneuvering to fix prices and cut off access to a competitive marketplace.[15] In 2013, in what was the largest-ever Chinese acquisition of a U.S. company, the Chinese company WH Group gained control of Smithfield.

Looking at the bigger picture, consolidation is the norm across major agricultural commodity groups. Dairy, soybean seed, and corn seed are other commodities that swiftly consolidated during a similar time frame. Between the years 2005 and 2010, eighty thousand independent farms in the United States disappeared. Then between 2011 and 2018, an additional hundred thousand farms in the United States were lost. In 2019 a feature article in *Time* about that year's farm bankruptcy crisis put forth a chilling proposition: "Farmers have always talked of looming disaster, but the duration and severity of the current crisis suggests an alarming and once unthinkable possibility—that independent farming is no longer a viable livelihood."[16]

What's so worrying about today's corporate ag economy is that as profits soar and corporations boast to shareholders about outputs and efficiencies, the entire system is a house of cards. The droughts and severe weather associated with climate change have pummeled crops. Trade wars and unstable commodity prices continually stress the system. Thanks to short-sighted federal policies promulgated under pressure from Big Ag corporations, large farmers rely heavily on subsidies. During the agriculture crisis that former president Donald Trump's trade wars played a role in triggering, $16 billion in aid went to farmers, and 40 percent of farm income in 2018 derived from federal aid and insurance.[17]

Farm subsidies have always been an important governmental tool for protecting producers and consumers from the inherent unpredictability of seasonal yields. Yet when subsidies are overused and funneled primarily to the wealthiest farm operations, the result is a highly unstable, top-heavy system that has no incentive to solve the pressing problems—such as climate change—that cause low and unpredictable yields.

As small farmers left the industry en masse, what has been the impact on rural communities and economies? One of the best efforts to probe this issue is Food & Water Watch's 2022 study of counties in Iowa, mentioned in chapter 1, that compares rural counties with high CAFO density to rural counties with both low CAFO density and more small farmers. The results show that between 1982 and 2017, personal income rose significantly in Iowa; even in the average rural county, income rose 41 percent. But in the top hog-producing counties, personal income fell by 8 percent. The report also found that while retail businesses in Iowa declined by a modest average of 2 percent across the state, counties with the highest CAFO concentration saw a decline of 33 percent.

Meanwhile, the study found that small, independent farms have the opposite impact: counties in Iowa with the highest proportion of small farmers actually experienced retail business growth, beating the state average.[18] (The economic vitality of small farms reminds me that hogs used to be called "mortgage lifters" because raising a small number of hogs on a diversified farming operation brought in some extra cash.)

CAFO approval in Iowa is all but assured by a combination of lax regulatory procedures, county-level industry infiltration, and state and national lobbying efforts. In this system, 97 percent of requested CAFO permits in Iowa are approved.[19] This overt friendliness to CAFOS is a main reason why Iowa produces more pork than any other state, surpassing Minnesota and North Carolina, which both have more regulations on the books.[20] That's good for the meatpacking conglomerates but bad for the people of Iowa. In 2019 a senior official at the Iowa Farm Bureau predicted to ag journalist Austin Frerick that "most rural communities will soon disappear." Frerick observed that the official seemed "accepting of this fate, even a bit happy about it."[21]

CAFO proliferation has disproportionally impacted communities of color and marginalized communities. African American, Hispanic, and Native American people are significantly more likely to live within three miles of a hog CAFO in North Carolina—a pattern that likely exists in other states as well. Writing for the *Sustainable Development Law and Policy* journal, attorney Christine Ball-Blakely showed that communities lacking political power, resources, and education are targeted as sites for CAFO development. Targeted communities "lack the resources to leave compromised areas, where they are trapped by decreasing property values and a plummeting quality of life," Ball-Blakely wrote.[22]

A CAFO's impact on property values depends on the size of the CAFO and whether the impacted property is downwind or upwind from the operation. The larger trend, however, is clear: factory farms cause surrounding property values to decline. A 2015 analysis of appraisal values estimated that properties within three miles of a CAFO lose 26 percent of their assessed value, and properties that are very close to a CAFO— within a quarter mile—lose as much as 88 percent of their value.[23]

This impact has a devastating ripple effect in rural communities, where many farm families are asset rich but income poor. The notion of losing a home's value is so frightening that families are forced to choose between taking a "wait and see" approach or being proactive by selling their properties and moving away before a CAFO goes up. I've seen this happen time and again.

I'm reminded of a small farmer and self-employed business owner in Goodhue County, Minnesota, whom I will call "Jack." I've contacted Jack several times regarding his community's resistance to area factory farms. Jack asked me to use a pseudonym, as he fears retaliation against his family and small business.

In 2015 he and his wife purchased a rural home on a few acres in Goodhue, an ag county adjacent to Dodge. Ten months after moving into the home with their children, they observed a hog CAFO going up nearby. They soon learned that while they were negotiating the purchase of their home, the Big Ag–friendly Goodhue County Planning Commission had approved the adjacent factory farm by a unanimous vote.

Jack also discovered that the previous owners, who had lived there for many years, were aware of the planned development. No law requires sellers to notify potential home buyers that a feedlot has been proposed or approved in the immediate area. The decision to cut and run before a CAFO is built and to not disclose such information—shuffling the property off to unwitting buyers—is yet another aspect of the factory farm takeover that corrodes social and community relationships.

After the facility went up and additional CAFO applications were submitted in Goodhue County, Jack joined with other neighbors to monitor the air quality near the border of the feedlot's property. The results showed concentrations of hydrogen sulfide far above state safety standards in the area near Jack's home. He is concerned for his kids, who frequently play outside.

Jack's family has been living in Goodhue County since the late 1800s. His father owns a small dairy operation nearby, but he's facing the decision to shut down. The operation is now surrounded by CAFOs, and the nitrate levels in his well have steadily increased. Soon he may be unable to give the water to his cattle.

The story of Jack's family is typical. In CAFO country, a small handful of feedlot operators profit, while their operations are under no legal obligation to abstain from rendering neighboring small farms inoperable and neighboring residences unlivable. Reflecting recently on his family's experience, Jack said, "The industry divides communities and divides families."

In general, there is an inverse relationship between industrialized farming and local economic vitality. A 2007 meta-analysis of the community impacts of industrialized agriculture found that among fifty-one studies, 82 percent concluded that the Big Ag model has a negative impact on rural communities across many economic measures, including poverty rates and population growth.[24]

This finding generally holds true in Minnesota. Urban counties in the state are growing, while rural counties' populations are declining.[25]

The majority of counties in the factory farm epicenter of southern Minnesota, along the I-90 corridor, have consistently reported population losses. Martin County in particular is a hotbed of CAFO construction, and its population fell more than 8 percent from 2000 to 2015. Neighboring Renville County suffered a population drop of 13 percent during the same period.[26]

Rural population flight and the poverty left in its wake pose major problems across the United States. In 2017 a widely read and debated *Wall Street Journal* analysis called rural America "the new inner city." The authors wrote, "For more than a century, rural towns sustained themselves, and often thrived, through a mix of agriculture and light manufacturing." Yet with the exodus of farmers and manufacturing jobs, rural America has suffered. The *Journal*'s data showed that rural areas trail urban and suburban areas by virtually every key measure of socioeconomic well-being: poverty, college attainment, death rates, population rates, teen pregnancy rates, and other benchmarks.[27]

The reasons for this are complex and interrelated: artificial intelligence (AI) and other new technologies slowing job growth, globalization, and manufacturing losses. The *Journal* highlighted that wage losses stemming from the 2008 economic downturn continue to impact rural workers disproportionately, while cuts to education and social services budgets during that recession were never regained. But among the many causes, consolidation of the agricultural sector has been significant. While the majority of rural residents are not farmers, farmers are an integral part of healthy communities and economies. Nearly one in five rural counties depends on agriculture as its primary income source. In the *Washington Monthly*, food economies researcher Claire Kelloway wrote, "In traditionally ag-dependent regions, even non-farmers' livelihoods depend, directly or indirectly, on farm income, which is often the only substantial source of incoming wealth."[28]

Assessing the situation from afar, economists are prone to talk about the economies of scale, the ascendency of automation, and the interconnectedness of the global marketplace. Taking a step closer, rural decline is about more than globalization, wages, and income. It's about the loss of community. As rural areas are hollowed out, the things that form the basis of a thriving community—good schools, amicable social relationships, civic participation, job opportunities, and health care—dwindle and diminish. When I think about how that has happened in my own community, I feel those changes are the most destructive and the most challenging to repair.

The Extinction of the Claremont Parrots and the West Concord Cardinals

Just six miles north of our family farm, one comes upon the tiny town of Claremont. Twenty-five years ago, Claremont was a quaint, bustling town with a local economy driven by small family farms. Today Claremont is a visibly degraded corporate outpost supporting area factory farms, largely devoid of local businesses save for the ethanol plant emitting its signature plume. The local high school—once home to the Claremont Parrots and its boisterous team mascot—closed years ago. The president of a major swine factory farm operation purchased the school following its closure and converted it to dormitory-style housing for immigrant laborers working inside the area factory farms.

Despite this influx of factory farm workers (it's rumored that many are undocumented), Claremont suffered a net population decline of nearly 15 percent between 2000 and 2016.[29] Even the mayor's offer of free residential lots has not attracted permanent residents or new businesses to Claremont.[30]

Douglas's hometown, West Concord, is another community in Dodge County that has become a shell of its former self. West Concord once featured a grocery store, a hardware store, two car dealerships, restaurants, a carpentry shop, and several businesses supporting independent farmers: two grain elevators, a cattle broker, and an implement dealer. All are gone. Community members once supported their local high school team, the West Concord Cardinals, but the local schools have all closed. Eventually, they merged with those of the neighboring towns of Claremont and Dodge Center to form the invented community of Triton and the aggregated school district of Triton Public Schools. Its pugnacious name masks the community lacerations from the corporate butcher's knife.

A small town with a sense of humor, West Concord hosts a "Survival Days" festival for three days each summer in a witty nod to the vanishing community. I once pointed out West Concord's population loss to a local Minnesota state senator, who shrugged off my concerns and smugly responded, "It's a good thing I own Hormel stock."

School and business closures are worrying indicators of community decline in rural counties across the United States where factory farm operators have replaced independent farmers. Between 2011 and 2015, around 4,400 schools in rural districts closed, while 4,000 have opened in suburban areas.[31]

While the CAFO-heavy counties undergo population declines, neighboring areas where the animals are slaughtered and packaged undergo population growth and increased poverty. The Family Farm Alliance says that meatpacking has been restructured from a dangerous, blue-collar union job to "an even more precarious working-class, non-union job, often staffed by marginalized female, immigrant, and refugee groups."[32] Beginning in the early 1990s, meatpacking jobs became less desirable as wage growth and rates of unionization fell, and as injuries increased. Slaughterhouse workers suffer twice the rate of injuries and illnesses compared to the manufacturing sector as a whole. The Economic Policy Institute categorizes meat slaughter and processing as "one of the most dangerous and exploitative industries in the country."[33]

In 2012 reporter Christopher Leonard partnered with a data analyst to uncover the local economic impact of Tyson Foods' slaughterhouses and production plants. Leonard called the findings "stark." In rural counties where Tyson plants are the most dominant, per capita income growth lagged significantly behind that of neighboring rural counties and state averages. "The data suggests that Tyson is a suffocating economic force on the communities from which it derives its wealth," Leonard wrote. "Without question, the company provides thousands of jobs and steady paychecks. But its cost-cutting ethos and the lack of competition restrains [sic] income growth in rural America."[34] (While poultry farming isn't my focus, poultry growers as a group are more impoverished and tend to have even less contractual freedoms than growers in other livestock industries do. The poultry industry has also been plagued by racial discrimination, as farmers from Black and other communities have been systemically excluded.)[35]

Today's slaughterhouse workforce comprises a higher percentage of immigrants than ever before,[36] as Big Ag grows its profit margins by underpaying and mistreating its workers. Immigrants—the majority of them undocumented—represent 37 percent of workers in meat processing and at least 20 percent in animal production.[37] (The slaughterhouse workforce is easier to track than the production workforce laboring inside CAFOs. The latter are often in off-the-books relationships with contract growers.)

In his investigation of immigrant slaughterhouse workers, journalist Eric Schlosser concluded that while U.S. Bureau of Labor statistics show that meatpacking is a dangerous job, the reality is even bleaker because injuries and illnesses are systemically underreported. "The meatpacking industry has a well-documented history of discouraging injury reports, falsifying injury data, and putting injured workers back on the job quickly to minimize the reporting of lost work days," Schlosser wrote. While speaking with workers in Nebraska, Colorado, and Texas, he heard many stories of those who were "injured and then discarded by their employers." Meatpacking towns include many residents who are permanently disabled by their years in the industry, left in chronic pain, unable to work, and reliant on public assistance.[38]

In recent years, the influx of migrants at the country's southern border, including migrant children who arrive without their parents, has created a steady workforce for the meat-packers. A devastating 2023 *New York Times* investigation followed a group of migrant children working overnight shifts at a Tyson chicken plant in rural Virginia. Many of the children went straight to school after working a full night shift, and they experienced chronic respiratory problems due to their exposure to fumes and toxins. Injuries were common yet went unreported because both workers and supervisors understood that their relationship was below board.[39] In one case, when a fourteen-year-old night shift worker nearly had his arm torn off by a conveyer belt, the supervisor hung up when the 911 dispatcher asked for the age of the injured worker. (While fourteen-year-olds are generally allowed to work in the United States, night shift work is barred for those younger than sixteen years old.)

Free school lunch eligibility is one of the easiest ways to track local poverty rates. In Minnesota, the list of top ten counties with free and reduced lunch eligibility for schoolchildren is essentially identical to a list of counties dominated either by Native American reservations or meatpacking plants.[40] Number 2 on the list is Nobles County, home to the JBS Foods pork-processing plant; 62 percent of its children are eligible. In Mower County, home to the massive Hormel facility, eligibility has increased to 51 percent. And in Watonwan County, equidistant between the JBS plant and the Hormel plant, 57 percent of students are eligible.[41]

As poverty soars in meatpacking towns and neighboring farming communities, multinational conglomerates continue to rake in record-breaking profits. Profits have remained healthy during today's era of post-COVID price inflation. Prices for meat products produced by the powerful four processors are consistently outpacing inflation rates for other consumer food products. In 2022 JBS Foods' net profit was an all-time record of $4.4 billion, a 70 percent increase over the prior year. Tyson also broke its own record in 2022 with $53 billion in revenue and $4.1 billion in net profit.[42]

In 2021 the White House's briefing room put out a special bulletin underscoring the administration's concerns about the meatpacking oligopoly. Not mincing words, the bulletin noted that gross margins among the top four meat-packers had "skyrocketed" since the COVID pandemic began, and it argued that these companies have "taken advantage of their market power in an uncompetitive market, to the detriment of consumers, farmers and ranchers, and our economy."[43]

In 2021 and 2022 the meat-packers settled a number of price-fixing and antitrust lawsuits, including litigation brought against JBS, Tyson, Cargill, and National Beef by grocery stores and wholesalers accusing the conglomerates of fixing prices by controlling the number of cows entering the marketplace.[44] In September 2022 Smithfield settled a $75 million lawsuit with consumer plaintiffs who argued that the company conspired to inflate pork prices by limiting the supply.[45] These lawsuits attracted rare bipartisan support on Capitol Hill, with lawmakers from both parties concerned about recurring antitrust violations by the meat-packers.

Despite these losses in the courtrooms, the meatpacking monopolists have enjoyed support in the larger regulatory and legal environment for decades. To understand why, it's necessary to go back to the year 2011, when one of the largest efforts to hold the industry accountable failed spectacularly.

8

In the Tank for Big Ag

"In all my years in the pork industry, I have never seen a regulation proposed that would do as much harm to America's pork producers as the GIPSA rule would do. There's no justification for imposing this rule on pork producers."—NEIL DIERKS, National Pork Producers Council CEO, 2010

When President Barack Obama hit the campaign trail during his first run for president in 2008, he won over Iowan voters, in part, by promising to stick up for farmers, saying he would fight the coercive and predatory contracts that were widespread in the livestock industry. His "Real Leadership for Rural America" platform promised to strengthen antitrust laws and "make sure that farm programs are helping family farmers, as opposed to large, vertically integrated corporate agribusiness."[1]

Keeping this promise wouldn't be easy. The meat-packers were accustomed to getting what they wanted.

The Bill Clinton and George W. Bush administrations operated under the philosophy that the major meat-packers and their models of vertical integration were a necessary component of the globalized, high demand meat market. Officials at the Packers and Stockyards Administration (PSA), the unit within the USDA tasked with regulating the meat-packers, had settled into a bureaucratic culture of systemic inaction. In *The Meat Racket*, Leonard describes the PSA at the beginning of the Obama administration as "hobbled by a series of loopholes and oversights that had been layered upon the agency. . . . The guiding doctrine for the previous decade seemed to be to sit on the sidelines and do nothing."[2]

In 2010 Secretary of Agriculture Tom Vilsack came out swinging with a plan to work with the PSA and the U.S. Department of Justice to enforce the antitrust regulations already on the books and to create new rules to address new types of industry abuses. Perhaps most worrying to

Big Ag was a proposed rule change under the Grain Inspection, Packers, and Stockyards Administration (GIPSA), the larger federal department that houses the PSA, that would allow contract growers to sue meatpackers and integrators for unfair, retaliatory, and deceptive practices.

The GIPSA rule was initially viewed as an easy win with bipartisan support. But according to Leonard, who spoke with the key players involved, "By releasing the GIPSA rule, Vilsack kicked into motion one of the better-funded, better-coordinated lobbying machines in Washington." These groups included some of the most powerful lobbying groups you've probably never heard about: the American Farm Bureau Federation, the American Meat Institute, the National Chicken Council, and the National Pork Producers Council (NPPC). Their lobbyists and advocates walked their rounds in Washington, telling congresspeople that regulating Big Ag would kill jobs and harm rural economies.

Their corporate propaganda flew in the face of reality. As noted in chapter 7, a slew of research has documented the negative economic impacts of corporate consolidation in the livestock industry, including a recent report showing that small pig farms "created more than three times as many jobs per 100,000 hogs marketed" as industrialized farms.[3] But when a congressperson representing a rural constituency hears the words "would kill jobs" from a person claiming to represent family farmers, the politician pays attention.

In late 2010 control of the U.S. House shifted from blue to red, and hopes for the GIPSA rule change dimmed. House Republicans were susceptible to the big business message coming from the meat lobby and began passing budget riders that would defang the GIPSA changes even if they went into effect. During the public comment period, the National Chicken Council sent out a memo asking Big Ag executives to recruit contract growers to submit public comments against the rule. "We assume that the above-average or more successful growers will be more likely than others to submit comments against the rule," the memo clarified.[4]

By late 2011, when the GIPSA update was passed as part of a spending bill, the majority of the proposed changes were not present, and the budget increase to allow the PSA to enforce existing regulations was not included. One rule that managed to survive the bill's passage was a provision for chicken contract growers, allowing them to sue over unfair contract practices and giving them other basic protections that are afforded workers in other industries. The meat industry spent the next several years lobbying to prevent the GIPSA rule from being funded or implemented, and in 2017 the USDA withdrew it.

The Obama administration woke up the sleeping giant, and the meat lobby handily won the day.

The defeat of the initially popular GIPSA rule is less surprising in light of the decades-long campaign to deregulate corporations in general and meat-packers in particular. It began during Ronald Reagan's administration, when the Department of Justice shifted its antitrust legal philosophy. While antitrust laws were previously used primarily to promote healthy competition, the new approach used the laws sparingly to increase efficiency and reduce prices for consumers.[5] While this effort saved money for middle-class families on the front end, on the back end it enabled a power shift between independent farmers and large businesses, leading to the multifaceted accumulating costs of increased economic inequality.

The courts sided with the corporations as well. In 1983 the Supreme Court decided in favor of Cargill—at the time, the country's second-largest meat-packer—in antitrust litigation when it sought to purchase Spencer Beef, the third-largest meat-packer at the time. "The decision set a precedent limiting competitors' ability to challenge mergers, and helped catalyze a rapid series of buy-ups across the agriculture industry. . . . With the balance of power upended, the companies were now free to dictate increasingly outrageous terms to the farmers," wrote Lina Khan, chairwoman of the Federal Trade Commission, in 2012.[6]

After years of the industry's exerting its political influence, the Obama administration's policy proposals were a decided shift, as they undertook a major effort to recast federal policy to protect farmers and workers rather than corporations. Many analysts believe that the collapse of these efforts was among the factors leading to hopelessness and anger in rural America and the election of former president

Trump. Small farmers continued to experience high rates of bankruptcy, foreclosures, and poverty, and frustration with global trade deals was arguably at an all-time high during the lead-up to the 2016 presidential election.

While researching for this book, I came across a most astonishing dataset compiled by OpenSecrets.org that is based on information from the Federal Election Commission. In the years 1990 through 2010, political contributions made by the political action committee (PAC) for the National Pork Producers Council, the main lobbyist group representing Big Pork, were fairly evenly divided between Republican and Democratic candidates (though Republicans received more in isolated election cycles). After the GIPSA rule's defeat in 2010, PAC funding from the pork lobby not only significantly increased overall but also favored Republican candidates by large margins in every election. The most pronounced difference was in 2016, when Republican candidates received three times more money from the NPPC than Democratic candidates did.[7]

The congressional maneuverings underpinning the GIPSA rule's defeat demonstrated that Republican lawmakers would reliably and consistently back corporate Big Ag. Ever since, Big Ag continues to place its bets with the Republican Party. Ironically, the more pro-corporation the Republican Party becomes, the more its base seems to believe the opposite. In 2017 a poultry contract grower told ag policy researcher Siena Chrisman that he'd been hopeful during Obama's tenure that the GIPSA reforms would save him from the predatory contract that was pushing him into bankruptcy, but the reforms never materialized. When he voted for Trump in 2016, he believed "the only light at the end of the tunnel was what Donald Trump said—we need to fight for the little man against the corporations."[8]

In 2018 the Trump administration's USDA, under the leadership of Big Ag advocate Sonny Perdue, further watered down the PSA's regulatory powers by eliminating GIPSA as a stand-alone agency altogether and transferred it to the Agricultural Marketing Service (AMS), a Big Ag–friendly outfit. According to a 2020 report from the Organization for Competitive Markets, "Subordinating the Packers and Stockyards

Division to AMS is the death knell for antitrust enforcement in the meatpacking industry."[9]

In 2021 President Joe Biden signed an executive order that encouraged the USDA to revisit PSA reform, including "unfair, discriminatory, and deceptive" practices, and to revive existing antitrust regulations. As of this writing, it's unclear if the USDA has made significant progress on these fronts.[10]

Operating in a political, judicial, regulatory, and legal environment granting them an open playing board, the meatpacking giants get away with practices that would be off the table in other industries. One little-noticed cornerstone of Big Ag's market dominance involves lending practices. The meat-packers have expanded their oligopolies by harnessing the Farm Credit System (FCS), the century-old financial entity that the federal government created to help small farmers. Today, the FCS operates as a major lender and insurer for contract growers, who have enabled the world's largest meat-packers to expand their market dominance.

The Easiest Loans in Town

Congress created the Farm Credit System as part of the Federal Farm Loan Act of 1916 and intended it as a reliable vehicle for small farmers to receive loans to create or expand farming operations. Today, the FCS is administered and regulated by the Farm Credit Administration, a federal agency, and its purported purpose is to provide "safe, sound, and dependable sources of credit and related services for all creditworthy and eligible persons in agriculture and rural America."[11]

The FCS has become a conduit for Big Ag to recruit its massive base of contract growers—once known as farmers—in rural America. Via a labyrinthine network of farm co-ops, feed mills, and partner banks, the FCS is now the go-to lender for factory farms.

In 2022 researchers at the University of Kentucky and the University of Wisconsin published a fascinating network analysis of the relationship between Big Ag and major financiers. Just as Big Ag has consolidated into a handful of market-dominating companies, the financial institutions supporting the sector have merged. Lending practices changed as big banks made loans easily available to those working within the Big Ag network rather than to small, independent farmers. "We find that Big Finance is closely tied to Big Ag, and that key players limit the capacity for more peripheral actors, like growers, equipment producers, and regional banks, to engage in the network," the authors wrote.[12]

The analysis found that Farm Credit Services was the most influential financier in the network. Today the FCS holds 41 percent of farm debt in the United States, as compared to 20 percent in the 1960s. The FCS itself has consolidated, morphing from a dispersed, horizontally organized network of more than a thousand associations in the 1970s to a vertically consolidated unit of sixty-nine associations and four major banks today. "FCS is at the helm," the authors wrote. "FCS enables or disables certain types of agriculture by choosing to finance it."[13]

These days, the FCS chooses to finance Big Ag. The American Bankers Association, which has long been calling for FCS reform, found that in 2015, the average FCS loan size was $24 million.[14] Even the group's smaller loans support the Big Ag system, as CAFOs nestled deep within America's forgotten rural areas are financed by banks that appear to be local but are actually partnered recipients of FCS funding. Let's take a look at how this works on the ground in Dodge County.

When CAFOs began to sprout up like invasive weeds across Dodge, a big head-scratcher was how all of the young farmers secured financing for their buildings. Even in the late 1990s, construction of a typical CAFO cost around $750,000.

My family spent many years piecing together the top-down financial relationships that prop up the CAFO system. During our yearslong legal battle with Big Ag—stay tuned for the next chapter—finding our footing was difficult, because we didn't know what we were up against. The novel financial relationships between the everyday contract grower in places such as Dodge County and the billion-dollar multinational financial entities supporting them are opaque, concealed in a Russian doll's aggregation of LLCs and banking partnerships.

Some of the CAFOs in Dodge County have been financed by AgQuest Financial Services, a Minnesota corporation that is owned by grain and farm supply retailers. This may sound bucolic, but today's grain retailers are big businesses and heavily invested in Big Ag partnerships. According to AgQuest's website, "AgQuest offers a variety of operating, real estate, and equipment loans for agricultural producers." Specifically, AgQuest provides facility loans for improvements such as swine finishing barns.[15]

In layperson's terms, this means that AgQuest finances CAFO buildings, farm equipment, and other inputs purchased by factory farm operators, thereby creating big business clients for their own constituency—namely, the grain and farm supply retailers. According to court testimony that unfolded during a contract dispute between contract growers and Holden Farms, a local integrator, "AgQuest is not a traditional bank, it's a financial institution that's owned by various players . . . to provide financing to farmers."[16]

AgQuest had been a mystery to my family. It seemed to materialize out of nowhere in Dodge County and began handing out loans for mortgages on CAFO buildings as if they were candy. How on Earth did AgQuest have enough backing to guarantee all of those loans? Where was it coming from? In 2020, during the annual meeting of the Central Farm Service (CFS), my brother Brad asked the vice president of business development at AgQuest Financial Services where the company receives its funding. "AgriBank," he responded, to finance "hog barns" (i.e., CAFOs).[17]

AgriBank is one of the four major national lenders in the Farm Credit System. So it appears that local financing entities such as AgQuest are acting as pass-throughs for the FCS to front money to factory farms, enabling contract growers to surpass the traditional banking system and typical lender requirements such as having a good credit history, a down payment, or sufficient collateral.

AgQuest is not particularly forthcoming about its relationship with the Farm Credit System. It took a bit of digging to discover the magnitude of the partnership delineated in the annual report of Farmward

Cooperative, a cooperative of ag input suppliers (retailers of fertilizer, chemicals, feed, and more) that formed in 2017 as a merger of Farmward, AgQuest, and Northland Capital.

The report shows that AgriBank (via the Farm Credit System) had extended $116 million in "notes and mortgages payable" to AgQuest as of 2018. A corresponding endnote on these liens states, "AgriBank, FCB [Farm Credit Bank] has extended a $160,000,000 line of credit, of which $116,688,551 had been advanced as of August 31, 2018."[18]

So it appears AgriBank was funneling loans to local contract growers who produce livestock for multinational oligopolies, while independent farmers have steadily lost access to such financing. Whatever happened to the Farm Credit System's century-old mission to help "rural businesses grow and rural families thrive"?

With such funding from AgriBank in hand, AgQuest partners with Minnesota farming co-ops to provide loans to contract growers. Again, "farming co-op" sounds downright bucolic, but in recent years, co-ops have become another tool to ensure an endless supply of CAFOs and contract growers. Take, for example, Interstate Mills, the local feed supplier in Dodge mentioned in chapter 5. Once upon a time, it functioned primarily as a supplier of feed for local hog barns. Today it's a lender as well, and as with many other rural co-ops, it has merged with a larger entity. It's been folded into the Central Farm Service, my father's former co-op, with a network of grain and farm supply retailers, and with more than a hundred locations across Minnesota.

The CFS provides loan guarantees to promote corporate factory farms. According to its website, the CFS "is a guarantor of loan obligations held by AgQuest Financial Services, Inc. . . . to induce AgQuest to make loans to the Company's patrons to promote production agriculture in the trade area."[19]

Co-ops such as the Central Farm Service assist the integrators and the financiers in prospecting CAFO sites and contract growers to operate them. The former director of swine services for Interstate Mills acknowledged in court testimony that he helped find contract grower "prospects" for Holden. Interstate Mills also helped guarantee the debt, running cash flow projections for prospective feedlot developments

```
                    Meat-
                   packer

                  Integrator

               Contract Grower
```

Contract growers are needed to support the pyramid. A financial system quickly evolved to provide easy financing for CAFOs that included the following:

- Farmer co-ops such as Central Farm Service
- Grain and farm supply retailers
- Finance companies such as AgQuest
- Major banks and Farm Credit System

CHART 2. "Big Pig" pyramid scheme with financing details. Created by the author.

on behalf of AgQuest. The director stated that if the contract grower needed a guarantee or an interest-free loan, Interstate would "put a budget together and see . . . if it met the lender requirements that AgQuest had . . . then present it back to the lender, back to AgQuest."[20]

Farmer-owned co-ops, originally organized to benefit independent farmers, have quietly played their role in the large-scale exodus of independent farmers by enabling easy financing for factory farms. With all of this in mind, the Big Pig Pyramid introduced in chapter 1 can be updated with more detail, showing how co-ops and financiers have joined hands to create a steady supply of CAFO operators. Within this system, profits continue to flow to the corporations at the top of the pyramid rather than circulate in local economies.

Similar to AgQuest, AgStar Financial Services is another financial entity that extends loans to build CAFOs in Dodge County. According to my own research, AgStar has been responsible for nearly $33 million in direct financing to swine factory farm operators in the county.[21] AgStar recently merged with a handful of other entities to create Compeer Financial, a huge conglomerate that is part of the Farm Credit System, holds over $18.6 billion in assets, and displays signage at University of Minnesota sporting events. AgStar's absorption is another example of once-local lenders being swept into mergers and consolidation, making it more difficult for independent farming operations to secure financing.

With AgStar Financial's merger, we arrive back full circle to the local officials in Dodge County who vote, again and again, to approve new factory farm projects. As discussed, some of these officials are factory farm owners, a fact that should constitute a conflict of interest when feedlot permitting applications come before the planning commission or the county board on which they serve. And some members of the board have a more direct interest in the proposed feedlots, yet they fail to recuse themselves from voting on such proposals.

One member of the county's board of commissioners is a high-level employee of Compeer Financial and, before the merger, of AgStar Financial. Serving on the board, this member voted to approve feedlot developments financed by AgStar Financial, his employer. A second member of the five-member board serves on Compeer Financial's Client Advisory Council and likely voted to approve feedlots financed by Compeer Financial.

Returning to the network analysis of the relationship between Big Ag and major financiers in the hog industry, the authors of that study came across a surprising finding: while the major meat-packers such as Smithfield Foods capture the majority of industry profits, the major local integrators—those who own the hogs and contract with the farmers— are the ones who uphold the system. "Their market power is greater because they leverage more authority over more peripheral actors," the authors write, "by bottlenecking producer-level LLCs . . . the feeding, finish, or gestation operations." The authors conclude that these "contract structures dominate the hog industry."[22]

Today, this network of lenders, feed and equipment suppliers, and government officials constitutes a system where only one type of livestock farming is easily accessible in farm country, and that is factory farming. This amounts to industry investment and rural disinvestment. As the consequences of this system have become entrenched in society, a citizen's resistance has quietly emerged in small towns across rural America. My own family's role in this resistance began in 2014, when we decided we just weren't going to take it anymore.

9
Getting to Know Your Neighbors

"Before buying a rural home, be aware of livestock farms in the area, and keep in mind that prevailing winds can carry odors. Getting to know your new neighbors is the fastest way to become accepted as a new arrival in your community. Building good relationships and talking regularly with your neighbors helps avoid potential future conflicts."—MINNESOTA FARM BUREAU FOUNDATION, "Moving to the Country"

In the summer of 2013, my mother, Evelyn, after years of suffering from Parkinson's disease, entered the local nursing home. This move was one of those "before and after" events. Henceforth for my family, the chronology of our memories was divided into whether something occurred before or after my mother left the homeplace.

This was a painful chapter in my father's life, as he dealt with Evelyn's departure along with the challenging consequences of then ten factory farms operating near our home. Fall harvest was no longer the unmitigated joy it once was. For Lowell, there were few pleasures on Earth as great as climbing into the bucket seat of his John Deere, fully equipped with cushy backrests, armrests, and climate control— all welcome upgrades from his first tractor, a 1935 Case CC with steel wheels and lugs. Previously, only bad weather got between Lowell and his fields. But now his days on the farm were unexpectedly interrupted when neighboring factory farms emptied their manure pits. On those days, the odor was so strong and the fumes so dangerous that he needed to stay inside with the windows closed.

Driving into town became an uncertain endeavor as well. There is one main route off our farm—the township road. Lowell could recall its construction in 1934, a road fit for a team of horses pulling a wagon filled with a hundred pounds of corn. This single-lane throughway was now frequented by semitrucks carrying hogs, manure, and feed associated with the thirty thousand pigs living in our farm's vicinity. It carried the traffic of a commercial highway yet had not been updated to bear this load. Frost boils heaped between one to three feet high inevitably scraped the underbelly of my father's vehicle each spring, try as he did to avoid them.

The problem had worsened. A mile to the north of our farm were two large swine operations owned by Roger and Rhonda Toquam, some of the earliest proponents of corporate farming in Dodge County (as noted in chapter 4, Roger had spoken with my brother-in-law Dave about becoming a contract grower). Roger's facilities, among the first CAFOS in the county, went up in 1993 and 1998. The stench from those barns was old news. But in 2011 the Toquams purchased a three-hundred-acre parcel directly west of our farm, just across the township road. They used the acreage for production agriculture—corn and soy—and Roger hired semi drivers to transport hog manure, presumably to be used as fertilizer, between his swine facilities and the fields. The additional traffic caused further damage to the road, leaving deep ruts and ruptures.

After my mother went into the nursing home, I spoke with Lowell every morning and evening on my way to and from work in downtown Minneapolis. While I traversed the metropolitan freeways amid the downtown office towers, we talked about the farm. I learned every last detail of the daily ups and downs of the operation; I supposed these things were what he would have spoken with my mother about. Of course, at times I missed his calls, but I received voicemails in his brusque voice, including, "Sonja, this is your dad. I suppose you're out honky-tonkin'!"

With two grown daughters, Douglas and I had shifted to caretaking roles for our aging parents. We also remained attuned to the challenges in the Dodge community since we'd cheered from the sidelines ten years prior, when my brother Brad was involved in the battle over Ripley Dairy. For the most part, though, Douglas and I were less affected by the constant feeling of encroachment on all sides that my family living and working near the farm had to endure. That was all about to change.

In late March 2014 my parents were the unfortunate recipients of a notice informing them that a farmer was seeking a conditional use permit to construct a CAFO across the township road from our farm. In many Minnesota counties, neighbors receive only ten days' notice of a public hearing for an industrialized feedlot. This arrangement gives neighbors little time to prepare a response, let alone hire an attorney if they plan to object.

In Dodge, the zoning ordinance requires the ten nearest properties to the affected property be informed, along with the township board, the municipalities within two miles of the affected property, the Dodge County Soil and Water Conservation District, and the Minnesota Department of Natural Resources.

That evening, my daily call with dad wasn't the typical recitation of happenings at the farm but a call to arms. Lowell felt blindsided. He was angry. According to the notice, the Toquams were selling a tiny portion—a postage stamp–size, six-acre parcel—of their three hundred acres to twenty-four-year-old Nick Masching for the purpose of erecting a swine CAFO. We didn't know Nick, but we knew that his family, the Maschings, owned several commercial feedlots in Dodge.

If approved, this operation would be the eleventh factory farm encircling our farm, and it would be the closest. Our family already had a taste (and a smell) of what living near these operations was like, and we dreaded the impacts of one being located just across the road, directly to the west, for the prevailing winds would bring the stench of the swine CAFO right over our building site and our farm home built in 1905.

There was a lot of swearing during that phone call. That's the kind of relationship my father and I had. We let it loose. With that out of the way, we started to make a plan. I would help my parents find an attorney. With just days to prepare for the public hearing, we had to move quickly. Before hanging up the call, Lowell said something with such an air of absolute conviction that I will never forget it: "Enough is enough."

The Insider's Club

As my family prepared to challenge the Dodge County Planning Commission, we knew that defeat was all but certain. I'm reminded of the lyrics from the musical *Hamilton*, when the American rebels prepare to defend New York from the British at the beginning of the Revolutionary War: we were "outgunned, outmanned, outnumbered, outplanned." Given those odds, we had to take an all-out stand.

The planning commission was an insider's club of factory farm operators. Of the seven members, four were feedlot owners or family members of feedlot owners, including some of the most prosperous CAFO operators in the county. One member later served on the Minnesota Pork Board and was appointed to the USDA's National Pork Producers Delegate Body. All four had conflicts and financial interests related to previous swine feedlot CUP applications. The planning commission, as well as the county board, had recommended and approved every factory farm proposal that came before it, no matter how egregious the environmental consequences or how vocal the public outcry.

This state of affairs was particularly irksome to Lowell, who as mentioned previously had served on the board of commissioners from 1973 to 1981. During the farm default crisis in the 1980s, many public officials in Dodge, including my father, stood in open opposition to the banks' predatory lending practices and exorbitant interest rates. In those days, populist public officials tried to protect residents from the very same big business interests that have now successfully permeated the county seat.

It pained my father to hear the factory farm operators use the language of a false populism to bolster corporate agriculture, claiming that those who stand up to Big Ag are hurting family farmers. In truth, Big Ag ran small family farms out of business, and the remaining "family farmers" are mostly CAFO operators and contract growers with financial ties to Big Ag. This is true for the Toquams, who engage in local governance and use their positions to bolster factory farm development and the continued centrality of factory farming in the local economy. Rhonda Toquam first served on the planning commission and currently serves on the board of commissioners. In both roles, she advocated for feedlot developments and pro-corporate zoning amendments, including those that intersected with her family's business dealings.

Interestingly, in March 2014, just weeks before Nick Masching's CUP came before the commission, one of the planning commission members and a relative of Nick's, Jessica Masching, abruptly departed.[1] An optimistic interpretation is that the commission cared about conflicts of interest, but just a month later, Jessica's vacancy was filled by Joshua Toquam, the son of CAFO operators Roger and Rhonda Toquam, who owned the property that Nick's feedlot would occupy.[2] Evidently Jessica was moving away, so the commission swapped one compromised individual for another.

During the days before the first hearing, my family learned more about the project. The feedlot would hold 720 animal units, or 2,400 pigs, half a mile west of our farm. No family or residence was associated with the proposed project, just the six-acre parcel of bare land upon which the CAFO barn would be built. While the Toquams owned the land surrounding the parcel, and Nick would eventually own the six acres, neither party would live there. The operation would produce manure equivalent to a town of nearly seven thousand people, or the urban equivalent of a seventy-story residential tower. Yet while a residential tower has indoor plumbing and nearby water treatment facilities, we had no idea what the plans were for the CAFO's manure management.

The Masching family operated ten swine factory farms in Dodge County, most of them located in our home township, Westfield Township. Nick's feedlot would bring the total number of hogs housed by the Maschings to twenty-one thousand, or nearly 57 percent of the estimated thirty-seven thousand hogs in a township that measures just six miles square.[3]

We discovered that this wasn't Nick's first rodeo. In 2011, at the age of twenty-one, he received a $600,000 loan for the construction of his first CAFO.[4] This time around, the same bank planned to extend a $778,000 loan for the new CAFO.[5] At the age of twenty-four, this young man was poised to receive a total of $1.4 million in CAFO loans.

As I scrambled to find an attorney for my family, Lowell and Brad had no choice but to attend the planning commission hearing on April 2 without adequate preparation, backing, or legal representation. The stakes of this meeting weighed heavily. Our family heritage, our family home, and our farming operation of the past hundred years—all was at stake. This was Lowell's garden, each square inch turned lovingly by hand. The Trom farm was a rare patch of remaining beauty, conservationism, and environmental stewardship in a countryside that had been converted to a wasteland of corporate ag and large-scale animal suffering.

My father always dressed well when he left the farm and was particularly meticulous with his church attire on Sundays. He was a handsome man, standing at about five feet eight, with thick black hair that didn't turn gray until his advanced senior years. Lowell dressed the same way for the planning commission meeting as he did for church, affording the proceedings a level of respect that was not returned. His dapper outfits were always topped with a black fedora.

They were such a contrast to Lowell's typical farm getup of denim bib overalls and a baseball cap bearing a John Deere or local seed corn logo. The overalls had a chest pocket that allowed him to carry a pen and small pad of paper, and he had pliers, a screwdriver, and other tools in the hip pockets. If it was cold, he switched into coveralls with long sleeves. And while the cap covered his head, it did not adequately protect Lowell from the sun. As with many farmers, in later years his multiple facial scars from skin cancer treatment served as reminders of a life spent outside.

When Lowell and my brother arrived at the first public hearing, they learned that the planning commission had already voted to recommend approval of the CUP.[6] We suspect that the commission anticipated Lowell's objection and hastily entered the vote in the several minutes between when the meeting was called to order and my father's arrival. The transcript shows that commission members entertained minimal discussion of the parameters of the CUP application—information that, according to the county's own zoning ordinance, must accompany feedlot approval.[7]

Upon arrival, my father wasn't allowed to speak or enter his objection on the record even though it was a public hearing; the intent was to hear input from the community. But members of the commission who were also in the Big Ag insider's club rushed the vote through, denying my father, who had lived in Dodge his entire life, any public comment regarding the installation of a huge factory farm across the road from his own house.

With the CUP green-lighted by the planning commission, the next step was to seek formal approval from the county board. Its meeting was less than a week away, on April 8. During the short interim, I contacted each commissioner to discuss my family's concerns about the feedlot development. While I knew this was unlikely to yield results, I'm a trained mediator, and my instincts are to keep lines of communication open whenever possible. You never know where a conversation might lead.

But as expected, it didn't lead anywhere.

Meanwhile, I located a lawyer with expertise in land use disputes, and my parents retained his services. Our attorney filed a letter with the Dodge County Board of Commissioners formally objecting to the feedlot. The initial objection stated that the feedlot would "alter the essential character of the locality, would cause an adverse effect on property values, and would cause injury to the health and environment of the residents."[8] In particular, my family was concerned about area waterways, many of which were already listed as impaired due to factory farm pollution. The proposed facility, located within the Cedar River Watershed District, was just a few hundred feet from a drainage ditch. This raised concerns about runoff.

The public health consequences of contaminated drinking water and air pollution were top of mind for my family. Numerous local residents suffer from diseases associated with environmental contaminants. This included my mother, who first developed Parkinson's—a disease proven to be associated with exposure to environmental toxins—in 1995, soon after CAFOs started going up nearby. Several cancer clusters also occurred in Dodge County, including one near our farm. Four of my father's cousins had died of cancer in recent years, and all four had lived within a mile of our farm, inside the ring of extreme CAFO concentration that entrapped us.

Our attorney asked the board to deny the CUP, to grant the CUP with certain conditions, or to postpone the board's decision until April 22,

2014, giving my parents time to prepare and present their objection in full.[9] The board did not grant the request; instead, it moved forward with the hearing as originally scheduled. My father and Brad hastily prepared to appear before the Dodge County Board of Commissioners just a few days later.

My heart ached for Brad, who works the farm as its groundskeeper. He was the Trom sibling most involved in the fight against factory farms in Dodge. He'd been very active in the defeat of Ripley Dairy and had started a homegrown newsletter, still operating today, devoted to news, analysis, and resources for members of the grassroots movement standing in opposition to uncontrolled factory farm development. Brad is extremely well read, particularly on factory farm issues, and we talk frequently, sometimes daily, on family and factory farm matters, politics, and current events. His vocal opposition to factory farms left him open to offensive comments and threats to his safety from certain members of the community. Though Brad has a gentle soul and spirit, he carries a baseball bat in his car, a sign of the fear he feels.

Tenderhearted and soft-spoken, Brad is a warrior. He endured cancer and multiple treatments and surgeries in his twenties, only for the cancer to recur more than a decade later. He is somewhat of a medical miracle, having fought off the aggressive cancer twice. He wears tinted glasses, as the treatments affected his vision, and he cannot tolerate bright light.

As the farm's groundskeeper, for some time Brad was able to indulge his love for dogs. He began raising them on the farm, eventually becoming a professional breeder. He also provided boarding and grooming services to local dog owners. Unfortunately, as the eighth and ninth and then the tenth factory farms encircled our home, his boarding business became untenable. His clients complained about the unbearable stench and did not return. Brad's own dogs became sick, vomiting at dusk—the time of day when area hog confinement facilities open their curtain-ventilated buildings, letting out the noxious air from the massive concrete pits of manure.

Brad has a great sense of humor, even during stressful times. His knack for keeping a quiet sense of determination in the face of hardship helped him and our dad get through their exasperating encounter with the county board.

Board meetings are held in the small city of Mantorville, the county seat, which features a historic downtown area with a stately courthouse standing atop a small hill. The courthouse is a source of pride in Dodge County; built in 1865, it is the oldest functioning courthouse in the state. County board meetings take place across the street in a one-story brick building that used to be a school and today serves various administrative functions. The public hearing room is a standard modern space, with gray walls, recessed lighting, and tables with microphones at the front where the commissioners, administrators, and county attorneys sit.

On April 8 the board members addressed all the routine matters on their agenda, and when the time arrived to discuss the Masching-Toquam hog confinement proposal, they allowed no public inquiry to take place. They neither allowed comments and questions nor acknowledged that Lowell and Brad were in attendance.[10] They skipped straight to voting, swiftly approving the CUP.

Even by Dodge County standards, this was a rush job. The board was required to confirm that the applicant submitted the information required on the CUP application form, including details about the site's geological condition and soil type, the manure storage and management plan, and the water drainage patterns on the site and their effect on nearby streams and waterways. *None of this* was included in Mr. Masching's application. The form was mostly empty. The only lines he had filled out were the name and address of the applicant, the name and address of the property owner, the size of the acreage (six), the animal type (swine), the number of animals (2,400), the barn type, the barn size, and the barn manure pit's depth.[11]

The county board approves all feedlot proposals that come their way. We knew this. But even with our low expectations, we were surprised that they abandoned even the minimum outward appearance of assessing and discussing the application. We wondered if the commissioners circumvented public comment to avoid creating a public record to memorialize our objections. All of them knew or knew about our family. After the meeting, one of the commissioners, a man who had served as commissioner for over thirty years after defeating my father in 1981, approached my father and said they didn't have any choice but to approve the project.

That comment is open to interpretation, but clearly many Dodge County officials decided long ago that CAFOS were the only way forward for the Dodge farming community.

The following month, in May, my parents filed a lawsuit, known as a permitting action, against the Dodge County Board of Commissioners and CAFO operators Roger Toquam and Nick Masching, challenging the board's issuance of the CUP and alleging that the Masching application was incomplete as it failed to include the information required pursuant to the local zoning ordinance. The lawsuit further asserted claims of an anticipated environmental nuisance based on the Minnesota Environmental Rights Act, and it requested an injunction preventing Masching from building the proposed feedlot.[12]

Like thousands of farm families across rural America, it was now my parents' turn to face off against corporate ag and attempt to protect their home and health with the limited legal tools at their disposal. They had no recourse other than the courtroom, an undesirable location to settle any dispute. Yet my elderly parents were not afraid. They approached the situation with open eyes and clarity of purpose. The die was cast. We were ready for whatever came next.

10

Industry Watchdogs

"Don't be afraid to ask for help. If a situation becomes controversial, it is nice to have allies. Ask for the support of other farmers in your area. Contact commodity organizations or farm groups you belong to and ask for their support.... Farm groups can also help encourage their members to attend public meetings in support of your project. If you are there to speak up in support of others, hopefully they will do the same for you."
—MINNESOTA FARM BUREAU FOUNDATION, "When an Activist Group Comes to Town"

After initiating my parents' lawsuit, we were immediately ostracized by certain community members. We expected it, but that didn't make it any easier. Those who opposed our cause sought to shame and intimidate us; those who supported us stayed silent.

Lessons learned during the previous decade made some folks in Dodge County afraid to say what they really felt. Many others simply didn't understand the parameters of the case and tended to naturally side with those claiming that our family's actions would hurt the local economy. Residents in Dodge, similar to most U.S. communities, are largely disengaged from local news and governance. Civic participation has been declining for decades, making it easier for factory farm operators in many rural communities to fill public official positions without anyone much noticing. The local news crisis, which began in the late nineties, hit rural areas hard. With fewer community newspapers, local corruption can more easily take root and flower. People can get away with a great deal when nobody is paying attention.

In Dodge, the folks who were paying attention included CAFO owners who wanted to keep operating on their own terms.

I made a point of accompanying my dad to church that spring and summer of 2014, as I knew he was getting the cold shoulder. Our family had attended First Lutheran Church in Blooming Prairie for as long as I can remember. Orlo Toquam, Roger's father, was also a member there, and over the years he and my dad had maintained a polite, if distant, relationship. My dad's first cousin was Orlo's second wife, and she was friendly to our family.

Yet when we attended church after the lawsuit began, congregation members avoided any conversation with my father, ignoring him before and after services. He was iced out. We quickly discovered who our friends were.

Community members sympathetic to our cause were out there but hesitant, afraid to receive the same treatment. We decided to create a community organization, similar to the local organization that had resisted Ripley Dairy in 2005, to serve as an organizing hub for those on the sidelines wanting to join our efforts. Brad was instrumental in creating the new group, which we called "Dodge County Concerned Citizens."

One of the early meetings was held at the family farm, and several friends and neighbors attended. Douglas and I drove in from Minneapolis that Saturday morning. As we neared the farm—driving south along the Claremont Road—we turned onto the township road leading to our farm and immediately spotted a pickup truck parked at the corner. We slowed as we approached, knowing that something wasn't right. We passed the truck, and who to our wondering eyes should appear but Rhonda Toquam, sitting in the truck's cab and making a note of every person turning onto the township road leading to our farm.

When Douglas and I arrived at the meeting, we asked the attendees if they, too, had passed Rhonda before entering. They had. Before the meeting even began, each participant had received an implicit threat, a warning that their actions were known to the Toquams and undoubtedly other hog operators.

Sure enough, one of the farmers in attendance that day chose to stop affiliating with our organization. We later learned that a local industry insider contacted him with questions about his participation in the meeting. The farmer in question held a prominent role on a local board, and an implied threat was made about his future position within the farming community.

Organizing in the community was hard, even harder than it had been a decade earlier. The industry's entrenchment in local governance was complete. Everyone knew the drill: don't try to fight the CAFO takeover; it won't work, and you'll regret it. While the Farm Bureau network made threats to the community under cloak-and-dagger, the Dodge County Concerned Citizens were very public in our organizing efforts. We worked proudly, in the light of day, publishing meeting notices in local newspapers and hosting meetings on Saturdays.

The meetings were intended to educate local residents about the dangers associated with factory farming, but area hog contract growers pig-piled into the meetings to disrupt and prevent our efforts. Their presence was immediately evident by their caps and jackets flashing corporate logos and, of course, by the scent of manure blanketing the room. This pattern of outright intimidation was established at our first meeting held in the Blooming Prairie City Hall.

Roger Toquam sat in the front row, where he was joined by another farmer whom I didn't recognize. The other farmer sat slumped in his chair, glowering. Within a few minutes of the meeting's start, he interrupted my presentation and blurted out, "When is your father going to file for bankruptcy?"

Afterward I asked a friend who the man was. He was Scott Masching, Nick's father.

As an attorney, I often see threats made between husband and wife in a divorce proceeding and knew such inappropriate actions can affect the parameters of the legal dispute. But I reacted to this intimidation not as an attorney but as a daughter of Dodge County. I was angry and sad that the CAFO operators acted as if they were kings of the county, free to expand their kingdoms at everyone else's expense without consequence or resistance.

At a second Dodge County Concerned Citizens meeting in nearby Dodge Center, factory farm operators stacked the meeting and tried to derail the discussion with frequent interruptions. As I did my best to retain control of the floor, one shouted, "Why do *you* get control of the mic?" It was a dumb question—I was the meeting's host and facilitator—but that comment sticks in my memory because of how revealing it was. Those who benefit from the industry's hold on Dodge didn't want me to have the mic. They wanted me to shut up and stay quiet. I had no intention of obliging.

Suspected Bribery in Dodge County

As we awaited a decision from the Dodge County District Court, I came upon something unexpected—another layer of collusion between local officials and the Masching family. Apparently, the Maschings and Westfield Township officials had made agreements contemporaneously with the CUP's approval in April 2014. These agreements concerned, of all things, manure.

As we put the pieces together, we realized, to our astonishment, that manure was likely a source of bribery in Dodge County. While that probably sounds odd, if not outright bizarre, to the uninitiated reader, it makes sense to farmers.

During the same period that CAFOs began to produce unmanageable amounts of manure, commercial fertilizer became exponentially more expensive. CAFO manure is an uncontrolled environmental disaster, but it's also a valuable commodity for farmers engaged in production agriculture who hope to save money on input costs by spreading their fields with hog manure rather than with expensive commercial fertilizer. CAFO operators who own land adjacent to their hog barns can spread the manure on their own land, but for those operators owning land miles away, hauling manure from point A to point B has become an important business in Dodge and, as we see in chapters 11 and 12, an additional source of pollution.

Some CAFO operators only own the few acres their CAFOs sit upon, so they enter into what are called "manure easement agreements" with area farmers who agree to take the manure to spread on their nearby fields. These agreements are lucrative for both sides of the deal: the CAFO operators offload and sometimes make money off the hog manure, which otherwise could become a huge burden to them, while the crop farmers save money on input costs. According to an article in *National Hog Farmer*, "As the price of corn and the cost of production rise, primarily the cost of commercial nutrients, the value of hog manure rises as well. That interest has resulted in a growing number of crop farmers becoming interested in either raising hogs or entering into agreements that would gain them access to hog manure."[1]

Primary crops in Dodge County and throughout southern Minnesota include repetitive rows of field corn and soybeans. Minnesota is the fourth-largest producer of corn in the United States. While some farmers plant corn on corn, most alternate corn and soybeans every other year. An occasional field of sweet corn or peas breaks up the monotony. Demand for land in Dodge is now driven, in part, by the need to apply millions of gallons of manure from area factory farms to neighboring fields. And today's farmers, struggling with ever-rising land and input costs, farm every square inch. Many encroach upon areas reserved for road easements, working the land immediately adjacent to utility poles stretched along the roadways. While these violations are illegal, the law typically isn't enforced. Some farmers also work the land immediately adjacent to area waterways, violating the buffer zones intended to safeguard the water.

I find it amusing that the hog industry, primarily via educational materials produced by the American Farm Bureau Federation and the National Pork Producers Council (the industry's lobbying group), have begun to sing the praises of hog manure, arguing that CAFOs provide nutrients for area farmers during an era of skyrocketing fertilizer costs. While this is true, it's also true that the symbiosis between livestock manure and crops has existed as long as farming has existed. This association didn't begin with CAFOs. Instead, CAFOs introduced a disconnect between manure and crops since many operators don't own adjoining acreage and must either store or haul away their manure.

Further, with the extreme geographic concentration of CAFO manure, there will always be an excess, with myriad environmental, ecological, and health consequences. The most common effect of manure overapplication on too little land is the seepage of excess nitrogen, phosphorus, and other contaminants, such as antibiotics, into the groundwater and runoff into area waterways.

A standard 2,400-hog CAFO holds an estimated 1.1 million gallons of manure per year, and Nick Masching's proposed CUP cited the standard size. Per a 2022 analysis by a South Dakota State University swine specialist, a swine finishing barn of that size produces an estimated $35,000 worth of nitrogen, potassium, and phosphorus per year.[2]

Here's where the suspected bribery comes in.

As per Dodge County's zoning ordinance, the county is required to obtain input about feedlot proposals from the pertinent township officials before the CUP's public hearing. The township must acknowledge, in writing, that it has reviewed the staff report prepared by the Dodge County zoning administrator regarding the land use proposal and must provide comments, concerns, and opinions regarding the proposed land use.[3] In the case of the Masching proposal, its oversight was the purview of Westfield Township, a small township. At any given time, only five Westfield officials are serving: three township supervisors, a treasurer, and a clerk.

On March 28, 2014—one week prior to the April 2 planning commission's meeting to consider the Masching CUP—records show that three ten-year manure easements went into effect between three Westfield Township officials and Nick Masching's uncle, James Masching.[4] A CAFO owner, James hauls manure for feedlot operators in Dodge County, including for family members who also own CAFOs. While the easement agreements went into effect on March 28, they were not *executed and recorded*—that is, made visible via the Dodge County Recorder's Office—until April 12, four days after the board of commissioners formally approved the CUP.

Something stinks in Dodge County, and it's not just the pigs.

The township officials and James Masching signed the three easements, but it's unclear whether the officials expected to receive manure *specifically* from Nick Masching's future CAFO or from James Masching's CAFO (the agreements state that James Masching and his "heirs, successors, and assigns" are recipients of the ten-year easements). Regardless, the officials clearly expected to receive it from somewhere and entered into the agreement just days before performing their township duty of assessing Nick Masching's CAFO proposal. We saw in chapter 6, when the Ripley Dairy's CUP was overridden at the township level, what can happen when township officials oppose a feedlot.

When the time came for Westfield Township to offer feedback at the April board and planning meetings, the township officials were absent. They spoke neither for nor against the project.

Nick Masching was later required to complete a manure management form provided by the Minnesota Pollution Control Agency.[5] This form included the following question: "How will you ensure that enough land owners in the area are willing to purchase your manure or otherwise receive your manure?" His response? "Long term written agreements." He didn't provide additional information. Why would he? The barebones requirements and regulations in the state don't require details about manure easement agreements.

As mentioned, the estimated annual value of manure from a 2,400-head hog farm was $35,000 in 2022. What was the value of manure in Dodge County in 2014? The best guess I have comes from a 2013 lawsuit, when a local swine factory farm operator estimated the value at $19,000 per year.[6] The three Westfield Township officials entered into ten-year agreements, so if they're receiving manure from a standard operation, that's up to $190,000 in input costs. That's real money.

If only one township officer was involved, it would look suspicious but could feasibly be chalked up to coincidence. But three officers, all three of whom are farmers in Dodge with corn and soy acreage? And merely days before the CAFO was approved?

Has this type of quid pro quo become an industry strategy for steering factory farm projects to persuadable township and county officials? Free manure is an easy perk to dangle before farmers who serve on local township boards, planning commissions, or county boards. Given the well-known lack of reporting and poor supervision of manure storage, management, and land-spreading plans, these arrangements would easily fly under the radar. Indeed, many manure easements aren't written but exist as oral agreements between the two parties.

This type of scheme backfired in 2019 in the town of Trade Lake, Wisconsin, where local residents opposed the installation of a gigantic twenty-six-thousand-hog CAFO. It was discovered that James Melin, the town's chairman, who had publicly supported the project, had failed to disclose a number of personal financial ties to the proposed feedlot. They included an agreement with the CAFO developers to receive free manure for himself or his immediate family members with an estimated value of $42,000 per year. Town residents sued for Melin's removal, citing the Wisconsin Code of Ethics and violations of its bribery statute.[7] In response to the scandal, Burnett County, where the town is located, issued a one-year moratorium on new CAFOs.[8]

Not all bribes take the form of cash in brown envelopes passed under a table. They can take many forms: gift certificates, prepaid credit cards, free travel and entertainment, free meals, or other noncash transfers. Offering free manure to be spread on an elected official's land is an easy, non-traceable method to encourage officials to fast-track factory farm approval. No checks. No bank wires. No cash. No paper trails. Just a trail of stench—and I'm not talking about the manure.

With the Trom lawsuit still pending that summer, I received a call from my dad that something unexpected was taking place across the township road. Apparently, Nick Masching was preparing to break ground on the CAFO.

I drove home that weekend to see it for myself. Sure enough, the crop had been removed from the six-acre parcel even though it was too early to harvest. I stared in disbelief at the six acres of dirt and the excavator in the middle digging a huge hole to make way for yet another swine factory farm.

As an attorney, I was stunned. Who the hell proceeds with construction of a project when a pending lawsuit might strip the underlying permit? The audacity of this action told me that both the Maschings and the Maschings' lender didn't expect them to lose the lawsuit, or in the event that they did, they must have felt very confident about a plan B.

For the umpteenth time, I wondered why the Toquams had decided to sell this tiny parcel of their three hundred acres. Easy access to CAFO manure was certainly a perk, but they didn't necessarily need it; they were already spreading their crops with manure hauled from their own facilities one mile to the north. I imagined they did stand to save money in trucking costs. Still, it felt personal. This CAFO would be as close to our farmhouse as is legally allowed. Was it payback for our family's opposition to factory farms over the years?

Or perhaps they simply wanted to stink us off the land. In Dodge County, land is in very short supply. As each individual farming operation grows larger, the amount of available land diminishes. This situation creates cutthroat competition among the small number of remaining local farmers and the burgeoning array of faraway investors who purchase land in Dodge and pay people to work on it. It's akin to a game of Monopoly, a zero-sum game of acquisition at all costs.

As my parents grew older, interested renters began to circle them like vultures. My brothers Brad and Jim had spent their lifetimes working on the farm, and my family's ties to the land were well known, but that didn't stop avaricious farmers from giving it a shot anyway. One of our neighbors, an area farmer who was always looking to expand, showed up one day with a contract and handed it to my father to sign. How bold.

Another area farmer wrote a letter to my father asking to rent our land. When my father didn't respond, this young man—who had no prior relationship or connection with my father—worked up the courage to approach him in person and asked where he stood on the list, apparently presuming that such a list existed. It did not. As my father loved to recount to us kids, "Well, can you believe it? I told him, 'You're at the bottom.'"

It must frustrate the hell out of folks who are determined to expand their operations or to find more land to spread their manure that our farm remains an intergenerational family farm—something that only two decades ago would have been the norm and would have been assumed. It's a sad state of affairs. Everyone has to worry that the farmer next door is conspiring to chase you off the land. And now we were being ostracized by our community for standing firmly to preserve our family legacy, our own health, and our livelihood.

That year was a very difficult one for my family, particularly because we were not confident that our legal actions would lead anywhere. But we wouldn't let the odds stop us from doing what we knew was right.

On November 18, 2014, my parents' lawyer called. The decision was in. The Dodge County District Court ruled in favor of my parents and vacated the CUP issued by the county board. Focusing on the requirements in the local ordinance and the accompanying application form, the judgment stated:

> The application submitted by Defendant Masching was clearly incomplete. The application form asks for a description of the geological condition, soil type, and seasonal high-water table for the proposed site. This was not provided. . . . The application form asks for manure management planning information. This was not provided. The application form asks for a map of the proposed site showing the location and dimension of any manure storage facilities, the location of any well, and drainage patterns on the site. This was not provided. . . .
>
> The application contained only a fraction of the information required by both Dodge County ordinance and asked for on the application form itself. . . . The CUP was therefore issued in violation of the requirements of Dodge County Ordinance § 16.24.3, and is hereby vacated.[9]

Our feeling of triumph was deepened by emerging signs that fellow community members not only supported us but also recognized the difficulty of what we were going through. One day that autumn when I accompanied my dad to church, a member of the congregation who had a leadership role in the community approached after the service and pulled me aside.

"Thank you for your work on behalf of your family and on behalf of our community," he said firmly with a tone of assurance and conviction. Encouraged by this thoughtful comment and brave public action, I realized that sympathetic parishioners had been sitting among us all along.

11

Risk of Pollution

"An increase in animal numbers does not mean an increase in pollution potential. As long as new or expanded livestock facilities are sited properly and follow Minnesota Pollution Control Agency (MPCA) feedlot rules, there is minimal risk of pollution and odor problems."—MINNESOTA FARM BUREAU FOUNDATION, "When an Activist Group Comes to Town"

On July 2, 2015, a piece of farm equipment fell into a manure pit inside a CAFO in the small rural community of Woodmohr, Wisconsin. Rodney Seibel, age forty-seven, climbed down a short ladder into the pit area to retrieve it but was immediately overcome by the noxious fumes. His son Jeremy climbed in after him. Jeremy, too, was overcome. While witnesses were present and immediately called for help, father and son could not be revived. First responders pronounced both dead at the scene.[1]

A few weeks later, on July 25, 2015, another father and son were repairing a pump in a hog confinement at their family farm in Cylinder, Iowa, when a piece of equipment fell into the manure pit area. Austin Opheim, the son, went in first. He immediately lost consciousness. His father, Gene, went in after him and started to carry his son out on his back. Gene almost made it out before he, too, lost consciousness. Gene and Austin became the second father-son pair to die from hydrogen sulfide poisoning in livestock confinements during the month of July 2015 alone.[2]

Stored manure emits ammonia, hydrogen sulfide, methane, and carbon dioxide, among many other toxic air pollutants. These emissions occur at higher rates when the manure is disturbed—or "agitated," as the industry calls it—and releases greater concentrations of the gases, particularly hydrogen sulfide.[3] This typically happens when manure is transported, such as during pump-out, when it's pumped from the concrete pits inside the CAFOs, or when manure is removed from the massive outdoor storage lagoons and spread or sprayed onto fields. Manure is also agitated when something falls into it; this likely explains why the situations in Wisconsin and Iowa were so deadly.

Hydrogen sulfide is a particularly menacing threat for feedlot workers because while the notorious rotten egg smell can be detected at lower concentrations, the odor is undetectable at potentially lethal concentrations. When hydrogen sulfide gets above five hundred parts per million in the air, collapse can occur within seconds. According to one Occupational Safety and Health Administration (OSHA) accounting, 125 hydrogen sulfide–related worker deaths occurred at CAFOS between 1984 and 2009.[4] This number is likely an undercount, and no updated numbers exist. Despite clearly meeting the requirements, feedlots are not categorized as *permittable confined spaces prone to a hazardous atmosphere* under OSHA; therefore, OSHA is not able to appropriately track injuries and deaths or to implement safety measures within CAFOS.

Poisoning deaths are but the extreme outcomes of the widespread air pollution problem that industrialized livestock facilities cause. The global agrifood system, which includes concentrated livestock operations, is responsible for "one-third of global greenhouse gas emissions" contributing substantially to climate change.[5] Particularly worrisome is the *type* of gases emitted by the mass, concentrated storage of manure. Nitrous oxide, for example, is three hundred times more potent as a greenhouse gas than carbon dioxide, and livestock manure management is the fourth leading emitter of nitrous oxide in the United States.[6]

Feedlot emissions also adversely affect the ambient air quality of surrounding areas, impacting not only the environment but human health as well. Ammonia is a respiratory irritant that can cause chemical burns to the respiratory tract and severe lung disease. Hydrogen sulfide causes headaches, nausea, respiratory problems, confusion, and, in high concentrations, permanent neural impairment and death.[7] The fine, inhalable particulate matter associated with industrialized feedlot operations also poses several health risks: chronic lung conditions and respiratory disease, heart disease and heart attacks, links to several cancers, and increased rates of spontaneous miscarriage, infant mortality, and premature death.[8]

Dozens of studies show higher rates of asthma, chronic headaches, lung disease, bronchitis, depression, fatigue, and cancers among farm workers and those living near concentrated feedlots.[9] One study in the San Joaquin Valley in California found that dairy CAFOs were responsible for 44 percent of total ammonia emissions in the area.[10] This is typical for agricultural areas since agricultural operations are the single largest source of U.S. ammonia emissions. According to the Environmental Working Group, 1,292 deaths *every year* in the San Joaquin Valley are attributable to fine particulate matter of less than or equal to 2.5 microns (PM 2.5), and ammonia emitted from livestock operations is a precursor to the formation of PM 2.5.[11]

One global study found that emissions from farms "outweigh all other human sources of fine-particulate matter air pollution in much of the United States, Europe, Russia and China."[12] Agricultural practices lead to the formation of airborne particulate matter because agricultural outputs (including fumes from manure and fertilizer) combine with existing industrial emissions. It's a deadly combination.

A truly eye-opening study published in 2021 by the *Proceedings of the National Academy of Sciences*, one of the world's premiere science journals, found that ammonia emissions contribute to 12,400 deaths per year in the United States and that animal agriculture is the leading cause of these emissions. The study examined how changes in farming practices could significantly reduce such deaths. "On-farm interventions can reduce PM 2.5-related mortality by 50%," the authors estimated, and such interventions include "improved livestock waste management and fertilizer application practices that reduce emissions of ammonia."[13]

Given the grave impacts of CAFO-caused air pollution, one might assume that these facilities operate within a responsible, commonsense regulatory regime similar to what is expected from other polluting industries. Sadly, it isn't so. Minimal regulations exist, and their adherence and enforcement are likewise minimal. The industry labored for decades to lobby and litigate their way into gaping loopholes and generous exemptions.

CAFOS technically qualify as a "stationary source" of air pollutants under the Clean Air Act (CAA), yet they are exempted from reporting air emissions and other types of CAA compliance measures.[14] In 2017, under the Trump administration, the EPA exempted all CAFOS, even the largest known polluters, from reporting under two major laws governing air emissions: the Comprehensive Environmental Response, Compensation, and Liability Act (CERCLA) and the Emergency Planning and Community Right-to-Know Act (EPCRA).[15] Congress formalized the CERCLA exemption in the Fair Agriculture Reporting Method Act, which was spearheaded by senators who were recipients of agribusiness PAC contributions.[16] Even before these outright exemptions, only the very largest CAFOS in the country had previously been required to track and report air emissions.

Legal scholars have deemed the industry's unusual freedom from regulation as "agricultural exceptionalism." "Nearly every major federal environmental statute passed since the 1970s has included carve-outs for farms," noted a 2014 analysis by ag law scholars.[17] The meat lobby found great success in arguing that feedlots should be allowed special privileges because agriculture is somehow more wholesome or important than other polluting industries. One report from the Environmental Integrity Project asserted that "the livestock industry has emasculated EPA's enforcement and regulatory efforts by manipulating the image of the small family farm in the media and on Capitol Hill."[18]

The few existing federal regulations only apply to feedlots that achieve the EPA's definition of a "large" concentrated animal feeding operation rather than a "medium-size" CAFO or an AFO; for hog operations, large CAFOS are swine feedlots containing 2,500 or more mature pigs.[19] For smaller CAFOS, the EPA kicks the regulatory ball to the states and counties, directing them to issue permits and collect information about where feedlots are located and how many animals they confine. Even for the largest feedlots, the EPA allows many states to administer the permitting program on the agency's behalf—as in Dodge County.

An analysis by the Natural Resources Defense Council (NRDC) found that only a handful of states—including Maryland, Tennessee, and Indiana—do a moderately acceptable job of collecting feedlot data, let alone regulate the feedlot's pollution.[20] Minnesota ranked "low" across all categories, including on transparency of manure management plans and feedlot permitting status.

Here's where the absurdity of this system comes full circle. The EPA regulates large CAFOs, but how does it determine where they're located? That information is reported by the states, which often receive it from the counties; however, the counties might or might not inform state agencies that a large CAFO has been constructed. It's a neat little loop in which oversight often does not occur. A decade-long, court-mandated investigation by the NRDC estimated that the EPA had records for *fewer than half* of the existing CAFOs.[21]

With feedlot tracking and regulation typically relegated to state environmental agencies, protection from feedlot pollutants depends entirely on where someone lives. Large CAFOs are supposed to obtain National Pollution Discharge Elimination System permits through state agencies, and procuring such a permit effectively means that state regulators then track the large CAFOs.

Yet whether feedlots are expected to actually obtain such permits depends on the state. In Oregon, NPDES permitting is widely enforced, but in Iowa, only 4 percent of CAFOs have an NPDES permit.[22] In the Texas Panhandle, where large cattle feedlots have caused drastic health problems in neighboring populations, an investigation found that the state's environmental regulatory agency, the Texas Commission on Environmental Quality, took no enforcement action, levied not a single fine, and issued no warnings in response to the many complaints formally filed with the agency.[23]

Feedlot owners prefer to avoid the risk of regulation altogether by limiting their capacity. As explored in chapter 7, an absurd number of hog operations in Dodge County house around 960 AUs, or 2,400 hogs. The difference in the environmental impact between a 2,400-head facility and a 2,500-head facility is minimal, depending on how each is operated, but the NPDES permitting requirement is an all-or-nothing threshold. Nor does the permitting system consider area CAFO density, an important determinant of public health impacts. A 1,000-AU facility operating in a region without other CAFOs is subject to EPA regulation, yet the area could have a dozen 995-AU facilities in close geographical proximity without one being subject to EPA reporting.

While feedlots of less than 1,000 AUs evade federal regulation, they must still comply with local regulations. In Minnesota, for example, they include the requirement to submit a manure management plan, along with information about soil conditions and the risk of runoff into lakes and streams, during the initial permitting process. My family brought its lawsuit because Dodge County failed to enforce even these frankly insufficient state and county regulations. When the presiding judge deemed Nick Masching's permit application "clearly incomplete" and in violation of the ordinance, for the briefest moment it appeared that accountability might be on the horizon for feedlot operators in Dodge.

Instead, the county's actions immediately after its loss in court showed how confident local officials really were in believing that feedlots would continue to enjoy the freedom from oversight that had somehow become the norm.

The Briefest Victory Lap

Following our victory in court, my family experienced what I would call "very cautious relief." We believed the justice system had done its job, but we'd also witnessed, up close and very personally, the plots and ploys Dodge County officials had performed in recent years to push feedlot permits across the finish line, transforming the ag district into a playground for multinational corporations. We were skeptical from the get-go, yet the breathtaking efficiency of the county's counteroffensive was nevertheless a spectacle to behold.

The court's decision to vacate Mr. Masching's permit came down on November 18, 2014. He didn't appeal the court decision. Instead, he behaved as though the judgment held no weight. Two days later, on November 20, Nick Masching reapplied for a CUP for the very same project.[24] It was an audacious move but a move one makes when local officials are believed to be in one's pocket.

By the morning of November 21, within twenty-four hours of receiving the new application, county officials completed and submitted a staff report recommending approval of the CUP. The report's instantaneous appearance suggests that information was flowing back and forth between the applicant and the county. It seemed to be a coordinated effort.

Likewise, that same morning, the county received comments from not one but three local agencies that were required to review the application and the staff report. It was as if the agencies already knew the report would be submitted that morning. The county also sent a copy to Westfield Township for review.[25] As described in chapter 10, three Westfield officials had entered into manure easement agreements with members of Mr. Masching's family just days before Nick filed the initial CUP application for this feedlot. These officials neither disclosed their arrangements with Mr. Masching's family nor entered any objections to the new application.

Attentive readers might well be asking, if the court vacated the original application based on its insufficient information, then did the new application include the required information? While that would be a reasonable conclusion, at this point Dodge County officials were acting outside the bounds of reason. Rather than requiring Mr. Masching to include the information, the county amended the application form by stripping out most of the questions.

County officials then scheduled a special meeting of the Dodge County Planning Commission for December 11 for the sole purpose of reviewing the new CUP. They also rescheduled the regular meeting of the Dodge County Board of Commissioners for the same day. This arrangement was the ultimate fast track.[26] By scheduling the recommending body (i.e., the planning commission) and the voting body (i.e., the board of commissioners) on the same day, the two groups would issue their decisions almost simultaneously, preventing any opportunity for public discourse or debate between the recommendation and the vote.

December 11 was an important date for my family but for different reasons: our elder daughter was scheduled for a C-section on the twelfth, and Douglas and I had already booked a flight to see her the morning of the eleventh. We rescheduled our flight for that evening instead, then joined my father and siblings to prepare for our second appearance before the Dodge County Planning Commission. With the help of our attorney and the Dodge County Concerned Citizens, we reassembled many of the materials from the lawsuit, including our sworn affidavits, letters, and scientific data. The day before the hearing, we submitted to the Dodge County Planning Office a five-hundred-plus-page detailed accounting of the hazards that would accompany the proposed feedlot.

Our submission stood against the county's own staff report, a ten-page assemblage of fluff recommending approval of the CUP without equivocation. A county staff report is meant to be an unbiased document compiled by public officials, yet it did not in good faith include the many concerns that local residents had raised about the feedlot.

On the morning of the hearing, Douglas and I practiced our public comments during the drive from Minneapolis. We knew that nothing we said would change any votes, but we wanted our words on the record for the public and the press. Five of the seven planning commission members were factory feedlot owners, children of feedlot owners, or industry supporters; in the year prior, the tally had stood at four of seven. At this point, they may as well have called themselves the "feedlot commission" rather than the planning commission.

We arrived at the little municipal building across the street from the courthouse in Mantorville, and upon entering the hearing room, we felt about as welcome as skunks at a garden party. The hostility coming from the front of the room, where the planning commission members sat, was palpable. We were informed that the "public" part of the public hearing would be truncated that day, with testimony from each person limited to three minutes.[27]

During my brief allotted time, I spoke about the conflicts of interest on the planning commission and asked members to recuse themselves. As a trained attorney, I recognized that two types of bias were present. First, the commission had a general industry bias, an implicit conflict of interest. Stricter feedlot permitting and oversight would affect feedlot operators in Dodge writ large, including the sitting commission members.

Then there were direct conflicts. For example, Joshua Toquam sat on the commission during the hearing despite his parents' direct involvement in the project under consideration. Not only had the Toquams sold the six-acre parcel to construct the feedlot in question, but we also later learned they had quietly entered into a manure easement agreement with Mr. Masching while the lawsuit against the project was pending that summer.[28]

Following my family's comments, the commission voted to recommend the permit. Minutes later, the county board rubber-stamped the CUP. Again.

The following month, my parents filed their second lawsuit against Dodge County, the Board of Commissioners, and Masching Swine Farms LLC. The lawsuit challenged the issuance of the second CUP and requested that it be vacated. It was essentially a rinse and repeat of the first lawsuit but further alleged that the county had whitewashed its feedlot application form, stripping away most questions in violation of the county's feedlot ordinance.

Soon after, in February 2015, the planning commission recommended changing the county's feedlot ordinance by drastically reducing the information required for initial CUP applications.[29] This action was a direct response to the court's order for Dodge officials to obtain all pertinent information from applicants. Judge Jodi L. Williamson, with chambers in the same tiny courthouse as the Dodge County Board of Commissioners, also held in her judgment that "the [CUP] application process was faulty from the very beginning, preventing the opportunity for a full public hearing."[30]

Instead of heeding the court's direction, the county amended the CUP application, betting it couldn't be disciplined for omitting information if the forms didn't include the questions to begin with. Amazingly, the gambit worked. The county board took up the planning commission's recommendation and adopted the ordinance amendment.[31]

There was just one problem: this maneuvering was illegal. Feedlot applications must include all of the information required under Minnesota law at the time of the initial public hearing.[32] This requirement itself was based on a compromise made under industry pressure. Years prior, the Minnesota legislature exempted feedlots under a thousand AUs from state environmental review. In making this change, the state established a public hearing requirement: feedlot permits brought before county boards must include everything required under Minnesota Administrative Rules' chapter 7020, which governs animal feedlots, and incomplete applications "must not be processed by the commissioner or delegated county feedlot pollution control officer."[33]

By creating an ordinance amendment that prevents public disclosure of the required information, Dodge County formalized a process that violated state law and would allow feedlot CUPs in the county to be issued without appropriate public discourse or oversight. This action not only circumvented the democratic process but also presented a clear danger to public health. My family was determined to continue our fight against it.

PART 3
The Resistance

The ultimate test of a moral society is the
kind of world that it leaves to its children.

—DIETRICH BONHOEFFER

12

Don't Drink the Water (or the Kool-Aid)

"America's pork producers are very pleased that the president ordered EPA and the Corps of Engineers to repeal or re-write this ill-conceived, overbroad regulation. The WOTUS [waters of the United States] rule was a dramatic government overreach and an unprecedented expansion of federal jurisdiction and control over private lands."—JOHN WEBER, NPPC president, celebrating pending repeal of Clean Water Act provisions, 2017

During the years of rapid CAFO expansion, something peculiar began to occur across midwestern farm country. Small lakes and streams were going dry. Water levels in wells were dropping. In the Central Sands region of Wisconsin, a popular fishing lake dried up completely in 2006, the fish by the thousands found dead in the mud.[1] In Illinois during the summer of 2012, the worst drought in decades caused waterways to go completely dry. Local towns and cities enacted emergency water-preservation protocols, farmers lost their crops, and livestock operators, unable to provide enough water for the animals, had to kill their herds.[2] Ironically, the CAFO owners who suffered the most during the crisis also had a role in causing it: concentrated animal feedlots and the intensive volumes of water they require to operate are a major component in today's groundwater depletion crisis.

In 2015 the Minnesota Department of Natural Resources sounded the alarm, releasing a report about substantially increased groundwater usage in the state. According to the report, large animal feedlot operations are a leading cause of groundwater depletion, with many counties in Minnesota doubling or even tripling their annual water usage during the previous two decades. The DNR warned that "an increasing reliance on groundwater may not be a sustainable path for our continued economic growth and development."[3]

Animal feedlot operations drawing more than a million gallons of water per year must be permitted by the DNR in Minnesota. A typical swine CAFO draws between two million and five million gallons annually; yet as per the DNR's own admission, most feedlots in Minnesota are not in compliance with DNR permitting. In March 2015 Dodge County, along with nearby Blue Earth and Freeborn Counties, was put at the center of a DNR compliance sweep. The department hoped that permitting would compel feedlot operators to track water usage and thus be incentivized to use less. In Dodge County at that time, only six of the dozens of qualifying feedlots possessed a water use appropriation permit.[4]

Groundwater depletion is a concern for many area residents who use private wells. Eugene Nilsen, a Dodge County resident, first encountered a problem with his well in the late 1990s soon after the first CAFOS went up near his property.[5] When his well's water table began dropping, eventually Eugene called the well company. The serviceman who came out told him to look around. The source of Eugene's problem was clearly visible, housed by the stark white structures standing gracelessly in the fields surrounding his home.

"Count the hogs," the serviceman said. "That's where your water is going."

Eugene spent thousands of dollars fixing the issues caused by the dwindling water supply, but by the winter of 2015, he concluded the well would be dry within a few years. Hoping to prevent this before it was too late, he filed a complaint with the local DNR office in Rochester. Coincidentally, that same month the DNR launched its investigation into southern Minnesotan factory farms that were lacking water appropriation permits. The DNR claimed that as part of this investigation, it would address complaints from neighbors such as Eugene Nilsen with drying wells.

Eugene's farm, similar to my family's farm, was surrounded by nearly a dozen hog CAFOS by 2015, with an estimated thirty thousand pigs living within two miles of his home. A 2,400-head hog barn—the typical feedlot size in Dodge—draws 3.5 million gallons of water per year.[6] Assuming this baseline estimate, the twelve confinements in our immediate vicinity were likely drawing nearly forty-two million gallons of water annually. It's a shocking tally.

Ultimately, nothing much came of the DNR's crackdown. While permitting briefly increased during the 2015 compliance sweep, the department was understaffed, and with feedlot operators accustomed to the long tradition of permitting noncompliance, the DNR was working within a system that wasn't structured to expect compliance. Spending between $10,000 and $30,000 on a new well is just another externalized cost of feedlot agriculture that folks living near CAFOs are expected to shoulder while the meatpacking corporations rake in billions of dollars from pork sales.

Depleted groundwater is troubling; perhaps more troubling is water contamination. With each additional feedlot going up nearby, Eugene became more concerned about his drinking water. He had seen with his own eyes that neighboring farmers didn't follow the manure land application guidelines. The rules are clear: don't apply at specified times of year, don't apply during "rainfall or snow melt events," and don't apply too much on too little acreage, which causes excess nitrogen and phosphorous content.[7] Farmers regularly breach all of these rules as the sheer concentration of area factory farms results in dwindling available acreage for land application of the manure.

One incident in particular stuck with Eugene. A neighboring hog farmer had about twenty acres of land near his home that didn't get planted. Eugene noticed and wondered about it. Why purchase land that's perfectly good for production but not use it? The answer became clear one sweltering August day, when he witnessed the farmer come out with a semitrailer filled with thousands of gallons of manure. The man didn't have the requisite applicator to knife it into the ground. He just opened the gate valve in the back and drove around that field, letting the manure run aground to the point where the truck's tires were inches deep in it. The manure sat pooled on the surface for days. Eugene believes that with the first rain that came, portions that hadn't already leached into the groundwater washed right into the nearby river.

This type of "manure management" was unthinkable in the days before CAFOs, yet factory farm operators routinely assure the public that such incidents don't take place. Don't trust your lying eyes, they say.

Dodge sits at the top of the watershed for two environmentally impaired rivers—the Zumbro and the Cedar. Little Dodge County, with twenty thousand citizens, produces raw sewage equivalent to a human population of nearly a million thanks to the easy CAFO permitting. While the local ordinance requires manure management plans for certain types of feedlots, no such file exists for many CAFOs that should be required to submit plans based on their size and other factors. I won't hold my breath for the county to follow up on that. I'm not sure it would matter anyway, because manure management plans tend to contain scarce details and because inspections aren't conducted regularly. In truth, no one knows where and how much manure is being lathered onto the land.

But we do know where some of it ends up, beginning with Eugene's well. In the fall of 2015, he submitted a water sample to a testing lab retained by the Olmsted County Department of Environmental Resources in Rochester, Minnesota. A few weeks later, he received the results: the water tested positive for coliform bacteria. "Your water may not be safe to drink," the report advised. Eugene carefully followed the department's specifications to disinfect the well, using bleach and following a process that took about six hours. He waited a few days, then submitted a follow-up sample to Olmsted County to verify that the water was disinfected.

While awaiting the results, Eugene attended a meeting of the Dodge County Planning Commission to share concerns about his well and water contamination. A humble man who prefers the simple pleasures, Eugene is not one to bring attention or conflict his way. Yet he's also a person of deep integrity who isn't afraid to speak the truth, and speaking the truth became unavoidable. In Dodge County, neighbors harmed by CAFO development have three choices: stay silent and suffer the consequences, speak up while suffering the consequences, or move.

Eugene submitted his public comments, including the positive coliform results, prior to the planning commission's meeting. At the meeting, the county's zoning administrator blindsided him by presenting the new water testing results, which now showed no detection of coliform bacteria. Evidently, in anticipation of Eugene's planned comment, the administrator had intercepted the results from the second water test and read them before Eugene did. The administrator conveniently failed to mention that Eugene had disinfected his well prior to submitting the second test.

Two years later, in 2017, Eugene tested his well again, and the results showed the presence of coliform bacteria at *fifteen times* the recommended safe level.[8] By then, after suffering gastrointestinal symptoms, he no longer drank the water. Unfortunately, unlike Eugene, many unsuspecting neighbors don't test their water and may fail to link their drinking water to bouts of illness. Why would they, when they are routinely assured that living near CAFOS is safe?

Since testing for every type of pathogen is difficult and costly, testing labs use the presence of coliform bacteria as a bellwether indicator that other dangerous microorganisms may be present in the water supply. One such microorganism, *E. coli*, can sicken people after a single exposure. Other pathogens that can cause severe gastrointestinal disease, kidney failure, and death include *Salmonella* and *Listeria monocytogenes*. Studies have linked disease outbreaks caused by such pathogens to livestock waste.[9] Additional by-products of CAFO-generated manure that can contaminate water include excess nitrogen and phosphorous, antibiotics, growth hormones, and copper sulfate.[10]

According to EPA records, "The drinking water of millions of Americans living in or near farming communities across the country is contaminated by dangerous amounts of nitrates and coliform bacteria from fertilizer and manure widely used in agriculture."[11] Private wells in farming communities are routinely found to have nitrate levels above the municipal drinking water safety threshold of ten parts per million. This high bar is based on when levels become potentially fatal to infants, but drinking water at even half this limit increases the risk for colon, kidney, ovarian, and bladder cancers; miscarriages; thyroid disease; and neural tube birth defects.[12]

A 2017 report showed that samplings of private wells in Dodge County between 1995 and 2016 found 24 percent contained coliform bacteria.[13] The county also published data collected between 1995 and

2011 showing that 21 percent of private wells contained nitrate "above background concentrations," and 7 percent contained nitrate above the legal drinking water limit of ten parts per million.[14] The county acknowledged that contamination was more prevalent in areas of Dodge "with shallow soils over limestone and over sand aquifers."[15]

I'm baffled that even with this contamination data, the county continues to permit feedlots over karst. Recall that in chapter 5, residents of Berne in northern Dodge, where karst topography dominates, fought hard against the first large swine CAFO in 2006. The community lost that battle.

In the years that followed, my husband's mother, Ruth, along with other Berne residents, watched as the nitrate levels in her private well shot up. Ruth encouraged family members to drink only bottled water at the farm. In the fall of 2013, she succumbed to cancer. For years, Douglas's family participated in the state's nitrate-monitoring program and dutifully submitted water samples to the local environmental services office in the spring and fall. The results were damning: nitrate levels regularly came back between twenty and twenty-seven milligrams per liter, or *three times* the municipal drinking limit. Douglas's family spent several thousand dollars to install a reverse osmosis system that removes contaminants from the water.

While pigs in the Berne area's factory farms drink pristine water drawn from a well drilled 480 feet down through multiple layers of porous limestone to the Prairie du Chien aquifer, residents drink water filled with nitrate from the pigs' manure. Today, locals refer to County Road B, the main thoroughfare north of Douglas's family farm, as "Cancer Road."

County Road B garnered international media attention following a 2023 news report that highlighted the nitrate contamination found in area water supplies. The reporter, Keith Schneider, spoke with four families who shared stories of twelve cancer cases and seven deaths concentrated along a short stretch of this single rural road. "Though the causes of the cancers are not proven, a key suspected culprit is believed to be the elevated levels of nitrates that have contaminated the drinking water for County Road B families," Schneider wrote.[16]

Contaminants deriving from livestock manure are also found in public water systems. A 2020 study found that the drinking water of an estimated half million Minnesotans is drawn from groundwater with elevated nitrate levels, citing "fertilizer and manure that runs off from farm fields and seeps into groundwater" as the primary contamination source.[17] In this and other ways, feedlot pollution is both a localized and a dispersed problem. Groundwater leaching impacts public water supplies in neighboring towns and cities, and pollution in local rivers and streams is an uncontained hazard.

Data from the EPA shows that as of 2018–19, 42 percent of the length of lakes and streams in the United States had elevated phosphorous levels, and 44 percent have elevated levels of nitrogen. The EPA attributes these elevated levels primarily to fertilizer and manure runoff.[18] In Iowa, where hogs outnumber people by seven to one, well over half of all waterways are impaired.[19] The widespread degradation of waterways not only impacts people's health, well-being, and leisure activities but also causes massive fish kills and contaminates the fish that we eat. This is, of course, only a broad summary of the impacts of concentrated livestock agriculture on wildlife and the health of ecological systems.

In 2019 the Minnesota Pollution Control Agency issued a report about pollution in the Minnesota River, which eventually flows to the Mississippi. The report identified livestock manure runoff as a primary culprit behind an emerging environmental emergency that, per local press coverage of the report, is "degrading our superstar Minnesota River to sewer status."[20] Worryingly, while the report indicated that the area of southern Minnesota included in the study contains 135 federally defined CAFOs (those holding a thousand-plus AUs), it did not specify the locations or the sizes of these feedlots—information that the public deserves to know. It also acknowledged that "while a full accounting of the fate and transport of manure was not conducted for this project, it is clear that a large portion of it is ultimately applied to the land surface and therefore, this source is of significant concern."[21] So the MPCA can identify the pollution and deduce that much of it derives from factory farm manure, but lacking oversight capabilities, the agency is unable to pinpoint the most serious offenders or hold them accountable if identified.

Another MPCA study concluded that in Minnesotan regions dominated by agricultural land, "just half or fewer" of the area lakes "do not fully support swimming" due to excessive phosphorous levels, which are likewise caused in part by manure runoff.[22] My family's beloved home of Minnesota, the "Land of 10,000 Lakes," has become the land of 4,600 impaired waterways. The meatpacking industry uses local rivers and streams as its own personal toilet. It's no wonder that my father used to proclaim, "I don't call them 'pork producers.' I call them 'shit producers.'"

In 2019 the American Public Health Association, in response to an avalanche of research connecting concentrated animal feedlots to serious environmental and public health hazards, recommended a moratorium on all new or expanding CAFOs nationwide until the federal government "removes such operations from reporting exemptions related to environmental emissions." The association specifically called for ending air pollution reporting exemptions under CERCLA and asked the federal government to "enforce the Clean Water Act as it pertains to CAFOs."[23]

In making this request, the association presumably knew perfectly well that the EPA has its hands tied as far as the Clean Water Act (CWA) is concerned yet hoped the public denouncement would instigate some kind of change. Under the CWA, pollution "point sources" that discharge pollutants into U.S. waters are subject to certain permitting requirements; the EPA identified CAFOs as point sources as early as the 1980s. Back then, when CAFOs were few, they were designated a low enforcement priority, and the EPA asked the states to issue permits and regulate feedlots on the agency's behalf. Many states ignored this direction. Well into the 2000s, some states weren't even issuing permits.

By 2003 CAFOs were the dominant form of livestock agriculture, and the EPA finally published a comprehensive rule concerning CWA enforcement via the National Pollution Discharge Elimination System permit program. The new rule required most types of feedlots to obtain NPDES permits. But soon afterward, a handful of court decisions stripped down the rule; a 2012 decision exempted CAFOs that don't "actively discharge" pollution. This judgment disqualified the vast majority of CAFOs, because the actual building sites—namely, the barns—do not "actively discharge" waste. Manure is discharged off-site during land application or when fields are sprayed with the liquid manure from outdoor storage lagoons. A similar loophole exempted "precipitation-related discharges," effectively disqualifying manure runoff, one of the primary forms of CAFO-caused water pollution.[24]

Among CAFO owners, as well as the state agencies tasked with monitoring the facilities, there is a culture of disregard for following the rules that accompany permitting. As a result, the EPA is unable to carry out even those few regulations that haven't been rescinded via judicial decisions and legislative loopholes. If a state doesn't collect information about a CAFO, then the EPA drives blind. In 2010 an investigation by the nonpartisan U.S. Government Accountability Office concluded that the EPA "could not fulfill its regulatory duties under the Clean Water Act" because the agency lacked "facility-specific information" about feedlots. The EPA agreed, stating that "unlike many other point source industries, the EPA does not have facility-specific information for all CAFOs in the United States."[25]

Nonenforcement continues, and the consequences accumulate. Dodge County is but one among many farming communities that suffer due to the industry's environmental reporting exemptions. Evidently public officials are largely unwilling or unable to pursue the clear solution—that is, limiting CAFO development and requiring existing feedlots of all sizes to monitor and mitigate pollution.

Reimagining the Grassroots in Dodge

When the government fails in its duties, the public has many avenues for pushing back: casting a vote, exercising First Amendment rights to free speech and assembly, or becoming a public servant and creating change from within. Such is the great tradition of U.S. democracy, and in Dodge County, we weren't about to lose sight of that.

When the county board approved the ordinance amendment to remove public disclosure requirements for feedlot CUP applications, members of the Dodge County Concerned Citizens realized it was time to launch a new effort to curb unbridled development. Our first idea was to push for local planning and zoning regulations in Westfield Township, as had been done a decade prior in neighboring Ripley Township. Given the lack of top-down industry regulation, hyper-local regulation is one of the few existing tools for keeping industry abuses in check. Regulations might limit feedlot size, increase the minimum acreage requirement for feedlots, or require an owner/operator to live on the site where the CAFO will be situated.

In the spring of 2015, the Dodge County Concerned Citizens wrote and circulated a petition calling for a special township meeting for residents to vote on a single question: Should Westfield Township adopt local land use and zoning regulations? As per Minnesota law, townships must convene a special meeting if 20 percent of residents sign a petition. In tiny Westfield, we needed thirty-two signatures.[26]

We collected them the old-fashioned way, going door-to-door. This process told us a great deal about where the community stood. The feedlot operators were openly hostile, going so far as to chase us away and shouting obscenities—so much for civil discourse. Many neighbors supported the cause and signed without question. A few residents weren't sure, or they supported feedlot restrictions but were afraid to openly support the cause.

Early in the process, one township resident confessed that she supported local feedlot regulations but feared harassment from the hog clique. She offered to sign the petition only if we failed to reach the thirty-two-signature threshold. "I'll risk my job," she said. Another resident likewise said he feared retribution. He referenced an argument he'd recently had with a prominent member of the feedlot crew. "It didn't come to blows," he said, "but it was close."

It turned out we didn't need those two signatures. Despite the fear-based reticence of many residents of Westfield Township, within a few weeks we collected sixty-nine signatures, nearly half the township. We presented the petition at the annual meeting in early March. The town clerk slowly read all sixty-nine names on the petition aloud. This recitation was not standard procedure, nor was it required. It was a public broadcasting of the signers. The hog gang took note.[27]

Right after the meeting, several feedlot operators surrounded one Westfield Township resident as he walked to his car, demanding an apology for his recent complaint with the DNR over his dwindling well water. This incident was the first indication that the hog people fully intended to intimidate township residents. They did so with gusto during the three weeks between the petition's presentation and the special township meeting prompted by the petition, scheduled for March 31.

Also immediately following the meeting where the petition was presented, a locally prominent swine factory farm operator whose family owns more than seven thousand hogs sent a threatening email to a resident who had signed the petition.[28] This operator has many connections with the national Big Ag network and is one of the de facto heads of the hog gang in the immediate area. He copied several local swine operators on the email, which stated, in part:

> Your name was read as one of the people who signed the petition being circulated. . . . I realize it is well within your personal rights to do as you wish. However, it will not be good for the [local] businesses and community if you lose any further credibility because of this issue. A feedlot battle is not something you should be involved in. I highly recommend issuing a public statement apologizing . . . and you are going to refrain from future involvement. It is your reputation and also it reflects negatively upon the business community and the local ag community. Your job should be to unite, not to be in the dividing lines.[29]

The threat worked. The resident, whose job relied heavily on relationships with the local business community, understandably chose to remain silent.

Other residents received harassing telephone calls, including from the wife of a Westfield Township supervisor who pressured citizens to remove their names from the petition. Some residents yielded to the pressure and removed their names, but the majority held firm. The special township meeting to consider the issue moved forward as scheduled.

The meeting was held at Westfield Town Hall, a simple, rectangular white steel building situated along the banks of the Cedar River. As with many of the homes in Westfield Township, not much is in the hall's immediate vicinity save for trees and fields. The building is easy to access, set back several yards from the main road, Highway 30. To this day, an antique yellow road grader with steel wheels sits out front—a reminder of the crude roads constructed decades ago in the township.

The town hall is a small building for a small township, but on the evening of March 31, attendees made it painfully clear that this meeting wasn't for the township. It was yet another showdown coordinated by the swine industry.[30]

Pulling into the parking lot, I was immediately struck by the number of cars there, with overflow onto Highway 30. I entered the town hall as I'd done many times before and was confused to find that the meeting area was empty. Instead, I was ushered through an internal doorway leading to a large storage area where road equipment is usually stored. Two Dodge County sheriff's deputies stood near the doorway. I was shocked to see that the storage room had been cleared out and now contained over two hundred folding chairs. Apparently, this would be our meeting's venue. Searching for a familiar face, I saw few.

The people present were not residents of Westfield Township; members of the swine industry occupied the chairs. Contract growers had descended on Westfield to intimidate residents, fulfilling one of the unwritten obligations that comes with signing the contract. With the click of a button, industry bosses can send mass emails to hundreds of hog growers in southern Minnesota, activating the network of corporate soldiers to harass a township that's attempting to adopt local zoning rules. Similar to a political rally, supporters are summoned from near and far.

The meeting was called into session, and the township supervisors distributed a meeting agenda that invited "comments from Westfield

Township residents *and people with taxable interests* [emphasis mine]."[31] This wording was a big red flag. Special meetings convened by a citizen's petition are meant for township electors, for residents. The odd revision led me to believe the township was consulting with an attorney. "People with taxable interests" is a broad mandate that opens the floor to anyone operating land in the township, including feedlot operators.

As per Minnesota statute, during a special electors' meeting, only matters listed in the meeting's notice can be discussed. In this case, the sole matter listed was local planning and zoning. Township supervisors had one job that evening—to set up the ballot box and allow residents to vote on the following question: Shall the township adopt zoning regulations and restrictions? It was a yes or no question designed to launch the process of discussing, debating, and potentially drafting local regulations.

After supervisors handed out the meeting agenda, who should appear but Jack Perry, the industry lobbyist who was also the attorney for swine operator Nick Masching in my parents' pending lawsuit. The township supervisors introduced Perry and promptly held a vote to secure his representation. That was a new one—hiring an industry attorney to represent the township, as if the industry's interests and the township's interests were one and the same.

Jack Perry was someone I knew peripherally outside of my family's lawsuit. For many years, we both worked at different law firms located in the IDS Center in downtown Minneapolis. (Readers of a certain age may be familiar with the iconic building, made famous in the opening credits of the *Mary Tyler Moore Show*.) Perry was the perfect representative for an industry that follows a scorched-earth policy of running independent farmers out of business and evading responsible regulation at all costs. He is the quintessential litigator, projecting confidence and self-assurance in every setting, whether at a tiny township gathering, arguing before the court, or lobbying before the Minnesota legislature. With a generic handsome face and an upright military posture, Perry practices law in a way that I would describe as thorough yet detached. He's there to get the job done and doesn't seem particularly interested in the larger repercussions.

That evening, his job was to prevent the residents of Westfield Township from voting on local planning and zoning. Immediately assuming the role of township attorney, he took the floor and introduced Westfield Ordinance No. 2015.01, which calls for "a temporary prohibition on the establishment of (1) new land uses and (2) land use and zoning regulations and restrictions within Westfield Township."

The township supervisors approved the interim ordinance then and there. It temporarily barred any changes to local zoning regulations even if residents voted that evening in favor of making such changes. (Having served its purpose, the interim ordinance was promptly rescinded the following month.)

Ironically, this type of ordinance was created as a legal tool for townships to place moratoriums on CAFO projects. The industry had turned a shield into a weapon, degrading a law designed to protect communities from unwanted development into one wielded by developers to fight against community oversight.

My parents' attorney was in attendance that night, and he responded on his feet, trying to counteract the unexpected meeting takeover. He stated that township supervisors were acting illegally by conducting business outside the parameters of the special meeting and refusing to hold a vote via the ballot box. Where were the ballot sheets to hand out to the township residents in attendance?

In response, Perry asked the attendees whether the township should skip the vote on zoning, asking for a raise of hands. The room was dominated by feedlot operators from outside the township, and, of course, the majority of hands shot up. It was quite the show, an orchestrated spectacle giving the appearance of public input to the numerous journalists present.

The meeting ended with no vote taken and with the democratic process in Westfield Township dealt a wounding blow. Westfield residents were denied the opportunity to vote, our efforts thwarted by old-fashioned intimidation paired with extra-legal maneuverings. We later learned that Westfield Township paid almost $19,000 in attorney's fees to fight local planning and zoning, with the majority of that expense going to Jack Perry for "legal fees and phone calls."[32] The supervisors recklessly used public funds to game the democratic process, suppress CAFO opposition, and support the financial interests of a handful of local families involved in the swine industry.

As I watched these maneuverings unfold, my resolve to stand up to the industry solidified. This marked the beginning of my involvement in the national grassroots movement for ag reform and commonsense CAFO regulation.

FIG. 1. TOP: The Trom farm in Dodge County, Minnesota, is the heart of this story. The land was originally acquired in 1925 by my grandfather Elmer, who was raised on a neighboring farm. Photo by Laurie Schneider.

FIG. 2. BOTTOM: Siblings Jim, Peggy, Sonja, Brad, Shelley, and Randy (*pictured in reverse birth order*) operate the Trom family farm today. Photo by Laurie Schneider.

FIG. 3. Imagine the mixed emotions Great-grandfather Ed Trom (*right*) must have felt as he left his home in Hemsedal, Norway, generations deep with family history, and embarked upon a new continent. He boarded the *Thingvalla*, a passenger ship with a direct line from Scandinavia to Ellis Island, where he arrived on April 21, 1892. A sepia-tinted photograph shows a clean-shaven Ed dressed in a heavy wool coat, standing beside his mustachioed cousins donning impressive, heavy furs. Courtesy of the author.

FIG. 4. Great-grandfather Ed Trom was an industrious man. He constructed several homes, barns, and other structures throughout the Blooming Prairie area, many of which still stand today. His legacy remains the Westfield Lutheran Church, for which he served as the chief architect. Photo by Laurie Schneider.

FIG. 5. OPPOSITE TOP: Township meetings were typically held at Ripley Town Hall, a small venue originally serving as a one-room school for local children. During the battle over Ripley Dairy, nearly two hundred factory farm proponents from all over the county, the state, and even the country descended upon tiny Ripley Town Hall in Dodge County. Photo by Laurie Schneider.

FIG. 6. OPPOSITE BOTTOM: The Land Stewardship Project joined with local citizens to organize a protest on the county road bordering the Trom family farm. Local citizens learned that the Minnesota AgriGrowth Council, a pro-industry group, had planned a bus tour of the area. Its first stop was the Hormel Foods meatpacking plant in Austin, twenty-three miles south of our farm. The second stop was the proposed site of Ripley Dairy, three miles north of our farm. This route would take the tour bus right past our farm and the project's protesters. Courtesy of the Land Stewardship Project.

FIG. 7. ABOVE: Roger and Rhonda Toquam's first two-thousand-hog CAFO went up in 1993 and still stands today, one mile north of our farm. A second went up alongside it in 1998. Today, the twin CAFOs produce an estimated ten thousand hogs per year. Photo by Laurie Schneider.

FIG. 8. ABOVE: The Masching family owns several swine CAFOS in Dodge County, including these facilities owned by Scott Masching. Photo by Laurie Schneider.

FIG. 9. OPPOSITE TOP: The Al-Corn Clean Fuel ethanol plant dominates the town of Claremont, six miles north of the Trom farm. The large vapor plume is the result of the conversion of corn to ethanol, which is then transferred into dozens of black rail tankers and shipped elsewhere for further processing. The residue, distiller's dried grains, is used as an ingredient in the feed given to animals confined in area factory farms. Photo by Laurie Schneider.

FIG. 10. OPPOSITE BOTTOM: Following its closure, Claremont High School was converted to dormitory housing for area factory farm workers. Photo by Laurie Schneider.

FIG. 11. TOP: This controversial swine factory farm owned by Nick Masching was the subject of two legal actions and constructed a half mile west of the Trom farm. Photo by Laurie Schneider.

FIG. 12. BOTTOM: Nearly two hundred members of the swine industry appeared at the Westfield Town Hall in the spring of 2015 to fight citizen efforts to adopt local planning and zoning to limit the proliferation of area factory farms. Photo by Laurie Schneider.

FIG. 13. In November 2017 we were trapped in the center of an endless loop of
manure tankers transferring manure to field applicators. The semi tankers loaded
up at the Toquam swine feedlots. The waste was pumped from tanker to applicator;
then the tankers drove by our farm before heading back to the Toquam farm for
another load. The vehicles made countless laps that day around the same square
mile while my father attempted to finish his fall harvest. Courtesy of the author.

FIG. 14. LEFT: In November 2017, during manure pump-out, a manure tanker attempted to force our vehicle off the road near the Trom farm. Courtesy of the author.

FIG. 15. BELOW: In the fall of 2017, while picking corn, Lowell had to step off the combine to vomit due to dangerous gases emitted during manure pump-outs of neighboring swine CAFOs. Courtesy of the author.

FIG. 16. Blooming Prairie's Main Street is lined with a number of empty stores, and a sea of gray hair fills area church pews on Sunday mornings. A generation of farmers is ominously absent, and we know the source of this sorrow. Photo by Laurie Schneider.

13
The Corporate Bully

"Be there to support other farmers in your community if they apply for a permit for a new or expanded facility. Make the time to get involved. We are all busy, but there are some meetings that are so important that farmers can't afford to not have representation at them. Work with your farm groups to educate local elected officials about modern agriculture."
—MINNESOTA FARM BUREAU FOUNDATION, "When an Activist Group Comes to Town"

On a sunny June morning in 2015, Douglas and I departed the Twin Cities and embarked on the familiar, well-worn route to our family farms in Dodge County. We had traveled this road many times before, but our trips home were no longer the carefree family visits of years past. They were imbued now with a sense of purpose, even urgency. My family's second lawsuit against the Dodge County Board of Commissioners was pending in the courts, and our reputation for speaking out against factory farms was stretching beyond southern Minnesota. As our fight continued, much to my surprise, I received numerous phone calls from citizens in rural farming communities in northern Minnesota, Wisconsin, and North Dakota—all asking the same question: How do I fight the installation of a factory farm?

Each person had a unique story to tell, but I began to recognize the commonalities, the telltale anxiety and feeling of disorientation when rural constituents realize their community is about to be changed forever and that a well-financed corporate army stands against anyone trying to prevent it. At first, I felt like an unwitting soldier in a war I hadn't signed up for. My family just wanted to protect ourselves, our land, our livelihood. Yet as I learned more about the battles occurring in rural counties across the Midwest, my natural tendency to fight for what's right was stirred. I became animated with purpose. Folks were asking for help, and I needed to respond.

I wasn't alone. The Trom siblings weren't about to stand idly by while international meatpacking conglomerates made billions, leaving independent famers in the dust and running rural residents off the land.

When Douglas and I arrived in Dodge that morning, our first stop was his family's farm, the Eayrs farm on the northern end of the county. I dropped him off—he was helping with tasks on the farm that day—then continued south to the Trom farm, where my brother Randy and I planned to begin work on a short documentary about the hog war unfolding in Dodge County.

Randy, the eldest Trom sibling, has always been the creative one. He worked for many years as a radio and television professional. As befits this public-facing career, he is gregarious and articulate, as well as tall and handsome, with the serious yet approachable demeanor of a television host. He's also a gifted musician. As kids, we loved listening to his renditions of Herb Alpert and the Tijuana Brass on trumpet. Just as Douglas and I do, Randy and his wife, Karen, have two daughters, but their family lived in neighboring Wisconsin, within driving distance of the Trom farm.

Though Randy wasn't as involved in the day-to-day operations of the farm as our brothers, Brad and Jim, were, ours is a family farm through and through: we all help in whatever capacity we can. With our mom in the nursing home and our father soon to become a nonagenarian, seeing each of us step into our roles was incredibly gratifying. My youngest brother, Jim, was becoming the heart of the operation as its devoted operations manager. An electrician, Jim knows how to repair, maintain, and operate all of the equipment, and works with our agronomist to select our seed and crop inputs. He attends to the day-to-day operations; I handle the budgeting and work with our accountants. Jim and I both watch the markets daily, always looking for the opportune moment to sell grain. My brother Brad serves as the groundskeeper, maintains the farmyard, and assists with the spring planting and fall harvest.

Randy thought a short film could be a good way to promote our citizens group, the Dodge County Concerned Citizens, and to raise public awareness about the community and environmental impacts of industrial-size factory farms. Prior to filming, I drafted the questions and brainstormed ideas for whom we might interview. Randy would conduct the interviews and produce the film, and Karen worked behind the scenes on the production team.

As we loaded my SUV and prepared to visit the first location, I was surprised to discover the extent of the production equipment that Randy transferred to my vehicle: a digital movie camera, a tripod, audio cables, headphones, and other electronics that I couldn't identify. I felt like a little kid again, admiring my older brother's cool gadgets. I remembered another adventure I'd gone on with Randy, when he let me ride the back of his emerald-green Yamaha motorcycle. I will never forget that ride, as we flew down the Claremont Road at ninety miles per hour. I'd never been so afraid in my life. That was the first and last time I joined him on a motorcycle.

Ironically, despite Randy's fondness for riding, he's always on the lookout for imminent dangers. His daughters call him "Safety Dad."

With the equipment loaded, it was time to depart. We drove along the township road and admired the gorgeous green carpet of corn and soybeans on either side of us. I told Randy to expect a Dodge County sheriff's deputy to pull us over at any moment. I'd learned in recent months that factory farm owners were large and in charge, and they did not want anyone to so much as look at their operation even from a distance. Randy shrugged off my concern. He'd spent his career interviewing people and tracking down stories; this time was nothing different.

We turned south onto the Claremont Road and stopped at the local hub for newborn baby piglets, a massive sow gestational unit. Randy set up his tripod on the side of the road, making certain that we didn't intrude on private property. The huge industrial complex was heavily fortified with security cameras. Randy waved to the cameras and filmed the property's exterior and adjoining composting station piled high with dead pigs hidden under wood chips. He explained that this footage would serve as an extreme long shot, also called an "extreme wide shot," to give contextualizing visual information to the viewer.

We reloaded the vehicle, drove less than a mile south to Highway 30, then turned and drove past two nurseries on either side of the highway.

We continued east to 150th Avenue, where several swine factory farms owned by members of the Masching family are located. We didn't stop at these locations; instead, Randy pointed his camera out the passenger window and filmed as we slowly drove by.

No sooner had we passed the first factory farm than we noticed an all-terrain vehicle and a pickup truck following closely behind us. Refusing to be intimidated, we calmly drove to our next location. We returned to the Claremont Road, drove north to the city of Claremont, and turned east onto Highway 14 toward Dodge Center, where we passed turkey factory farms the size of several football fields.

Randy was satisfied with the footage, so we turned around to head back home. Lo and behold, as predicted, a sheriff's deputy pulled us over. Concerned that his video camera would be confiscated, Randy removed the memory chip and slid it into his pocket as the deputy approached. The young officer appeared nervous and uncertain of the task at hand.

"Uh, are you filming a documentary?" he asked.

We readily answered his questions and produced our names and driver's licenses. He let us go quickly. We later learned that a member of the Masching family had called to complain about people filming in the area.[1] Our conjecture was that someone had seen us on the security camera at the first facility and sent out a message to area factory farm operators.

Filming along public roadways is perfectly legal, and we weren't loitering, littering, or behaving suspiciously. The local hog gang was using groundless complaints with the sheriff's department to intimidate us and gather information about our activities. This unnerving and arrogant pattern to secure local law enforcement to serve as corporate guardians would continue for years to come.

I spent the night at the Eayrs farm and rose early the following morning to drive back to the Trom farm. Our film only needed two days' worth of footage, and on day 2, Randy and I planned to interview a handful of folks about their experiences with area factory farms. During my drive over, Randy called, sounding alarmed. In the middle of the night, he'd seen a car drive into our farmyard. In farm country, you have to drive down a long driveway to reach the front of someone's farmhouse.

I hung up and turned onto the township road leading to the farm. As I approached our driveway, I saw a pile of loose garbage along the side of the road. Someone had dumped it sometime after I had departed the farm the prior night and before my return that morning.[2]

This wasn't the first time in recent months that garbage was dumped near our farm. It began about a year before, in the spring of 2014, when my parents first sued the county board and area swine operators. At one point Brad was picking up at least a bagful of garbage per week. My parents and siblings had their theories about who was behind it, worrying that the activities would escalate. In July 2014 my dad saw a man snooping around our property in the middle of the night. That time he was prompted to call the sheriff's office and request an extra patrol in the area. These activities continued, with vehicles driving around the farmyard in the middle of the night and garbage regularly left along the road outside our farm.

Just two weeks before Randy and I shot the documentary, my brothers witnessed a Westfield Township supervisor drive right into our farmyard and continue in a slow circle around the building site. Then he left. This bizarre showing could only be interpreted as some manner of threat or intimidation.

And now this morning, more garbage. I had planned to accompany my father to church that morning, but instead Randy and I discussed the incident and took footage of the garbage along the road. We knew the best way to protect ourselves was to continue to document and shine a light on what we experienced. We weren't the only ones.

Harassment on the Prairie

The harassment and intimidation that rural residents experience when they speak out against factory farms follow a familiar pattern that can only be understood when one considers the culture of factory farm owners and operators. Feedlot operators are an insider's club, a good ol' boy's network, a community within a community. Many strive to appear wealthier than the average rural resident, masking burdensome debt as they compete to get big. They tend to be active in local sporting events, at school events, and at corporate-sponsored events disguised as community events to bolster their image, such as the annual Ribfest in my hometown, Blooming Prairie.

While some area residents likely believe Ribfest is a homegrown affair that's been around for ages, Ribfest is a more recent "tradition" that was originally sponsored by Hormel. The industry recently recruited additional corporate sponsors, including the Minnesota Pork Board, Holden Farms, Cargill, and others in a corporate show of force in the small town. Each summer, sponsors donate racks of ribs and encourage teams to compete in a barbecue competition. The neighboring town of Claremont holds a similar annual gathering, Hogfest, which features a tractor pull, a street dance, mud bogs, and other events. The Dodge County Concerned Citizens participated in one of the first Hogfest parades, pulling a wagon decorated with black-and-neon-yellow "NO FACTORY FARM" signs. Immediately following the parade, one of the organizers yelled at Brad and forbade the group from participating in any future parades.

Creating and sponsoring these types of local pork-centric events helps ensure corporate dominance and a positive public image, allowing the hog industry and feedlot operators to continue making money in a way that harms the community and often ruins neighbor's lives.

This might sound cynical, but it's the plain truth. The Minnesota Farm Bureau Foundation's "When an Activist Group Comes to Town" urges feedlot operators to be active community participants as a way not only to promote their business but also to pave the way for continuous feedlot expansion. "Every community has opinion leaders. Identify them, address their concerns, and they may become valuable allies in your efforts to expand," the publication advises. It continues: "Perhaps you can invite the community to a pot-luck dinner or Sunday picnic. An event like this can generate positive public feelings, and give you an opportunity to talk about your farm and your family. . . . Being active in local civic organizations puts you in contact with opinion leaders, and helps them recognize you as a concerned member of the community. Supporting community church activities and contributing to youth organizations like 4-H and FFA [formerly the Future Farmers of America] also helps show your family's importance to the community."[3]

Feedlot operators position themselves as local protectors who uphold the economy and shield the community from the dangerous outside world with its dirty cities and corrupt politicians. The psychology behind this has a very mafioso quality to it. Factory farm operators like to convince others—and, to be fair, have deeply convinced themselves—that Big Ag and industrialized agriculture are necessary to feed the world. Without them and their sacred, overpopulated hog barns, the farming community would collapse. In this system of logic, anyone who opposes factory farming is a threat—not only to the feedlot operator's personal business and profits but to everyone else as well.

It's classic doublethink, and it's created a toxic social environment that divides farming communities, with far-reaching implications.

Dead animals left in mailboxes and on front stoops; death threats, raised rents, social ostracization; fires set in front yards; threats to local businesses; getting fired from your job—these experiences are common among rural residents who speak out against new CAFOs or proposed feedlot expansions. When choosing a site for a new CAFO, the industry targets remote rural areas often inhabited by poor or undereducated residents who are likely to either drink the industry Kool-Aid or lack the resources to effectively fight back. In an industry game of Whac-a-Mole, these isolated battles—strategically targeted in remote or impoverished locales—are part of a systematic strategy to permanently anchor the corporate Big Ag factory farm economy.

In 2004 in Swift County, Minnesota, farmer Orvin Gronseth received a midnight call from a neighbor, advising him that four round hay bales had been set on fire at the end of his driveway. Gronseth had a yard sign displaying his opposition to the new factory farms coming into the area.[4]

In Kewaunee County, Wisconsin, Lynn and Nancy Utesch, specialty farmers in rotational grazing for grass-fed beef, are part of a citizen's group fighting the expansion of industrial-size hog, dairy, and beef CAFOs in the area. The couple reports that intimidation from fellow community members is a "daily occurrence" that "just comes with the territory of speaking out against CAFOs."[5]

In Clear Lake, Iowa, lifelong independent hog farmer Chris Petersen has been speaking out against CAFO development for over twenty years. He has received numerous death threats. "It's the price you pay for doing the right thing," according to Chris.[6]

In Iowa, the top pork-producing state, agriculture is the only major industry that is projected to lose jobs over the next decade. Environmental reporter Brian Bienkowski poignantly wrote about Iowa's incongruencies—more pork production with fewer farmers and in declining rural economies—when he visited its hog country in 2017. "Japan, Canada, Mexico and South Korea love pork and represent the leading customers for Iowa, which, in 2016, exported about $1 billion of pork," he wrote. "It's hard to see all that as I drive past classic Iowa scenery—corn, and some soybeans, as far as the eye can see. Interspersed are the long hog barns. But I don't see pigs. In fact, you can drive for hours through farm country in the state that raises a third of the nation's hogs, and not see a single one."[7]

In his travels across the state, Bienkowski spoke with many rural residents who stand in opposition to swine CAFOs out of pure necessity: their friends and neighbors have been driven out of business, swimming in local waterways or drinking from wells is dangerous, property values have plummeted, and the stench is unbearable. "I never thought I'd become an activist" is a refrain that Bienkowski heard from "almost everyone I visited in Iowa."[8]

And for this, the local hog bosses make sure there's a price to pay.

In south-central Michigan, Lynn Henning grows corn and soybeans with her husband, Dean, on a fourth-generation family farm in Lenawee County. Lynn was pulled into the hog wars in 2000, when a neighbor reported that a CAFO operator was dumping manure into a local creek. Alarmed, Lynn and Dean learned more about the pollution of area waterways and joined a local environmental group to test the waters. They learned that the twenty thousand dairy cattle and ten thousand hogs within a three-mile radius of their farm produced more waste than the city of Chicago. In the years to come, more CAFOs went up in Lenawee County, and the pollution worsened. As in Dodge County, Lenawee's independent farmers all but disappeared.

In 2008 Dean had a heart attack while cutting wood outside. That day operators were spreading manure on the surrounding fields, a practice that poses immediate, life-threatening health risks—including cardiac events—to anyone who happens to be outside. Despite this, operators are not required to alert neighboring residents when they're planning to haul and spread manure. Dean's parents, who live nearby, were both diagnosed with hydrogen sulfide poisoning. An elderly couple living in the area told Lynn they were considering suicide because their water was undrinkable, the smell around their home was so bad they couldn't open their windows, and they wanted to move but nobody would buy their house.

"They felt they were worth more dead," Lynn told a reporter for *Oprah* magazine.

For daring to speak out against the destruction of her community, Lynn says she's found dead animals on the hood of her car, stuffed in her mailbox, and on her porch. She was run off the road by a car following and harassing her.[9] Worst of all, her granddaughter's bedroom window was shot out while her granddaughter was inside sleeping.[10]

These examples are just a handful among hundreds, perhaps thousands, of harassment, intimidation, and outright threats and violence among neighbors that have become all too common in farm country today. The vast majority of these incidents go unreported because the threats are effective. People decide to stay quiet when they realize that speaking against factory farms will put their jobs, businesses, and families at risk. Livestock operators make it very clear that one's position on the latest factory farm development is a purity test that measures the loyalty of the locals.

This power imbalance is exacerbated when local governing bodies are infiltrated by CAFO owners and those with other vested financial interests in the local Big Ag economy. A 2015 anthropological analysis of four counties in rural Illinois examined how county boards have enabled corporate power grabs. The paper compared two Illinois farming counties that have become inundated with CAFOS to two farming counties that have staved off the CAFO takeover. In the CAFO-heavy counties, businesspeople with connections to Big Ag dominate local governance. Social relations have deteriorated, and economic inequities have grown. Many residents oppose feedlot development yet stay quiet, fearing the retaliation of those in power.[11]

One resident told the researcher that anyone who attends a public meeting over a CAFO permit risks being "run out of town." Another resident, a business owner who publicly opposed a CAFO development, confided that someone tore down the business's signs in the middle of the night. A farmer who spoke in a public hearing concerning a CAFO expansion ended up moving after the rent was raised in retaliation.

"We had to move," yet another small farmer said. "Me and my husband couldn't handle the smell. I complained to the EPA, but they didn't do a damn thing. I complained to the county board and wrote a few letters to the paper, but same thing—not a damn thing. We lost a lot of money, and they're making a boatload."[12]

With nowhere to turn for assistance, rural residents feel disempowered, helpless, and harassed. Despite this, and knowing the risks, some choose to fight back.

The Threat to Lake Country

In December 2015 I received a panicked call from Mariann Guentzel, a woman in her early seventies who lives in the famously beautiful segment of central and northern Minnesota known as Lake Country. Mariann, along with her handicapped adult daughter and her partner, Al, had recently moved into a home in a remote, wooded area of Byron Township, Cass County. The family bought eighty acres, including a large barn to house Mariann's horses. A lifelong rider and enthusiast, she owned five and finally had a larger property to house them.

But soon after moving in, they learned that a developer planned to construct a swine gestational facility in the immediate area. The proposed facility would house an estimated five thousand piglets and supply them to neighboring feeder operations. Its manure pit would be located just four thousand feet from Mariann's property.

The neighbors in Byron Township were caught completely off guard by the news of this coming industrial complex. Many of them didn't get word until the legally required notice of the public hearing was distributed. They had little time to prepare or react.[13]

In my work as a family law attorney, I'm accustomed to dealing with individuals in distress. The sound of worry and uncertainty in Mariann's voice was similar to what I hear when my clients face the unforeseen and painful end of a marriage. For Mariann, this unexpected end to her dream of spending her retirement outside with her horses was painful. It was a familiar story, but the unfamiliar part was where it was unfolding: Cass County is in north-central Minnesota, not the southern part of the state where most factory farms are sited.

But this tracked with recent developments. The swine industry had saturated Iowa and southern Minnesota. Corporate expansion was now radiating out into Illinois, the Dakotas, Nebraska, Wisconsin, and northern Minnesota. Mariann's community was undergoing what Dodge had experienced twenty years earlier. The proposed facility was a gestational complex, which typically serves as an anchor for further CAFO development.

Disease outbreaks in swine CAFOs in southern Minnesota were another factor pushing developers into other parts of the state. This was certainly the case with the Cass County developers, who stated in a township meeting that the "reason they are looking in this area is they need a clean environment for the pigs, as the areas in southern Minnesota have disease that affect the pigs."[14]

I shook my head in sadness and disbelief as Mariann told her story. Lake Country was a region with countless creeks, rivers, and small lakes. Tourists drive to northern Minnesota to experience the pine forests, the pristine waterways, the quaint shops, and the miles upon miles of hiking and bike trails. I travel there often for work and pleasure. The thought of millions of gallons of manure making their way into those clear waterways was maddening. It was beginning to feel as if Big Ag would invade every unspoiled region until there weren't any remaining.

I decided to drive to Byron Township and attend the public hearing. The residents had been blindsided. They needed the perspective of someone who had been through this fight before.

14

In the Trenches

"It is important that county commissioners, county staff, township supervisors, and other elected and appointed local officials, be trained in recognizing and dealing with issues related to growth and development. When a new development such as a subdivision, business operation, or a new or expanded feedlot is proposed in a rural area, it may encounter opposition. Local decision-makers must be prepared to handle controversial issues."—MINNESOTA FARM BUREAU FOUNDATION, "When an Activist Group Comes to Town"

On a bitter cold, subzero evening several days later, Douglas and I departed the Twin Cities right after work and drove north. I felt out of my league. I understood the politics of Dodge County but didn't know what to expect in Byron Township. During the drive, we took notes and developed a game plan. The days are very short in Minnesota in December, so I sat crouched under the car's interior lights for most of the drive.

We were particularly troubled by the question of manure application. Unlike southern Minnesota with its sweeping corn and soybean fields, forests and lakes cover this part of the state. We assumed the feedlot developers were making a variety of empty promises about responsible manure storage, removal, and land application, as this is their modus operandi during permitting. In truth, they likely had only sketchy plans for how to handle the millions of gallons of excess manure.

Despite engaging the GPS to lead us to Byron Town Hall, we had difficulty locating the building. We turned off a major highway onto a dark county road, then made several wrong turns before spotting the small structure in the middle of a dimly lit, heavily wooded area. We were a few minutes late. We quickly got out of the car and signed into the meeting. I noticed several names on the sign-in sheet were from

Spring Valley, Minnesota, five hours to the south, near the Minnesota-Iowa border.

"What are *they* doing here?" I whispered to Douglas, winking. We quickly ascertained the situation: the swine industry knew about this meeting and had activated the corporate posse to pressure the citizens of this tiny, remote township. Scanning the room, we noted that the hog mob outnumbered the residents. In a township of fewer than a hundred registered voters, this was an easy task. We stayed in the back of the small, bustling room and quietly introduced ourselves to a few of the locals, including Mariann Guentzel. She was sociable and as sharp as a tack.[1]

The township supervisors were seated at two long tables at the front of the room. The nearly three-hour proceedings were similar to public feedlot hearings in Dodge, with the exception that the supervisors listened attentively to Byron's residents and gave them more time.[2]

The project developer spoke first, making the usual assurances about odor mitigation techniques and environmental stewardship—all while failing to mention, of course, that many of these mitigations are not required by law, and operators don't face consequences for failing to fulfill promises made during the public hearing. A number of factory farm operators who had driven up from southern Minnesota spoke in support of the project.

Several members of the Cass County Concerned Citizens Alliance (cccca), including Mariann and other area residents, spoke in opposition to the development, citing evidence of health risks, odor problems, and pollution.[3] Prior to the meeting, cccca members had canvased the township and collected about eighty signatures from township residents, seasonal nonvoting residents, and landowners on a petition to request a two-year feedlot moratorium to allow further research on the impact of the proposed facility. The goal that evening was for township officials to consider the petition and vote on the question of a moratorium.

Douglas and I patiently observed the proceeding, absorbing the comments from industry insiders and blindsided neighbors. When it was our turn to speak, we shared our family's experience living near several factory farms. We voiced our opposition to the proposed cafo and encouraged the township officers to consider the well-being of their constituents rather than only the business interests of the developer.

At the end of the marathon public hearing, the township chair made a motion to adopt a six-month moratorium. The two other township officers did not second the motion, and the effort to enact a moratorium failed.

Afterward, Douglas and I stayed for a while to join the conversations that were abuzz in the room. We automatically eased into our respective roles: as in countless times during our marriage, I wore the black hat and he, the white hat. I approached the project developer and spoke frankly, expressing my concern that industrial-size swine CAFOs would ruin our beautiful northern Minnesota Lake Country. I can still recall the smirk on his face.

Douglas chatted with township officers in the opposite corner of the room. Two of the officers shared that they had experienced intimidation in advance of the meeting, and they were afraid of a lawsuit if they prevented the CAFO's permit from moving forward.

That night we were struck by how blindsided the township officials and residents had seemed. They had been subjected to a classic hog mob sneak attack. We felt we had made a difference by providing our advice and perspective.

We drove the three hours back home that night, arriving around two o'clock in the morning. Our experience had been exhausting yet invigorating. This trip was the first of many Douglas and I would make in the coming years, as we crisscrossed the state of Minnesota to testify in the Minnesota legislature and local court houses, to speak at colleges, and to help residents stand up to corporate infiltration.

A few weeks later, Mariann called with frightening news: her former home in a town not far from Byron Township—the house her family had recently left and put on the market—had burned to the ground. They'd had buyers lined up and were scheduled to close on the sale. On a Monday morning, the buyer's inspector showed up for the scheduled visit and discovered there was no house to inspect, only embers.

Mariann was contacted by the local sheriff's deputy as well as the state fire marshal, whom she happened to know personally. She had worked for many years as a paramedic and at one point in her career had conducted death investigations. The fire marshal asked if she'd made any enemies recently, expressing his belief that a professional arsonist had started the fire. He saw telltale signs of arson, yet because he couldn't find the accelerant, he was forced to list the cause of the fire as "unknown."[4]

Mariann and her family no longer felt safe. They eventually decided to relocate. Sadly, another Byron Township family who had vocally opposed the CAFO also chose to move over safety concerns.

Within days following the project's approval, the township official who had consistently supported the development was seen driving a new pickup truck. Soon enough, residents discovered he had a direct financial interest in the CAFO development that he had never disclosed. The same official had told several residents who opposed the CAFO, "Do you want what happened to Mariann to happen to you?"[5]

As for the factory farm, it was constructed in a different location just a few miles from the original site near Mariann's home. Interestingly, the family that sold the land for the facility's ultimate development site had multiple connections to Byron Township officials. And despite assurances during the permitting process that the developers weren't interested in expanding, the facility doubled in size after its permit was approved.

Meanwhile, a wealthy area businessperson with six hundred acres nearby bought the land originally sited for the project.[6] He took this defensive tactic to prevent CAFOs from eventually being permitted in the immediate vicinity of his business, essentially creating a buffer zone around his property. I've seen landowners in other counties use the same tactic, and it really highlights the socioeconomic and racial dynamics that can come into play. Most rural residents aren't in a financial position to create these buffer zones, nor can they count on being taken seriously at township or county meetings.

Racism and exclusion based on limiting people's access to opportunity, capital, and land are major problems in farm country, and these dynamics play out very differently depending on the locale and the commodity group. In North Carolina, the hog industry targeted farming regions with majority-Black property owners and renters who often lacked the resources or political clout to effectively fight back. The triumphant saga of a group of property owners in North Carolinian hog country who sued Smithfield Foods is documented extensively in *Wastelands*, a recent book by novelist-turned–nonfiction writer Corban Addison.

In Minnesota, industry giants do not rely on blind luck to find geographically distant rural communities for CAFO siting. The Minnesota Department of Agriculture (MDA) created an industry cheat sheet for targeting "prime locations for livestock operations that want to sell to local, national, or international markets." Known as the Animal Ordinances Web Map, the online tool provides information about local feedlot ordinances, allowing corporations and developers to easily find counties with lax feedlot rules.[7] As per the MDA's website, the map "includes the most common kinds of regulations, such as setbacks and separation distances, conditional use permits, feedlot size limitation, and minimum acreage requirements."[8]

Frequently revised with up-to-the-minute information, the interactive map identifies counties, townships, and cities that adopt or change a livestock-related ordinance. It's a vacancy sign for industry giants with a system that identifies the counties and townships most susceptible to infiltration by multinationals such as Hormel, Smithfield, JBS, and the like.

This tool is just one small piece of the larger institutional and regulatory machine that evolved to support Big Ag, which stamps out small-scale farming. When residents dare protest, they are subjected to heavy-handed intimidation tactics so severe that it's not uncommon for Big Ag opponents to be forced to move. Such coercion is "corporate cancel culture," and it has been perfected and fine-tuned in many of today's rural farming communities.

Voices That Won't Be Silenced

As I became more involved with feedlot battles outside of Dodge County, my family's lawsuit awaited judgment. In June 2015 the district court in Dodge County determined that it had subject-matter jurisdiction over our case. This important decision allowed the lawsuit to proceed. We expected a decision around the end of the year.

That summer, a few weeks after Randy and I shot our documentary, the cornfield across the Claremont Road from our farm was sprayed with a chemical that left a dead patch spanning nearly a mile and caused thousands of dollars of damage. The property owner didn't know where the spray came from or who the perpetrator was. We strongly suspected the perpetrator thought the field belonged to us.

Later that summer, Brad and I were pulling weeds from the bean field near the Claremont Road, as we often do that time of year. We noticed several area swine operators drive by on their way to an event hosted by the Minnesota Corn Growers Association at the Toquam farm one mile to the north. Hours later, when Brad left the family farm to drive to his home in Blooming Prairie, he saw fresh bullet holes riddled the stop sign just a few feet from where we had been picking weeds. The chances that this was a coincidence struck us as extremely low.

Meanwhile, the garbage left in the roadside near our driveway, the harassing phone calls, and the nighttime intrusions remained a regular occurrence. Feeling unsafe was wearing on us. We had never experienced anything like this before. I came to deeply understand why this breed of low-level yet protracted, relentless intimidation often works. There's only so much a person can take.

By then I'd heard many stories from folks whose jobs and livelihoods were threatened by Big Ag industry operatives hell-bent on silencing the opposition. As a respected attorney working in a major law firm in the Twin Cities—not in farm country—I didn't think this was a particular danger for me. I was wrong.

In the summer of 2016, an ethics professor at an area university who was organizing a speaking panel on factory farming requested my input and collaboration. I was more than happy to oblige. We met at the university several times to identify panel members and develop the content.

We scheduled the event for September, calling it "Factory Farming in Minnesota—Time for a Change?" Speakers included representatives of the Socially Responsible Agriculture Project and the Minnesota Center for Environmental Advocacy (MCEA), as well as the professor and me. To promote the event, we emailed information to several local newspapers and publications.

Within a few days of sending the emails, someone contacted the managing partner of my former law firm to complain about my affiliation with this public event. To this day, I don't know who it was or the exact content of the message, but I do know that my law firm included a group of attorneys representing agribusiness as well as food processing and renewable energy clients. My managing partner let me know about the situation, indicating that my involvement was "being noticed by existing clients in the ag industry." He clarified that I was free to pursue my interests in my personal time, but I was to refrain from sending emails related to them from my work email address.

Whoever they were, these "ag industry" folks apparently felt threatened by our simple university event. They had the audacity not only to contact my law firm but to interfere in other ways as well. The night of the event, we included a PowerPoint presentation with a prominent slide thanking our sponsors, including Catholic Rural Life, a major national nonprofit organization "promoting Catholic life in rural America." The organization set up a table in the hallway and shared its literature with attendees as they arrived. Within days following the event, someone contacted the organization and asked it to refrain from getting involved with any future similar event.[9]

Big Ag interests are so entrenched that it's impossible to say who the errand boys might be for this manner of interference with institutions of higher education and religious organizations. Perhaps area feedlot owners and operators are tasked with making the unsavory phone calls. Or perhaps it's a white-collar job involving meatpacking or integrator executives, or even higher-ups at one of the industry groups such as the Minnesota Pork Producers Association or the Minnesota Farm Bureau that are intent on silencing "activists."

Not long after the first panel event, we convened a similar panel at Assisi Heights, a beautiful Franciscan convent that sits at the top of a hill in Rochester, Minnesota. The night of the event, industry attorney

Jack Perry, along with several prominent industry businesspeople, sat in the front row just feet from the panelists. Another classic industry power play.

We held a third panel event the following year at Minnesota State University in Mankato. We were apprehensive. Doing my due diligence, I warned the panel participants to expect pushback from the swine industry. The small city of Mankato is Big Pig central, home to the Minnesota Pork Board and the Minnesota Pork Producers Association.

As expected, the industry reacted in standard fashion: threats, intimidation, and attempts to stonewall public discourse and free speech. This time, they went straight to the top rather than merely threatening panelists and event sponsors. Industry representatives contacted administration officials, asking the university to pull the plug on the event. The school did not succumb to this intimidation. Our event proceeded as planned, though the format seemed to indicate extra caution on the university's part.[10]

At our prior events, to preserve their anonymity, attendees submitted written questions directly to the panelists. With this event, university officials vetted the questions, adding a layer of oversight that struck me as bizarre. These panel events tended to be small affairs attracting interest mainly from particular academic departments and members of the public with niche intellectual interests. They were barely on the radar of the universities' top brass. But in our case, we felt as though we were being monitored. The school set up two microphones and asked participants to approach and ask a question while university officials stood by each mic. This arrangement contrasted with our previous standard informal format, where panelists passed the mic between themselves and solicited anonymous written questions. Swine industry superstars, including the CEO of Christensen Farms, one of the largest pork producers in the United States, again sat in the front row.

We had originally envisioned the event as an unremarkable but important discussion of factory farming and its impacts on rural communities, the economy, the environment, and the welfare of the animals. It's amazing that Big Ag interests are so threatened by the truth that they'll go to such lengths to silence or control the conversation.

They know the truth stinks, but much like the hog manure, try as they might they can't contain it.

The Dismissal

In May 2016 the district court in Dodge County issued its ruling in favor of the defendants, Masching Swine Farms and the Dodge County Board of Commissioners. The judge put forth his opinion that the county's approval of Masching's factory farm was "reasonable" and not "arbitrary or capricious," as our lawsuit alleged. He also sympathized with our situation, writing, "I uphold Dodge County's approval of this CUP; and I do so despite the fact that I think Lowell Trom's description of the smell of hog feedlots in Westfield Township is, at least at times, entirely accurate. In this situation, what recourse, if any, do the Troms and similarly situated parties have?"[11]

The judge further observed that complaints such as ours would typically fall under the tort of nuisance, or nuisance lawsuits. In our case, we didn't pursue nuisance litigation; instead, we focused on the defendants' failures to comply with state feedlot permitting rules and the requirements of Dodge County's zoning ordinance. But the truth is, despite the judge's speculation about the tort of nuisance, nuisance suits against CAFOs are infamously impotent thanks to the loopholes and exemptions in many states' nuisance laws that have been carefully crafted and endorsed by Big Ag lobbyists and their affiliated politicians.

With the ruling in, my parents promptly appealed to the Minnesota Court of Appeals.[12] During the case's consideration under the appeals justices, several organizations filed amicus briefs in support of our position, including the Minnesota Center for Environmental Advocacy, the Humane Society of the United States, Environment America, Food & Water Watch, Animal Legal Defense Fund, and scientists affiliated with Johns Hopkins University's Center for a Livable Future and the Johns Hopkins Bloomberg School of Public Health.

We were blown away by the extent of their support. We knew being concerned about factory farm pollution wasn't a fringe position, but with the way Big Ag proponents gaslight folks in farm country today, it's easy to lose that reference point.

One of the key allegations of my parents' lawsuit was that the county board's approval of the feedlot's permit was unreasonable and arbitrary (these are legal terms of art) because the commissioners failed in their public duty to assess whether the project adhered to Dodge County's zoning ordinance. Perhaps most relevant was chapter 18 of the ordinance, including a requirement that the "operation will not be detrimental to or endanger the public health, safety, or general welfare." Another key provision stipulates that the commissioners are obligated to assess whether "existing groundwater, surface water, and air quality . . . are or will be adequately protected."[13]

The commissioners approved the CUP despite the applicant's failure to fill out portions of the form relevant to these matters. Upon losing the first lawsuit in November 2014, the county solved the problem by omitting those questions from the application form, thereby institutionalizing a process that defies the zoning ordinance and fast-tracks feedlot approvals. Further, minutes from both the planning commission and board of commissioner's meetings show that public health issues weren't seriously discussed, despite Dodge County residents' having submitted hundreds of pages of pertinent concerns.

The amicus briefs were instrumental in showing that the proposed operation would indeed endanger public health, as expressly prohibited in the zoning ordinance and in the state's feedlot rules. One of the briefs, authored by scientists affiliated with the Johns Hopkins Bloomberg School of Public Health, noted that odors associated with feedlots are not only a "nuisance," as treated under the nuisance tort, but also a grave public health issue. One study found that human subjects exposed to air simulated to replicate the air within factory farms were four times more likely to develop headaches and nearly eight times more likely to report nausea.[14] These results are worrisome for feedlot workers, many of whom are allegedly undocumented.

The Johns Hopkins scholars also discussed a 2013 study's finding that people living near fields spread with CAFO manure are significantly more likely to experience MRSA and other soft tissue infections.[15] The steady diet of antibiotics fed to confined animals results in the proliferation of antibiotic-resistant pathogens affecting the pigs, and those agents can then jump to the human population through the air in the form of dust, from the soil via crops, and through groundwater and surface waterways.[16]

The amicus brief submitted by the Humane Society likewise focused on antibiotic-resistant bacteria, to an extent that initially surprised us. At that time, scientists around the world were beginning to better understand the role that factory farm confinements play in the worldwide crisis. In 2016 the World Health Organization (WHO) identified the misuse of antibiotics in animal agriculture as a major driver of antimicrobial resistance, describing it as "one of the biggest threats to global health." The WHO published a formal recommendation urging farmers to use antibiotics only to fight existing disease rather than routinely giving them to prevent disease and promote growth.[17]

In the United States, the Food and Drug Administration and the Centers for Disease Control and Prevention have echoed these recommendations to various extents. But as with nearly all commonsense Big Ag oversight, judicious usage of antibiotics is recommended, not mandated with enforcement power, even given the seriousness of the public health threat. Scientists estimate that by 2050, ten million deaths per year will be attributable to antimicrobial-resistant bacterial infections, overtaking the current rates of cancer-related deaths.[18] Despite this conclusion, a recent meta-analysis of the effectiveness of U.S. policies on antibiotics use in meat production found that such policies "have been implemented voluntarily or incompletely.... The political will, robust systems for collecting and integrating data, and cross-sectoral collaboration have been notably absent in the USA, especially at the federal level."[19]

The authors of the Humane Society's amicus brief noted that the Dodge County commissioners didn't once mention antibiotic resistance during the CUP approval process. Nor did they ask the developer the obvious question of whether he planned to feed his animals antibiotics and whether he would do so for growth and disease prevention purposes or only for disease treatment. To my knowledge, commissioners have not asked this question of *any* feedlot operator in Dodge.

This concern isn't theoretical. Antibiotic resistance caused by feedlot operations affects hyper-local health, which is squarely within the purview of the commissioners' oversight obligations. Multiple studies have shown that bacteria with genes resistant to antibiotics are found at higher rates in local soils in areas with dense feedlot clustering. One study found that people living within one mile of a feedlot are 88 percent more likely than the control population to be carriers of *Staphylococcus aureus* (staph).[20] Other studies have found that feedlot workers and people living near feedlots are more likely to be exposed to bacteria resistant to antibiotics.[21]

Finally, the brief submitted by the MCEA and Food & Water Watch contained a comprehensive overview of the multitudinous local environmental impacts of factory farming.[22] The authors examined how the specific siting of the Masching CAFO puts waterways at risk. Selecting a site that minimizes such impacts is meant to be a basic parameter of feedlot permit approval, but the relevant section wasn't filled out on the CUP application.

Unfortunately, Masching's CAFO is on an elevated site, where manure is likely to run off into waterways that are already impaired. The brief's authors wrote, "A few hundred feet from the CAFO, the ditch turns and runs less than a mile downstream and empties into the Little Cedar River, which is an impaired water listed as 'non-supporting of aquatic life for aquatic macroinvertebrate communities' due, in part, to low oxygen caused by high concentrations of nitrogen and phosphorus. The Little Cedar River, in turn, empties into the impaired Cedar River, a tributary of the impaired Iowa River."[23]

Predicting the nitrogen and phosphorus levels that would result from a facility's manure application is one of the key objectives of a responsible manure management plan. Food & Water Watch went ahead and ran the calculations that Dodge County's zoning administrator failed to compute. The county had estimated that Mr. Mashing needed only 244 acres for land application of his CAFO's 1.1 million gallons of annual manure. Using standard recommendations for the acreage needed to absorb the given levels of nutrients, the brief's authors noted that "if manure is applied at [this] suggested rate, more than 225 pounds of nitrogen and 196 pounds of phosphorus would be applied to each acre, well in excess of MPCA recommended guidance that determines feedlot rule compliance. This suggests that land application . . . is unlikely to comply with the manure management requirements of the feedlot rules."[24]

Dodge County failed to consider or discuss these inconvenient facts during the CUP approval process. While reading the amicus briefs, I was overcome with relief that our valid concerns were finally taken seriously rather than elided over or outright dismissed as they had been at the public hearings.

Sadly, these supportive efforts were all in vain thanks to a procedural technicality that won the day for the defendants.

When my parents first moved forward with their second lawsuit in early 2015, the Dodge County sheriff was charged with the service of process to the defendants. In layperson's terms, the defendants needed to be personally served with the appeal document to start the clock on the time for appeal. Following standard procedure, my parents' attorney mailed the summons and complaint to the sheriff for personal service to Masching Swine Farms and the chair of the Dodge County Board of Commissioners.

At the time, we believed the board chair was Rodney Peterson, who indeed had been the chair during a county preceding just a few weeks prior and who was listed as the board chair on the county's website. The sheriff delivered the summons to Peterson, but apparently he was no longer board chair, having vacated this role *one day* before he was served. The sheriff didn't tell us this information. Nor did Peterson, who, being an attorney himself, likely understood the potential implications of serving the wrong person.

By the time the county informed us that a new chair had been seated, the period to serve the summons by the applicable Dodge County ordinance had passed. The defendants raised this issue in 2016, but the judge didn't address it until the court's final opinion in April 2017. In an opinion dated April 17, 2017, the Minnesota Court of Appeals vacated my parents' appeal on the grounds that the sheriff had not properly served the chair of the Dodge County Board of Commissioners and that therefore the appeals court lacked subject matter jurisdiction over our case.[25]

By so doing, the court dealt a fatal blow to my parents' request to prevent the construction of yet another swine factory farm. But more significant, by vacating the case on a procedural technicality, the important arguments put forth were never tested. The appeals court did not address either the merits of my parents' appeal or the public health and environmental concerns raised in the amicus briefs. It was an unnecessary and regrettable circumvention of the serious zoning and land use dilemmas that frontline communities across the country, not only in Dodge County, continue to face.

15
The Three-Day Stink Out

"Livestock manure is a valuable source of organic nutrients for crops; however, manure can cause odors. Livestock facilities are engineered to minimize odors. Farmers follow best management practices when applying manure to crop land in order to limit odors and protect water quality."
—MINNESOTA FARM BUREAU FOUNDATION, "Moving to the Country"

After the appeals court's decision, my family's feeling of unease in the Dodge County community continued but with new contours and nuances of psychology. Industry insiders already acted as if Dodge County was their mini fiefdom, and now they had proven that resistance was futile. Despite the transparent machinations, despite the mounting evidence of local pollution, despite the illegal maneuver to strip required information from feedlot applications, the county prevailed. We settled into the certainty that the newest and nearest feedlot to our farm wasn't going anywhere, and it wouldn't be subject to adequate oversight.

It didn't take long for the implications of this situation to be made known in spectacularly smelly fashion.

In mid-November 2017 Douglas and I went home for the weekend to join my father on the combine for the fall harvest. We stopped at the grocery store on our way out of the Twin Cities and loaded up on the typical staples required for a weekend visit. With my mother in the nursing home, I frequently made homemade carrot cake, apple crisp, or cookies to leave at the farm for my father and brothers. We also brought the basics, including organic eggs, organic milk, and other healthy items that Lowell didn't have access to at the local grocery. Such a dreadful irony—right in the center of America's heartland, the shelves of area stores were filled with industrial foods that are "not fit to eat," according to my father.

After quickly unloading the groceries, Douglas drove me to the field and dropped me off. I eagerly waited for my father to approach in the combine. He understood my passion for fall harvest and this special time together, and he readily accommodated the annual father-daughter proceedings. Some daughters join their fathers on annual fishing trips; Lowell and I bonded over combine rides.

It was the end of fall harvest. I admired the progress my dad and brothers had already made, as many of the fields were bare and ready for tillage. The northern portion of our land, though, awaited the combine. Cornfields, a pure deep green during the summer months, turn a deep yellow as fall approaches. The corn stalks stand upright while the ears of corn bend down to the ground, a sign of maturity. Against this honey-gold backdrop, spotting the green John Deere was easy as my father traversed the field.

Lowell, wearing his legendary blue-and-white striped overalls, beige coveralls, and matching beige seed cap, opened the heavy cabin door to greet me. I bent over to give him a kiss, then buckled into the jump seat next to him. My father lowered the corn head, adjusted the throttle, engaged the autosteer function, lined up the corn head with the corn, and expertly maneuvered through the dense ocean of gold.

The late-autumn day was particularly gorgeous. The sun shone brightly, and the air was crisp as we made several rounds in the 360-acre field we lovingly refer to as "the Ponderosa." We were working from east to west, picking the final 100 acres or so of corn. I took a moment to admire the rich rural landscape stretching before me as far as the eye could see.

And then I was hit with the overpowering stench of CAFO manure. It was not the normal farm smell we all know and accept. This was the concentrated, liquified olfactory output of millions of gallons that have been stored for months before being released all at once onto land that can't hold it. It's the kind of odor that's not just a smell but a toxin-laden health hazard that leads to dizziness, headaches, and vomiting if you don't get out of its way. It's a malodor that has destroyed lives and livelihoods, chasing people out of their homes and robbing them of the value of their land.

Beyond the northern edge of our Ponderosa was a 240-acre parcel that the landowner rented to Roger Toquam so he could spread manure from his factory farm one mile to the north. Scanning the landscape, we soon spotted the manure crew doing their work. I was appalled, but not surprised, that they were spreading an estimated two million gallons of manure on frozen ground. It was too late in the season for such large-scale spreading because frozen ground increases risk of runoff. The best time to land apply manure has a very small window— that is, after all the fields are harvested but before the ground freezes.

With the loss of pasture-grazed animals and the conversion of farmland to strictly corn and soybeans, punctuated by the occasional CAFO, manure is now commonly spread on the land all at once later in the fall, when the land is more likely to be frozen. This problematic practice, necessitated by the combination of CAFOs and monoculture, causes polluted lakes, degraded ambient air quality, and contaminated waters.

I called Douglas to ask if he could pick me up. Evidently Toquam was emptying his manure pits, and I wanted to see for myself how the manure was transferred from the pits to the semi tankers and then to the field applicators, which injected it into the soil. While I'd been smelling these epic pit cleanings for years and understood the timing of the process, I'd never had the chance to observe the full scope of it in action.

Douglas showed up in short order, and we drove north. Through the partially harvested cornfields bordering the road, we could easily see Roger Toquam's swine facilities and spotted the manure being transferred from an underground pit to several manure semi tankers. These tankers are a specialized type of semitruck with equipment to transfer the liquified waste from the tanker to the field applicators. We slowed for a moment on the township road and observed the proceedings. We were a good quarter mile away but could see the basics of the process even from our distance.

We continued west on 690th Street, a narrow township road, and observed a field where a tractor was pulling a manure applicator, a massive vehicle with specialized machinery that injects manure into the ground. Minutes later, we watched as a manure semi pulled up to the side of the road, then slowly extended its long hydraulic boom to the waiting applicator sitting at the edge of the field. The waste was transferred via the semi's discharge pipe into a large rectangular fill opening at the top of the applicator. With the two massive vehicles briefly connected in this way, thousands of gallons of liquid manure were transferred from the tanker to the applicator.

The applicator then discharged the waste to concave discs that incorporate manure with the top layer of the soil. As the applicator went back and forth in the field, the sharp disks sliced the harvested ground, turning the soil laced with manure a pure pitch black. I was amazed by how quickly the manure was laid down—a deceptively fast process with such far-reaching and harmful consequences.

Our curiosity sated, we headed in the direction of Blooming Prairie to visit my mother at the nursing home. Douglas turned around in a large circular drive near the intersection at 690th Street and 120th Avenue so we could return back east. As we made the turnaround, we realized a manure semi tanker was headed toward the same circular drive. Soon enough, the tanker was in our rearview mirror. Up ahead, a tractor with an attached manure applicator waited at the edge of the field for the tanker to arrive and transfer manure. We passed the tractor and headed toward the Claremont Road.

Looking in the rearview mirror, we were startled to see the semi tanker still behind us. It had not stopped to transfer the manure. Instead, the tanker picked up speed, tailgating us. As it came within a few feet of our vehicle, hurled dust enveloped us. Was the driver trying to run us off the road?

Douglas began to panic. I rolled down my window and stuck out my digital camera, showing the driver, only a few feet from us now, that we intended to document the unfolding event. I quickly managed to snap a photo or two.

It seemed to work. The driver slowed down, and the tanker receded in the rearview mirror. My heart continued to pound for several minutes afterward, the adrenaline pumping. Thankfully, we had a fifteen-minute drive to Blooming Prairie and time to regain our bearings before visiting with my mother.

Within a few minutes of arriving at the nursing home, I received a text from my brother Jim asking why a Dodge County sheriff's deputy was pulling into our farmyard. I called to quickly explain what had happened. We were both amused and infuriated. This wasn't the first time feedlot operators had used the sheriff's department as an instrument to intimidate us. Jim relayed that the deputy drove around the yard, likely searching for our white suv, then left.

I subsequently obtained a copy of the call for service, which identified Roger Toquam as the complainant. The notes specified that the complainant "states there are protestors blocking his path down the road. They are trying to spread manure. . . . [Complainant] is not currently on the scene but states that the people are using their vehicles to block the road. . . . 2–3 people taking pics and blocking the road refusing to move."[1]

There was not an ounce of truth to this complaint, but we knew that the sheriff's department tended to believe feedlot operators, many of whom serve as community leaders. That the Toquams were willing to call in a false report to law enforcement was unsettling. If they were willing to bend the truth on this occasion, what else did we have in store?

That night at the Trom farm, Douglas and I settled into the master bedroom upstairs to discuss the day's troubling events. My father routinely slept in a recliner in the downstairs family room, so we always slept in my parents' bedroom during weekend visits. The space is elegant and dignified, yet cozy and warm—a reflection of my mother's refined style. Before Parkinson's limited her day-to-day functioning, my mother, Evelyn, had loved interior design and redecorated the entire house. The master bedroom had gold-pleated drapes, gold-and-white wallpaper, a bright red-and-gold damask bedspread, and a small chandelier.

I fell asleep that night to the hum of the grain dryer operating fifty yards away. Jim was still at work. During the fall harvest, he diligently watched the settings on the grain dryer and dried the corn to the proper moisture content. Farmers don't risk storing grain if the moisture content is too high, which can cause moldy grains. The process of drying corn is slow and tedious. It takes several hours, and the hum of the dryer can be heard until 3 or 4 a.m. After drying, the corn is transported via an auger system to tall steel storage bins, where it remains for several months.

Douglas and I woke up early the following morning, a Sunday, and drove half an hour north to attend Douglas's home church, United Church of Christ, in Berne. Afterward I dropped him off at the Eayrs farm and drove back home to continue helping my father with the last of the corn.

I was dispirited to discover that the manure-spreading activities were continuing for a second day. To my astonishment, the same 240-acre parcel just north of our cornfield appeared to have been coated with a second layer of manure. If so, it was a flagrant violation of the most commonsense parameters of land applying manure and the exact kind of violation that feedlot owners swear up and down during permitting that they won't commit. The area was pitch black; the manure pooled on top of the ground. Dozens of gulls pecked away at the surface.

For a lifelong farm girl who'd seen many a field fertilized the proper way, I thought the birds' appearance was a strange sight. Gulls do not eat manure. Later I learned that CAFO manure attracts the birds because of the mixed-in pig carcasses. Pigs packed into CAFOs are prone to fighting and even cannibalizing one another, and the body parts fall through the slats in the floor to the manure pit below. A soup of decomposed bones, muscle, intestines, and flesh likely dotted the field's surface, along with nitrates, phosphorus, growth hormones, and antibiotics—all lying atop frozen ground just a mile upstream from the headwaters of the Cedar River. The stench coated my nose and throat.

As these manure-spreading activities continued, Lowell and I had no choice but to return outside to finish fall harvest. Abandoning the fields at this time of year would be financially calamitous. Knowing that hydrogen sulfide poisoning was a real possibility, I covered my face with a cloth and advised my father to do the same.

The manure crew moved operations across the road to the old Bass farm. During my youth, Ray and Audrey Bass sponsored summer horse camps there. My parents owned farmland immediately adjacent to the south, our "northwest eighty." As with the final hundred acres of the Ponderosa we had worked the previous day, the northwest eighty had yet to be harvested. The manure crew set to work injecting manure into an area immediately bordering our field.

By this point, it was apparent that Toquam intended to spread millions of gallons of manure that weekend. We were trapped in the center of an endless loop of manure tankers and field applicators. The semis loaded up at the Toquam swine feedlots, drove south along the Claremont Road, turned west onto 690th Street, and turned south to the manure applicators waiting in the fields. The waste was pumped from tanker to applicator, then the tankers drove by our farm before heading back for another load. These vehicles made countless laps that day around the same mile square where my father was finishing fall harvest. Brad was likewise caught in the dangerous cloud of noxious fumes and dust as he moved grain wagons to and from the field and our farm.

At one point I took a break from the combine and drove over to survey our northwest eighty, just across the road. I pulled into the field driveway leading to our land and sat in my vehicle for a few minutes, watching the manure applicators do their work in the adjacent field. I got out of my SUV and quickly took a few photos, then got right back in, and made certain the windows were rolled up as the fumes were overwhelming.

As I shifted into reverse to head back home, the first semi driver had just finished unloading his toxic cargo into the field applicator. There was a good hundred yards between us. He pulled into the middle of the road, exited the semi cab, and ran toward my vehicle. As he approached the passenger side, I checked that my doors were locked and opened the passenger window a few inches.

"What's your problem?" he shouted, waiving both arms in the air. "I'm calling the sheriff!"

I calmly responded, "What's your name?" He didn't respond but ran back to his semi, got in, and began to drive toward me.

I pulled over to the side of the road, rolled down the driver's side window, and waved my hand to the driver, signaling him to pass my vehicle. Given the false report to the sheriff's department the day before, I wanted to make clear that I had no intention of interfering with his activities. It's a narrow road for semis. Thanks to the constant commercial activity associated with the area CAFOs, driving on rural roads in Dodge has become harrowing. They are used as two-lane roads, but nothing is demarcated. When you see a semi or tractor pulling machinery coming from the other direction, you really don't have much room to spare to avoid a head-on collision.

After the semi passed, I drove to our farm, pulled into our driveway, and went into the house. Within fifteen minutes, a sheriff's deputy arrived, informing me that he had received a complaint that protesters were blocking the road. I laughed at this version of events and explained what really happened, as well as what occurred the day prior when a truck tried to run us off the road. I offered to share photos documenting the events that weekend, but the deputy declined. Determined to show my unwillingness to be bullied, I stated emphatically to the deputy, "They're calling *you* to get to *me*, and you tell them it's not working!"

Once again the call for service later identified Roger Toquam as the complainant. The report states, "2–3 people protesting again. . . . Subjects are blocking the road so the manure spreaders are unable to get by."[2]

The deputy left after our short conversation, and that marked the end of my long-anticipated daddy-daughter fall harvest weekend. It did not go the way I'd imagined.

When the Regulators Don't Regulate

As Douglas and I drove back to the Twin Cities early that evening, my father called from his cell to report that he had become dizzy while picking corn and had stepped off the combine to vomit. I advised him to leave the field immediately and get to the house. I was disgusted and didn't know whether to cry or yell.

Factory farm operators receive education and training—though inadequate—on safety precautions to take when stored CAFO manure is agitated and moved, including when the manure is pumped from the pits, transferred to the applicators, and spread onto the fields. These safety measures represent an implicit acknowledgment of the dangers associated with these activities. As noted in chapter 11, manure releases concentrated quantities of hydrogen sulfide when agitated, and the gas has caused dozens of deaths among factory farm workers along with health problems in neighboring populations.

Yet CAFO operators are not required to alert immediately adjacent neighbors about a planned pump-out, and the industry frequently underplays and ridicules the complaints of area residents who experience poor associated health outcomes. Its prevailing philosophy amounts to this: there's nothing you can do about it, so get the hell out of our way!

The great stink out of 2017 did not end with the weekend. The next day, Monday, my dad called to inform me that the brand-spanking-new CAFO across the road was pumping out manure. It appeared that Nick Masching had chosen this day, of all days, to empty his million-gallon-plus manure pit and spread the contents on the Toquams' land immediately surrounding his six-acre feedlot.[3]

We suspected that Toquam and Masching had coordinated their schedules so that they would empty their manure on multiple fields surrounding our farm contemporaneously and during a time that interfered with our fall harvest activities. Toquam's three-hundred-acre parcel is directly across the road from our northwest acreage, the very field that my father had saved for last to harvest. He finally got to the parcel that Monday, and lo and behold, Masching emptied his pits and lathered the parcel immediately to the south the same day.

It was the grand finale of a three-day stink out, a juvenile yet dangerous payback for my parents' lawsuit. Manure canons laced with hazardous levels of hydrogen sulfide, ammonia, methane, and other gases blasted their target—elderly Lowell—just steps away from where he was picking the last few acres of corn.

That Monday night, my family and I talked it over and decided to contact the Minnesota Pollution Control Agency. My father's dizziness and vomiting were the last straws. Besides, we had witnessed manure spread on frozen ground. We also suspected that manure was spread twice on the same parcel and that with multiple operations unloading millions of gallons on a dense cluster of acreage, the hydrogen sulfide levels in the ambient air were likely well above 0.03 parts per million, the state's public safety standard.

The MPCA holds emergency powers under state law to "direct the immediate discontinuance or abatement" of polluting activities that pose an immediate risk to human health. Per the EPA, the MPCA's Air Emissions Planning document further states that the agency "is required to monitor feedlots for H_2S [hydrogen sulfide] and take enforcement action when needed," and adds that "inspection and enforcement of a CAFO's air emissions plan is largely driven by complaints received by MPCA."[4]

The MPCA's rules further clarify that "smaller feedlots also must comply with the H_2S standard." This distinction is important because only larger feedlots that exceed a thousand AUs, or 2,400 hogs, are required to obtain an NPDES permit and submit an environmental impact statement as part of the initial feedlot permitting process. Among other requirements, the EIS compels feedlot operators to submit an air emissions plan that delineates the mitigating methods the operator will use during manure removal and to create a plan "to mitigate air emissions in the event of an exceedance of the state ambient hydrogen sulfide standard."

By specifying that "smaller feedlots must also comply" with H_2S standards, the MPCA is communicating that any feedlot, regardless of size, cannot poison the air with hydrogen sulfide, whether the feedlot possesses an existing air emissions plan or not. While the spirit behind this clarification is commendable, its enforcement is another story.

The Toquams' CAFOs are large enough that they should have been required to submit an air emissions plan for them. The two facilities collectively hold 1,176 AUs, but for reasons that are unclear to me, the Toquams were not issued an NPDES permit for feedlots exceeding 1,000 AUs until 2011, nearly thirteen years after their facilities reached that benchmark. Regardless, it does not appear that the Toquams submitted an EIS or created an air emissions plan, so we assumed that the hydrogen sulfide emissions of their facilities weren't being monitored.[5]

If the MPCA couldn't bother with ensuring an EIS was submitted when the Toquams' feedlots were initially permitted and constructed, why would the regulators take our concerns seriously years later? We contacted the MPCA as a matter of principle and hoped that it could help us. But our expectations were not high.

I spoke with a feedlot compliance officer at the MPCA's southeast region office in Rochester and reported dangerous levels of hydrogen sulfide in the one-mile-square area where the manure spreading bonanza was taking place. We waited. Nothing happened. I later accessed our complaint file and found that the compliance officer had gone on vacation soon after our conversation and later left these notes: "MPCA did not investigate the land application site after returning from vacation on the 27th. The 27th was two weeks after the manure had been applied, as a result the possibility that any hydrogen sulfide would still be present would be eliminated."[6]

Where do you go for help when the regulators do not regulate? The following spring, I filed another complaint with the MPCA after family members experienced additional episodes of dizziness and headaches. I again spoke with a feedlot compliance officer. In May 2018 he suggested that my father complete an "odor log" and sent me a form titled "Oder Event Recording Log." This was a senseless exercise, as Minnesota feedlots are exempt from odor rules but not from ambient air quality standards. Besides, hydrogen sulfide is odorless when it reaches dangerous levels.

Nothing happened, or so we thought. Three years later, in 2020, I discovered unexpectedly that the MPCA had indeed conducted several tests at the property line of the Toquams' CAFO in 2018 and 2019 as a result of my complaints. Per the MPCA, these tests, called "H_2S Flex Surveys," are conducted based on neighbor complaints and "used to gather preliminary data on hydrogen sulfide levels." If a property fails the initial test, the MPCA is supposed to conduct continuous air monitoring at the facility and follow up with fines and compliance measures to reduce the facility's H_2S output.

The Toquam facility failed the first test, conducted in October 2018, with several readings over the safety limit of 0.03 parts per million.[7] A failure is meant to trigger continuous monitoring; instead, the MPCA returned the following week for another flex test. Presumably the agency wanted to confirm the finding before bothering the owners with results as apparently trivial as hazardous levels of hydrogen sulfide.

The result? Another failure.[8] And still nothing was done.

The MPCA returned to the property again in July 2019. The regulators appeared to be keeping their fingers perpetually crossed that the Toquams would pass the next test so that the agency didn't have to deal with the issue.

The results this time around, however, were significantly worse: thirty-five recordings registered above 0.03 parts per million, with the highest reading coming in at more than *seven times* the safety standard.[9]

Given the serious dangers associated with hydrogen sulfide poisoning, at this point the MPCA should have immediately ordered continuous air monitoring, which is required for any flex test failure, let alone a failure of this magnitude.[10] The agency did not. Instead, it tested the property again the following week and recorded another failure.[11]

I discovered the existence of these results only because a reporter with Minneapolis's *Star Tribune* was investigating the MPCA's feedlot oversight capabilities and contacted me to speak about my family's experiences. The reporter had obtained the monitoring data from the MPCA and shared it with me. Noting how odd it was that the agency conducted four tests when enforcement action was required after the first failure, the reporter surmised, "Either the MPCA was sitting on their hands, or they were trying to work with Toquam on a solution. . . . I don't know."[12]

The reporter asked the MPCA why it hadn't installed the required continuous air monitoring. In response, the agency said it planned to do so some time in 2020.

I waited patiently for an update. In September 2022 I drove by the Toquams' facilities. Nearly four years after the first failed test in October 2018, I finally saw a continuous air monitor equidistant between the two swine CAFOS.

Our experience aligns with how the MPCA systemically responds to factory farms that breach air emissions standards. Complaints are ignored; emissions tracking, on the rare occasion that it occurs at all, only occurs after a disaster, a tragedy, or a series of complaints have been lodged. In our case, apparently the MPCA took the matter seriously only after our repeated complaints and the inquiries from a reporter. It's very rare for a CAFO to be fined or asked to enact measures to mitigate emissions. The agency's after-the-fact compliance system does little beyond creating the illusion that the industry is being regulated.

I find it difficult, though, to lay blame at the feet of the MPCA or even frankly at the feet of the feedlot operators. Human nature is what it is, and people are unlikely to spend extra money on hydrogen sulfide monitors unless they're told they must. The animal livestock industry is exempted from reporting emissions under the multiple relevant federal air pollution acts. In the absence of federal regulation, air emissions reporting and standards are left to state or local governments. For the most part, the states don't go beyond what is required federally, although they absolutely should. A small handful of localities have required emissions analyzers and detailed manure management plans, or have implemented a ban on new CAFOs after a series of local disasters, as occurred in North Carolina. But they are the exceptions.

The great tragedy of the government's continuing failure to regulate is that simple regulations would undoubtedly save lives. While hydrogen sulfide is the air pollutant most likely to cause emergency health situations, the fine particulate matter (PM 2.5) and one of PM 2.5's precursors, ammonia, cause the most mortality and morbidity among the livestock industry's prevalent toxins. Chronic exposure to fine particulate matter and ammonia can lead to lung diseases, heart diseases, and a number of cancers. As mentioned in chapter 11, a groundbreaking 2021 report found that ammonia emissions contribute to 12,400 deaths annually in the United States, and animal agriculture is the leading cause of such emissions. The scientists concluded that changes in farming practices, most importantly in manure and fertilizer management, could reduce these deaths by half.[13]

In Dodge County, feedlot operators would not accept these findings as truth, nor would county officials. At least I hope they wouldn't. Otherwise, I find it impossible to understand why the county doesn't require the mitigations that residents consistently advocate for during feedlot CUP public hearings: installations of odor-reducing biofilters on all factory farms; inspections to ensure that biofilters, once installed, are in proper working order; hydrogen sulfide analyzers to test air emissions; limits on the size of factory farms in the county; a cap on the concentration of factory farms in the county; and increased setback requirements beyond the state-mandated minimum so that CAFOs are sited farther from the nearest neighbor.

I prefer to believe that county officials, who refuse to implement these measures time and again, reject them out of ignorance rather than other motives.

PART 4
The Reclamation

Big Pork is king in hog country, and its advocates and apologists get their just reward in this story. Goliath has never looked so bad.
—JOHN GRISHAM, referencing North Carolina residents' win in their lawsuit against Smithfield Foods

16

Corporate Indoctrination

"At any given moment there is an orthodoxy, a body of ideas which it is assumed that all right-thinking people will accept without question. . . . Anyone who challenges the prevailing orthodoxy finds himself silenced with surprising effectiveness.

If liberty means anything at all, it means the right to tell people what they do not want to hear."—GEORGE ORWELL, original preface to *Animal Farm*

In the early years of the CAFO takeover, Big Ag faced a unique public relations challenge. Concentrated animal feedlots are too small for the animals living inside of them. From the perspective of animal health and well-being, one can't reasonably claim that it's the ideal way to raise livestock. It's right there in the name—*concentrated*. The truth of how the animals live is unpalatable. They're genetically engineered to grow large quickly, causing illnesses, defects, and chronic pain. They experience continuous stress. They never go outside, and they're fed a daily diet of hormones and antibiotics. Confined as they are, they're prone to fighting and killing one another.

The CAFOs look bad, they smell bad, and contained within are inconceivable amounts of animal suffering. They are not representative of the bucolic image of the family farm that once anchored the PR and marketing of essentially every agribusiness corporation, from the seed, equipment, and chemical companies to those that package and sell food.

Initially, images in livestock industry publications continued to show animals grazing outside, romantic windmills, and serene red barns. The veneer was plausible because few knew the truth about CAFOs and how they operate. In the 1990s the industry passed state-level "ag-gag laws," known in industry doublespeak as "farm security laws." Some of these laws prohibit people from taking photographs or videos inside a factory farm without the owner's permission. Others criminalize employees—potential whistleblowers—for sharing images or videos that capture animal abuse or safety regulation violations. Ag-gag laws have been struck down as unconstitutional in several states, including Wyoming and Kansas, yet they remain in effect in key ag states such as Iowa and Arkansas.[1]

Despite these laws, the tenacious efforts of animal rights groups have made the public generally aware of what happens inside the factory walls. The industry shifted from pretending CAFOs don't exist to claiming that animal rights groups that gain access to CAFOs doctor their images or handpick the worst offenders. Big Ag crafted a counternarrative in which factory farms are not warehouses where animals grow fat until they're slaughtered for profit but are modern, cutting-edge incubators of scientific progress where animals are cared for by highly trained veterinarians. In the pork industry, company websites are especially fond of using images that feature a veterinarian examining an adorable piglet and holding an iPad while surrounded by nondescript machinery.

With time, the challenge to such whitewashing widened. Evidence mounted that factory farms drive climate change. They poison rivers and streams. They affect the drinking water of neighboring cities. People living near them are more likely to develop cancer and a host of other health problems, from emphysema to depression.

The greater the challenge, the greater the response. The industry now positions factory farming as not only the *best* method of livestock production but the *only* viable method to feed the world (see chapter 18). Referring to George Orwell's quote at the beginning of this chapter, the supposed inevitability of CAFO agriculture is becoming part of the popular orthodoxy—that is, among the pantheon of "ideas which it is assumed that all right-thinking people will accept without question."

The best way to anchor the orthodoxy is to start them young.

Ag in the Classroom

Big Ag communicates with young people by sponsoring booths and events at state and county fairs, encouraging Farm Bureau members to volunteer with local 4-H clubs, and waging targeted television and social media ad campaigns. The industry increasingly uses National Agriculture in the Classroom (NAITC), a public-private partnership founded in 1981, to develop school curricula that teaches large-scale corporate agriculture as the default type of agriculture in the United States. NAITC materials systematically ignore, gloss over, or malign alternate models of agricultural practice.

NAITC was created in 1981 under the direction of the USDA as a partnership between ag businesses, educators, and the government to promote strong agriculture education and career pipelines in an era where most students no longer have direct exposure to the practice of agriculture. The mission is essential and laudable. Unfortunately, the organization is so tied to the Farm Bureau and Big Ag corporations that its K–12 curriculum is indistinguishable from industry propaganda.

In 2017 the long-standing union of the NAITC with the American Farm Bureau Foundation was consummated. They announced a partnership to "strengthen collaboration between the two groups" and to "partner on communications and promotions." At the time, the groups already clearly worked in lockstep: the chairperson of the NAITC, Zippy Duvall, was also the president of the American Farm Bureau Foundation.[2]

The formal marriage of the Farm Bureau to an organization that produces lesson plans for public school students is troubling. Farm Bureau leaders regularly go to Washington to lobby against environmental regulations and legislation that combat climate change and promote clean air and water. The organization consistently supports and funds Republican candidates at all levels of government, and its membership is a pipeline for up-and-coming conservative politicians. The Farm Bureau is manifestly not the type of unbiased, apolitical organization that traditionally develops public school curricula.

According to NAITC's 2021 annual report, the nonprofit's donors included the Iowa Farm Bureau, Farm Credit System, and Smithfield Foods among others.[3] In Minnesota, industry giants such as Compeer Financial, Minnesota AgriGrowth Council, Minnesota Corn Growers Association, Minnesota Soybean Research & Promotion Council,

Minnesota Farm Bureau Foundation, Minnesota Pork Board, Christensen Farms, and others fund the classroom materials that the Minnesota Agriculture in the Classroom Foundation develops.[4]

In alignment with industrial farming practices, the corporate educational materials familiarize students with the terminology that practitioners of corporate ag use. For instance, farmers are no longer farmers; they're "producers." NAITC provides educators with a range of reading passages, worksheets, activities, and tests for students in each grade level. In a worksheet for the younger grades, students must determine if a series of true or false questions about pigs are "Truth or Hogwash." An example: "Most hogs are raised in temperature controlled buildings." The answer: "Truth. Pigs live in clean, modern buildings that protect them from weather and predators and provide optimum temperatures. Fans and sprinkling systems cool pigs in the summer. Heat lamps and heaters warm them in the winter."[5]

In a recent edition of *Ag Mag*, the industry's magazine tailored for each grade level, sixth graders are asked to match the corporation to its raw and processed products: Hormel matches to hogs, pepperoni, and ham; General Mills to milk and ice cream; and so on. Each magazine features an accompanying quiz with questions that repeatedly highlight the monocultures of the Midwest: corn, soybeans, hogs, beef, chicken, and ethanol.[6]

Ag Mag for fourth graders devotes a cheerful page to the importance of clean water in Minnesota, the Land of 10,000 Lakes. Platitudes about environmental stewardship abound in NAITC's education materials, with frequent passages proclaiming how deeply farmers care about sustainability, ecological balance, and healthy soils, clean air, and clean water.[7] Yet the lessons typically don't go deeper than these vague assertions. If they did, NAITC would be forced to explore the complex, challenging realities of modern agriculture's impact on the environment.

NAITC frequently features hog production in its lessons. First graders, for example, are taught that pigs are kept happy by living in CAFOS, where they are sprinkled with water to keep them cool: "Pigs have no sweat glands. When they get hot, they cannot sweat to cool off like you can. . . . So, to naturally keep cool and not get sunburned pigs dig in the earth and make mud wallows. Today, producers keep the pigs and hogs shaded and sprinkle them with water to accomplish the same goal, but help the swine stay clean."[8]

The notion that CAFOs are a luxury destination for pigs because they're kept "shaded" and sprinkled with water is absurd, yet this particular claim is repeated ad nauseum in NAITC materials. The materials fail to mention that the water-intensive industrial method of raising hogs uses four gallons of water per day per pig, stripping aquifers of valuable resources that should be preserved for future generations. The corporate fairytale converts a looming water sustainability crisis into a spa service for pigs, which have the privilege of being sprinkled while they're imprisoned in a crowded facility until the day of their slaughter arrives.

Almost any corporate educational pamphlet about hog production, whether it's published by the Farm Bureau or the National Pork Board, repeats this bit about CAFO barns protecting pigs from predators and keeping them cool with sprinkling systems. Rinse and repeat so the students accept the message—that's indoctrination 101.

An Ag in the Classroom publication in Illinois states, "Here in Illinois, we have very extreme weather! We can't control the weather, but barns can. Keeping the pigs in the barns keeps them out of these varied conditions and away from predators and harmful infections and diseases." The lesson goes on to promote the preventative use of antibiotics in hog barns, although major health organizations both globally and nationally have come out against this practice.[9] Similarly, a children's coloring book produced by the Minnesota Pork Board and handed out at the Minnesota State Fair features a child speaking to his friend Billy about pigs. Each assertion is accompanied by a picture to color:

> Pig barns don't have any mud, Billy. Producers keep all of their barns clean so the pigs stay healthy and happy.

> Pork producers also take care of the environment when they are raising pigs. They plant trees and bushes that help reduce dust and possible odor.[10]

I must admit I chuckled when I leafed through the coloring book. I would truly like to see the facilities that Billy's friend references. Most of the factory farms in Dodge County and elsewhere have absolutely no tree perimeter despite the industry's very frequent claim that this buffer is an industry-backed solution to odors and air pollution.

In recent years, NAITC has developed programming designed to fulfill curriculum requirements in specific states. The operation is becoming more sophisticated. Through a partnership with the National Center for Agricultural Literacy, NAITC now provides an ever-growing number of students and teachers with individualized state, standards–based lesson plans. It's more convenient for elementary and high school teachers to use NAITC materials when they're prepackaged to align with the state's testing standards.

Big Ag's role in higher education is equally trenchant. University agriculture departments are tied to corporate donors, and research priorities are often influenced by agribusiness corporations that either support the university directly or are helmed by CEOs with connections to the government agencies funding the research. Looking at the hog industry specifically, agribusinesses commonly give generous support to universities in their home states. (Agribusinesses also regularly donate to the state-level Farm Bureaus and pork councils.)

In Iowa, Deb and Jeff Hansen, the politically connected owners of Iowa Select Farms, the country's eighth-largest hog processor, donated $2 million to Iowa State University for a new building. After construction was completed in 2014, the building was dedicated as the Jeff and Deb Hansen Agriculture Student Learning Center.[11]

Closer to home, Hormel Foods continues to influence the direction and priorities of agricultural research in Minnesota. In 2023 the University of Minnesota purchased 80 acres just outside my hometown of Blooming Prairie and unveiled plans to buy another 750 acres in Mower County, where it will build a state-of-the-art facility, the Future of Advanced Agricultural Research Minnesota (FAARM) center. The Hormel Foundation pledged $60 million to the project.[12]

The month after the FAARM announcement, the University of Minnesota named former Hormel CEO and current Hormel Foundation board chair Jeff Ettinger as the interim president of the university after the departure of its prior head, Joan Gabel. One member of the university's board of regents voted against Ettinger's selection, citing concerns about corporate influence in higher ed.[13] Shortly after his appointment, university students and faculty members protested outside a board of regents meeting. A representative for the American Association of University Professors questioned the premise behind Ettinger's selection, given that he is a "former CEO of a meat processing company with no academic credentials."[14]

When public funding for ag research declined in the late 1980s, private funding from agribusiness began to fill the gaps. The food sustainability firm FoodPrint released a white paper on the pork industry that summarizes the chilling effect this connection has had on academic independence: "[Private] funding not only determines what research gets funded or not (e.g., research on breeds that do well in confinement rather than expanding knowledge on pasture-based systems), but it can make the institution and its researchers fearful of engaging in inquiries that could reflect negatively on the industry."[15]

Researchers with prominent positions at major universities are not protected from Big Ag's influence. Jim Merchant, the former dean of the School of Public Health at the University of Iowa, was unable to complete his research on the health impacts of hog farm emissions in Keokuk County, Iowa. In 2014 the university's administration killed the project. Merchant believes this wasn't the first time the industry's influence impacted his research. At Iowa State in 2002, a study he coauthored on CAFO air emissions was published with conclusions that could have prompted industry regulation. His two dozen coauthors of the peer-reviewed report—respected scholars at the state's two major universities—all agreed on the findings. Almost immediately, leaders at the Iowa Farm Bureau met with Iowa State professors, then launched a PR campaign with anonymous sources maligning the study.[16]

"Big ag has a stranglehold over land grant universities," Merchant said in 2019. "Agribusiness has tremendous influence on their research."[17]

The first major, peer-reviewed scientific research paper on the health impacts of living near a CAFO was published in 1999 by Steve Wing, then an epidemiologist at the University of North Carolina–Chapel Hill. His findings—that people living near CAFOs are more likely to experience respiratory and digestive disorders—set off alarms for Big Pig. The North Carolina Pork Council asked Wing to hand over his dataset, which included the identities of the subjects. Wing was concerned for the safety of the people involved in his research. He refused. Eventually, under threat of arrest, he handed the data over but redacted the names of the study's participants.[18]

At a lecture later that year, an assistant professor at another university approached Wing and confided that he, too, had undertaken research on the health impacts of CAFOs, but he decided to pull the plug after hearing how the pork council went after Wing. As reported in Corban Addison's *Wastelands*, this professor believed that if he had to face the fallout of researching CAFOs, "I'll never get tenure."[19]

Big Ag's propaganda campaign combines academic suppression with relentless pro-industry messaging, creating a public that is minimally aware of Big Ag's impacts and suspicious that any negative claim about Big Ag's methods is "anti-farmer." The pigs are not sad; they are happy. Manure runoff does not pollute waterways with phosphorous, nitrogen, and antibiotics; to the contrary, feedlot operators are devoted environmentalists.

Once the falsehood is firmly anchored, it becomes the default belief. When faced with the truth, the truth is suspect. These are the trappings of doublethink.

The website for the National Pork Producers Council claims that "pork producers care deeply about the health and well-being of their animals and have a moral obligation to raise them humanely and compassionately."[20] While this may be true of individual pork producers, the humane treatment of animals is directly at odds with the advocacy of the NPPC, which aggressively lobbies against legislation to promote such treatment of farm animals.

For example, the NPPC determinedly opposed the Farm Animal

Stewardship Purchasing Act, a doomed Senate bill designed to discourage the use of sow gestation crates.[21] And in 2008 the council lobbied against the Downed Animal and Food Safety Protection Act, which prevents cattle that are too sick or injured to walk to slaughter from entering the food chain. The act was designed to both protect food safety and discourage animal abuse. While the act didn't cover hogs, the NPPC didn't want such a precedent in place. The law passed, and in subsequent years, the NPPC has played a pivotal role in repeatedly staving off efforts to extend the requirement to hogs.[22]

Yet the NPPC's oft-repeated mantra is that hogs are raised "humanely and compassionately." This message is heard so often in farm country that it seems suspicious when unknown "outsiders," such as university professors or Washington politicians, say otherwise. And if your own neighbor makes the claim, well, that neighbor has been brainwashed by environmental activists and is now considered an outsider as well.

When hundreds of North Carolinians sued Smithfield Foods in 2017, their stories stood against the gaslighting of very powerful state politicians and lobbyists. In North Carolina, hog manure from outdoor waste lagoons is sprayed into the air over adjacent fields (this practice is different than in Minnesota, where the manure is typically stored indoors and later injected into the earth). The noxious spray often carries in the wind, making its way to neighboring properties. Litigants testified that the odor and air poisoning would get so bad that they'd abruptly collapse in their yards. They had chronic headaches and vomiting spells, and developed respiratory diseases. As the manure spray accumulated as a thin film on their homes and even inside their kitchens, they could no longer have company over to visit. They rarely went outside.

Soon after the lawsuit began, state representative Jimmy Dixon, himself a factory farm owner, introduced House Bill (HB) 467, which would place restrictions on nuisance lawsuits against agriculture operations and would cap damage payouts. All eight hog industry lobbyist groups operating in the state supported the bill. The organizations financed a major PR campaign to counter the damaging claims about hog CAFOS that were exposed during the course of the Smithfield lawsuit. The bill was signed into law with some revisions, including, thankfully, one that allowed the existing litigation to move forward.[23]

Several of the House members who voted in favor of HB 467 had received substantial campaign contributions from the hog industry. In defense of the bill, Dixon wrote to a local journalist, "For people to say they can't go outside—I can't barbeque, I can't invite my neighbors over—those are exaggerations."[24]

17

The Pork Board

"Pork producers have long thought, based on anecdotal observations, that the substantial gains made in efficiency and productivity by modern swine farming systems were leading to major improvements in the sector's environmental performance."—NATIONAL PORK PRODUCERS COUNCIL, Senate testimony, 2018

In the spring of 2017, I learned about a policy change under consideration at the Minnesota legislature. It concerned Minnesota Statute 561.19, "nuisance liability of agricultural operations." Big Ag interests were pushing for a provision to exempt large-scale feedlot operations— those holding more than a thousand animal units—from public and private nuisance claims. The Republican-led effort would again place corporate interests above the health, safety, and fundamental rights of the people.

The industry had already successfully lobbied for prior changes to this statute, which is a type of right-to-farm law. Agriculture-based states across the country enacted such laws in the 1980s. The initial justification was reasonable: a wave of city folks relocating to farm country left farmers vulnerable to unwarranted nuisance litigation. Farmers feared they would be run out of business by rural newcomers surprised by the smell of manure. The interpretation of right-to-farm laws was initially guided by the "coming to the nuisance" doctrine, holding that nuisance claims are not reasonable if the offended party moves *to* the nuisance—that is, if newcomers move next door to an existing farm.[1]

When CAFOs overtook farm country in the late 1990s, this doctrine was glaringly unfavorable to CAFO operators and the meat-packers who served to profit from them, as the new factory farms were *bringing* the nuisance. As such, the industry sought to recast right-to-farm laws and exempt CAFOs from nuisance claims brought by preexisting farm families and rural residents—that is, farm families such as my own. Members of the Trom family have been on the land for longer than 130 years, yet the right-to-farm laws stripped our preexisting rights to bring a nuisance action against the newcomer, the factory farm next door. The laws were retooled from their original purpose of protecting independent farmers and now shield factory farms instead.

Today's rural residents have few options if a neighboring CAFO has destroyed the "use and enjoyment of their property," the classic benchmark of nuisance. According to a 2021 analysis of right-to-farm laws in all fifty states, many specifically protect commercial producers of particular crops, livestock, and chemicals; not a single one specifically protects traditional or family-owned farms.[2] The phrase "right to farm" has become yet another industry euphemism.

In Minnesota, an industry-backed provision introduced in 2004 shields most factory farms from nuisance claims once they have been in operation for two years. They are also exempted from such claims if they have been abiding by the stipulations of their permits. Yet there is an important exception: the largest CAFOs are not exempt after two years. This is logical, as the largest operations are the most likely to create odors, pollutants, and health problems substantial enough to meet the standards of nuisance.

Later, with the industry-proposed removal of the large-CAFO exception, neighbors would be robbed of this one remaining legal protection.[3] Douglas and I felt compelled to testify in opposition on behalf of the Dodge County Concerned Citizens.

Cozy Bedfellows

I testified five times before committees of the Minnesota House and Senate that spring. The process was contentious. While the majority of Minnesotans opposed the provision for exempting large CAFOs, the swine industry launched its brigade of attorneys, lobbyists, and contract growers in the direction of the state capital.

I could easily testify on short notice. It's a quick, fifteen-minute drive from my office in downtown Minneapolis, straight across the Mississippi River to Saint Paul, home of the impressive state government complex. The Minnesota State Capitol itself is one of the grandest structures in the Midwest. Architect Cass Gilbert designed it after he saw the architecture displayed at the Chicago World's Fair in 1893 and hoped to create something of equal grandeur in Minnesota. The result is a sprawling, white neo-Renaissance building with intricate murals, gold detailing, and a marble dome so reminiscent of the U.S. Capitol building that visitors sometimes ask if it's a replica.

During my visit to the legislature, I was accompanied by Douglas and Eugene, a Dodge County resident. The three of us had prepared remarks to testify at a house hearing, which would be convened in the State Office Building on the extensive capitol complex grounds. While I'm typically at ease in a courtroom, the backdrop of the capitol left me overwhelmed at the seriousness of the legislature's task. These are the halls of democracy in action, where representatives are the voice of the people. I learned they are also where democracy is contaminated by politicians who kowtow to donors and lobbyists rather than advocate for the constituents who elected them.

As we approached the hearing room, I ran into one of my business partners, Paul Thissen, who at the time was the minority leader of the house. His calm presence and our brief conversation were comforting. I knew him to be a devoted and good-hearted public servant. Our chance encounter was a timely reminder that many types worked in this building, including those who fight to preserve democracy and equality before the law.

At the time, Republicans controlled both houses of the Minnesota legislature. That didn't bode well for us. Minnesota's status as a purple state is the main reason our right-to-farm laws still leave space, though a shrinking one, for individual rights over corporate profiteering. Corporate agriculture, and its devoted network of Farm Bureau soldiers, does not *always* get its way in Minnesota.

We entered the hearing room and found Christine Coughlin, then the Minnesota state director of the Humane Society, who had initially told us about this hearing. Settling in, we watched as the house committee members entered and took their places in the black leather chairs surrounding a large horseshoe-shaped table. Situated nearby was a small table with a microphone where those testifying would sit and face the committee. Security officers dotted the room's perimeter.

The committee had several bills on the agenda, and I watched the proceedings with interest. It was a bit stressful from a constituent's standpoint. This pageantry was far removed from the daily realities of life in Minnesota, yet many lives were impacted by the actions of those seated there. I recall that one of the bills discussed was not controversial and drew support from both sides of the aisle, while others fell strictly along party lines.

When our time came, our testimony was limited to three minutes. Eugene spoke first, describing the odors and pollution the CAFOs caused around his home, including the contamination of his well water. He testified that he had personally witnessed violations of manure management regulations, as a nearby hog farmer lathered manure on the same twenty-acre parcel for three consecutive days. At one point a Republican house member challenged him and asserted that the MPCA, not hog farmers, is at fault if the regulations are not followed.

I testified after Eugene and described the twelve factory farms that were built within a three-mile radius of the Trom farm. The concentration of CAFO agriculture in such a small geographic area created the potential for nuisance, and the law had to continue to protect those residents at risk of severe impacts from these industrial operations. I took out a laminated color-coded feedlot map showing the high density of feedlots in southern Minnesota and passed it to the committee members. I watched as they examined the map and shook their heads in disbelief.

Although my time was limited, I also spoke about the harassment and intimidation my family had faced. I wanted the legislative record to reflect this conduct. I saw this testimony as a way to preserve the truth and protect my family.

A few years after my testimony, I read about former North Carolina representative Cindy Watson in Corban Addison's *Wastelands*. I felt a sense of relief and camaraderie when I learned that Watson had also sought to protect herself through public testimony. Watson was a Republican whose district included Duplin County, North Carolina, the epicenter of swine CAFOs and waste lagoons in the state. In 1994 she went to bat for impacted residents after meeting Elsie Herring, a Black resident who lived on the land her family had owned for more than a hundred years. Herring later became a leader in the grassroots fight against factory farms in North Carolina. When she reached out to Cindy Watson in 1994, Herring was in the early days of trying to stop the manure that was being sprayed on her home from a neighboring waste lagoon.

Watson began introducing bills in the North Carolina House to regulate the hog industry and mitigate its negative impacts on neighboring communities. One evening she came home to a voice mail stating, "If you don't back off this hog issue . . . you're going to find yourself floating facedown in the Cape Fear River."[4] She took the tape to the FBI and, the following day, brought it to be heard before the North Carolina General Assembly. She didn't face another death threat after that, and some space opened for her voice to be heard. In 1997 the moratorium on new CAFOs in North Carolina was signed into law.

The pork industry waged a political war on Watson, funding a broad effort in 1998 to unseat her. Corporate money funneled to a campaign called "Farmers for Fairness." A high-end firm created an ad campaign in which "family farmers"—that is, contract growers—spoke about their fear of regulation from supposed "outside" environmentalist groups. At the time, the funding behind this effort was very unusual for a state primary. Addison called it a "foretaste of the dark money campaigns of the future." Watson lost her seat by twenty votes.[5]

Our final day of testimony was before a senate committee. The Minnesota Senate is housed in a sleek, contemporary building with towering walls of glass alternated with slabs of Minnesota limestone. The hearing room itself is equally modern and majestic; with its soaring ceiling and walls of pinewood contrasting with the soothing, lake-blue fabric of the chairs, it's meant to elicit pride in our forests and lakes. Accustomed as Douglas and I were to rural town halls, the backdrops in Saint Paul continued to intimidate and inspire.

And yet the cast of characters was the same. Present that day were the ubiquitous industry attorney Jack Perry and other standard-bearers for the swine industry in Minnesota. One advocate of the nuisance law change was Pat FitzSimmons, a longtime board member of the Minnesota Pork Producers Association (MPPA) and a partner at Protein Sources, LLP. FitzSimmons and his brother Paul had been going to bat for this bill since it was initially introduced in 2015.[6] Their stake was personal: Protein Sources was a named defendant in a nuisance lawsuit in Todd County, Minnesota, in the northern end of the state, where neighbors were forced to move after a large swine gestational facility was constructed.[7] The CEO of Protein Sources, Bron Scherer, also happened to be the treasurer of the Minnesota Republican Party.

Just as we saw locally in Dodge County, the industry had many political allies in the state capitol.

I also spotted David Preisler, then executive director of the Minnesota Pork Producers Association, which is the state affiliate of the National Pork Producers Council, the swine industry's main lobbyist and advocacy organization. Interestingly, Preisler was also executive director of the Minnesota Pork Board, a USDA-sponsored entity funded by the federal pork checkoff program; thus, he was legally prohibited from engaging in political advocacy.

The industry players sat on the far right side of the room. We sat on the left and awaited our turn to testify. We listened to the familiar arguments. I was surprised when Preisler spoke in support of the bill. As the head of the state's pork board, he was obligated to abstain from such advocacy; yet, advocacy was one of his core duties as the head of the MPPA.

How confusing.

When it was our turn to speak, Douglas and I sat next to one another on the comfortable, padded chairs facing the committee. I shared my planned remarks, then brought the committee's attention to the unique conflict embodied by Mr. Preisler. Which hat was he wearing that day? Was he testifying on behalf of the Minnesota Pork Board or on behalf of the MPPA? If on behalf of the pork board, I advised the senate committee members that the use of federal checkoff dollars to influence policy constituted the misappropriation of federal funds.

I was keenly aware that I was speaking not only to members of an industry-aligned, Republican-controlled state senate but also to Jack Perry, David Preisler, and representatives of the swine industry. They were not accustomed to people speaking so candidly about their improprieties. I was determined to show that we understood how they operate. I knew it wasn't right, and *they* knew it wasn't right. As I spoke, I noticed some discomfort and a few red faces among the industry insiders present in the room.

Several week later, I was relieved to learn that the proposed change to shield large feedlots did not pass. Reason and fairness won the day in no small part because citizens refused to be silent.

The Pork Checkoff Program

Preisler's bizarre dual positions—heading both an industry group and a supposedly apolitical, USDA-sponsored organization—are the direct result of the unique workings of the federal checkoff program, a program that has strayed from its mission.

Under federal law, farmers of certain commodities are required to pay a portion of their sales into the respective checkoff program. My father used to grumble when delivering grain to the local elevator, watching as calculations were made to determine the checkoff to be docked from his payment. Funds that Lowell could have used to operate the farm were withheld and paid to the Soybean Growers Association as part of the federal checkoff, which increasingly forages on the incomes of family farmers and ranchers who are forced to support large corporate agribusinesses through this mandated tax.

The pooled fees are intended to be used to research and market commodities. The organizations tasked with the respective, well-funded, USDA-backed marketing campaigns have created some of the best-known slogans in the food industry, including "Milk: It Does a Body Good." In the pork industry, the checkoff program funded the blockbuster slogan "Pork, the Other White Meat."

Congress created the pork checkoff in 1985 under the Pork Promotion, Research, and Consumer Information Act (or Pork Act), part of that year's congressional farm bill. The intent was to "strengthen the pork industry in the marketplace" by funding research and marketing, and providing consumer information. The National Pork Board, administered by the USDA, oversees these activities. The pork board and its state-level affiliates are expressly prohibited from lobbying and advocacy, but the board maintains a close relationship with the industry's largest trade group, the National Pork Producers Council.

As of this writing, the federal pork checkoff rate is 0.35 percent, meaning that thirty-five cents of every $100 earned by pork producers goes to the checkoff. The checkoff regularly brings in between $75 million and $100 million annually to the National Pork Board.

When the program launched in 1985, it could plausibly be argued that all pork producers benefited from consumer education and marketing. At the time, the country had 388,000 hog farms, with the majority of them operated by independent small farmers.[8] Today there are about 65,000 hog farms, and the majority are large facilities operated by contract growers beholden to a handful of large integrator companies and ag corporations.[9] The marketing activities that these corporations prefer conflict with the interests of the remaining independent hog farmers. As an example, while the corporate producers oppose country-of-origin labeling, small farmers benefit by distinguishing their products as sourced locally. The NPPC, along with the trade groups for beef and other commodities, successfully lobbied in 2015 to repeal the USDA's country-of-origin labeling requirement.

Conflicting interests came to a head soon after the swine CAFO explosion in the late 1990s. In the year 2000, hog farmers demanded a referendum on the checkoff. Farmers alleged that the National Pork Board worked in lockstep with the NPPC, promoting the interests of big corporate hog farms—namely, the very ones running independent hog farmers out of business. Via the checkoff, independent farmers felt they were being forced to fund their own demise.

In the lead-up to the vote, the NPPC spent $4 million advocating in favor of the checkoff. More than thirty thousand votes were cast, and hog farmers voted, by a 5 percent margin, in favor of killing the program.[10] The secretary of agriculture put a process in motion to dismantle the checkoff while the NPPC challenged the vote in court. When the Bush administration took over in 2001, the new secretary of agriculture, Ann Veneman, unilaterally overturned the referendum vote.

Small farmers kept trying. In 2015 a group of hog farmers sued the Justice Department to probe the connections between the National Pork Board and the NPPC, alleging a corrupt deal on the licensing of "Pork, the Other White Meat." The board was still paying the NPPC $3 million annually to license the largely defunct slogan. A *Politico* article on the lawsuit noted that the deal "lets the Pork Board funnel money to the NPCC [*sic*] by assigning an absurdly inflated value to the . . . slogan; the money then goes to promote the NPPC's lobbying agenda."[11] The NPPC predictably launched an aggressive PR campaign characterizing the litigation as anti-farmer and a threat to the industry writ large. The district appeals court in Washington dismissed the case in 2019.

The checkoff program's abuses are most easily illustrated by looking at the state-level pork board affiliates. The National Pork Board reported whopping revenue of $110,570,528 for the period ending December 31, 2022. Chart 3 illustrates the *intended* use of federal checkoff dollars, with the National Pork Board distributing the checkoff dollars to state associations for their use in promotion, research, and consumer information, as well as administrative expenses. Minnesota's state share of checkoff receipts in 2022 exceeded $2 million.[12]

Chart 3 shows a closed loop. The Minnesota Pork Producers Association is not in it. Because the MPPA is an industry trade and lobbyist group, the Minnesota Pork Board can't fund it.

And yet the two organizations share the *same office space* in Mankato, Minnesota, and the Minnesota Pork Board's federal 990 tax forms suggest shared costs on internal operations.[13] In addition to working in the same office, the two organizations have *identical staff with identical titles*.[14] The CEO of the MPPA, Jill Resler, is also the CEO of the Minnesota Pork Board. (Resler assumed both roles when David Preisler retired in 2022.) The communications and marketing director at the MPPA is also the marketing director at the Minnesota Pork Board, and

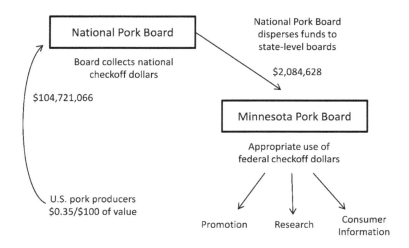

National Pork Board

Board collects national
checkoff dollars

$104,721,066

U.S. pork producers
$0.35/$100 of value

National Pork Board
disperses funds to
state-level boards

$2,084,628

Minnesota Pork Board

Appropriate use of
federal checkoff dollars

Promotion   Research   Consumer
Information

CHART 3. The intended framework: federal pork checkoff dollars, 2022. Created by the author. Source: 7 C.F.R. § 1230.60(a) and 7 U.S.C. § 4809(c)(1)(C).

so on. Thus, the inescapable conclusion is that the Minnesota Pork Board distributes federal tax dollars to the overhead costs of the MPPA.

Minnesota Pork Board staff members presumably assist with the MPPA's lobbying and industry advocacy efforts. With the same staff members serving the same role at the two organizations, how would they determine which part of their workday relates to appropriate expenditures under the Pork Act and which part relates to lobbying and policy advocacy that is prohibited by the Pork Act but practiced daily by the MPPA? David Preisler, for instance, had been a registered lobbyist for the MPPA since 2018, when he was still the CEO of the Minnesota Pork Board.[15]

It doesn't end there. A Greater Minnesota, a third affiliated organization incorporated in 2012, is an offshoot of the MPPA that is focused on electing pro-industry politicians and writing pro-industry legislation. Its website states that the organization "works to inform all candidates for the Minnesota Legislature about agriculture . . . and issues important to the industry." It further states that A Greater Minnesota "will be submitting high-priority policy proposals" to the state legislature. Records show that over a three-year period, from 2015 to

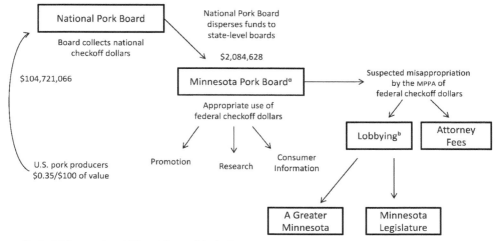

The Pork Act expressly prohibits certain use of the funds,
including for the purpose of influencing legislation.

CHART 4. The suspected framework: federal pork checkoff dollars, 2022.
Created by the author. Source: (a) 7 C.F.R. § 1230.60(a) and 7 U.S.C. § 4809(c)
(1)(C); (b) 7 C.F.R. § 1230.74(a) and 7 U.S.C. § 4809(e).

2017, the MPPA contributed over $205,000 to A Greater Minnesota.[16]
These funds represent a significant portion of the MPPA's total budget.

Until his retirement in 2022, David Preisler *also* served as the president of A Greater Minnesota.[17] So in Minnesota, there appeared to be a "four-hat" system, with one person wearing all four hats.

Chart 4 illustrates the *suspected* use of federal checkoff dollars. The ethical questions surrounding this four-hat system are many. As an example, the MPPA pays attorney's fees for agribusinesses and contract growers involved in lawsuits. Frequently, the defendants in these suits include hog contract growers, and the plaintiffs may include neighbors and independent hog farmers. The Minnesota Pork Board should be neutral; indeed, as a federally funded program that relies on mandatory taxes, it *must* remain neutral. Yet the pork board shares expenditures and staff with the MPPA as it actively defends the industry's side against permitting or nuisance actions initiated by independent farmers and neighbors, such as my family.

My family was always curious about the MPPA's role and possible contribution toward the payment of attorney's fees. During my parents' litigation with contract grower Nick Masching, we wondered how the young man was able to engage in protracted litigation and pay his expensive Minneapolis attorney. While my father struggled to pay his attorney's fees and my mother's expensive nursing home bills, we discovered swine industry pundit Trent Loos had written an article in the *High Plains Journal* about a Dodge County family that had "already spent over $200,000 defending a 2,400-head finishing building."[18] Loos was likely referring to Nick Masching, as the article was published years before the litigation concluded. Assuming the dollar amount Loos reported is correct, the attorney's fees incurred strongly suggest that Masching received outside financial assistance.

Other farm families engaged in isolated CAFO battles across the state, including in Freeborn, McLeod, Rock, and Todd Counties, consistently share the same observation: while local residents pay expensive legal fees out of their own pockets, the CAFO operators have ready access to seemingly limitless funding. In disputes relating to the CAFO next door, it's not farmer versus farmer. It's farmer versus industry.

The MPPA's tax returns offer a window into these activities. For the fiscal year ending September 30, 2019, the organization spent more than $678,000 on "strategic investment."[19] This is nearly one-third of its total reported revenue, and I'd bet dollars to doughnuts a portion of the funds was used to pay legal fees to help agribusiness developers stand against the democratic process as citizens attempted to adopt local planning and zoning regulations in their townships. The MPPA, which has three levels of annual membership fees for swine contract growers—$250, $400, and $750—affords the highest-paying growers access to the association's litigation fund.[20]

The misuse of checkoff funds is not unique to Minnesota or to the swine industry. In Ohio, the Organization for Competitive Markets conducted an analysis of the beef checkoff that revealed serious abuses.[21] Cattle producers, like hog producers, are mandated to pay a federal checkoff, and the Ohio Beef Council collects, administers, and expends these tax dollars.

Similar to the slick relationship between the Minnesota Pork Board and the MPPA, the Ohio Beef Council contributes to the state's industry trade and lobbying entity, the Ohio Cattlemen's Association. The two organizations share the same headquarters and the same staff. What's more, the political action committee for the cattlemen's association collects its PAC donations through the Ohio Beef Council's email address.[22] This flagrant violation of federal law shows how little the industry fears application of the law. The Ohio Cattlemen's Association lobbies against the interests of independent ranchers, who are nevertheless required to fund the checkoff, just as the NPPC lobbies against the interests of independent hog farmers.

At the national level, the NPPC recently expanded its capacity to back agribusinesses engaged in litigation and political advocacy in rural communities. In 2023 the organization launched a new initiative to increase the funding sent to its state affiliates to "enable state pork organizations to respond to threats on a state and local level."[23] The NPPC is vague about how this funding is used on the ground, aside from stating that it is "unrestricted" and to be used for lobbying, to advocate for public policy, and to combat local threats to Big Ag.

Lobbying under the Radar

Arguably the most powerful aspect of Big Ag's lobbying power is its facade of innocence. Big Ag would have us all believe that formidable industry groups such as the American Farm Bureau Federation are saviors of America's small farmer, not monied advocates for corporate agribusiness. Even obvious improprieties, such as the collusion between lobbyists and the distribution of the federal checkoff tax, enjoy a veneer of legitimacy—just enough to keep the public from prying.

Big Ag's advocacy against climate legislation, for instance, has been ruthless. The world's five largest meat and dairy producers create more greenhouse gas emissions than ExxonMobil, BP, and Shell combined, yet few people realize it.[24] There's a reason for that. The Big Ag lobby has been astoundingly successful at maintaining the image of the ecologically aware family farmer while keeping the truth—factories with animals crammed inside, manure lagoons, algae blooms, unswimmable rivers and lakes, and undrinkable water—tightly under wraps. Even environmentalist groups have apparently absorbed the industry propaganda; most spend only between 1 and 2 percent of their budgets on climate and environmental issues related to agriculture.[25]

Meanwhile, Big Ag lobbyists spent $2.5 billion in the past two decades.[26] The leading Big Ag industry groups are the American Farm Bureau Federation, the National Cattlemen's Beef Association, the National Pork Producers Council, the North American Meat Institute, the National Chicken Council, and the International Dairy Foods Association. The corporate giants, with Tyson Foods leading in lobbying expenditures, have their own fleets of advocates and lobbyists. These groups have banded together time and time again to oppose Clean Water Act and Clean Air Act regulations, to neuter antitrust activities at the USDA, and to kill climate legislation.[27]

While Big Oil is infamous for preventing U.S. participation in major international climate agreements, Big Ag was always working with Big Oil, side by side. Stuart Eizenstat, the chief U.S. negotiator of the Kyoto Protocol, the first major international effort to set emissions targets, said in 2018 that "the Farm Bureau was absolutely critical in derailing Kyoto."[28] The Farm Bureau also lobbied aggressively against the Obama administration's failed efforts to pass comprehensive cap-and-trade legislation.

The NPPC stands against almost any effort to regulate the pork industry. In its 2019 annual report, the group touted several legislative successes, including having "marshaled the effort to secure permanent U.S. Environmental Protection Agency rules exempting farms from [air] emissions reporting."[29] In 2021 the NPPC allied with the meat-packers to water down the USDA's attempts to protect meatpacking workers who become injured and chronically ill due to rapid assembly line speeds. The council boasted that it "aggressively campaigned in 2021 against a decrease in plant harvesting line speeds" and in favor of a pilot program to "restore faster speeds," which the NPPC is pleased to report may, according to one industry-aligned economist, "boost live hog prices by 6 percent."[30] The NPPC's "2021–2022 Policy Wins" fact page highlighted the group's success at blocking "Clean Air Act permitting requirements for livestock and a provision that would have required livestock facilities to report to EPA their greenhouse gas emissions."[31]

Industry lobbyists have also been very active in determining how their meat is labeled. A popular tactic is to confuse the American consumer, adopting such terms as "natural" and "no added hormones and antibiotics." Pork industry lobbyists successfully lobbied for changes to country-of-origin labeling that allowed foreign imported meat and meat products to be brought into the United States, processed through a USDA-inspected plant, and misleadingly labeled "Product of USA."[32] This practice, thankfully, may be coming to an end. In March 2024 the USDA again amended the rules so that beginning in 2026, "Product of U.S.A." labels can only be used when the product in fact derives from animals that were born, raised, and slaughtered in the United States.[33]

Through the federal checkoff program, the meat industry's lobbying efforts are funded, in part, by a mandatory tax on farmers. The meat lobby's destructive initiatives allow the largest ag corporations to create ever-expanding profits at the expense of public health, the environment, farmers, and consumers.

18
Feed the World

"We carry the awesome responsibility as American farmers to feed our country and the rest of the world. No one is better equipped to do that than we are."—ZIPPY DUVALL, American Farm Bureau Federation president, 2016

During the early days of the COVID-19 emergency in the spring of 2020, U.S. industrial meatpacking complexes owned by a handful of corporations emerged as the first, and the worst, COVID-19 hotspots. Many of us can still recall the frightening headline news as the pandemic took hold: by April, outbreaks among workers in meatpacking factories led to abrupt closures, causing a spike in meat prices, large-scale animal kills, and ultimately a presidential executive order to reopen the plants.

The bleak fact that our nation's first outbreaks occurred in the meatpacking plants is both revelatory and deeply unsurprising. Where else in the United States can one find thousands of workers packed into close quarters, working for low wages in under-regulated conditions? The vast majority of meatpacking workers have lost access to collective bargaining power thanks to the ruthless corporate opposition to unions. The Dickensian archetype of industrial-era factory work exists in the United States today, and you'll find it inside the meatpacking castles, where the prevalence of workers' injuries and poor health outcomes has risen in close tandem with corporate consolidation of the industry.

Here in Minnesota, some can still remember when Hormel Foods offered good union jobs. That was before the evolving ethos of the meat-packers placed profits above people, no matter the outcome.

Arguably the most consequential closure of the early COVID days was near the Minnesota border at Smithfield's Sioux Falls, South Dakota, pork processing plant, where some of the hogs raised in Dodge County see their last day. Smithfield waited several weeks after confirming its first cases to finally close. By that time, 644 positive cases were tied to the plant; however, until the closure, workers were ordered to show up—and that was before vaccines or known treatments were available. Smithfield also offered a "responsibility bonus" to workers who didn't miss a day before the closure in April. Employees said they felt as though they were being bribed to work while they were sick.[1]

In April 2020 Sioux Falls was the largest virus hot spot in the nation.[2]

The plant's temporary closure had immediate ripple effects. This single meatpacking plant processed 5 percent of all U.S. pork. It was the nucleus within a highly concentrated pork production system, where only thirty plants process 92 percent of U.S. pork.[3] After the closure of Sioux Falls and several other key meatpacking facilities, prices spiked. Americans feared meat would become as hard to find as toilet paper. Bending to these fears and the corporate meat-packers' lobbying, former president Trump signed an executive order for the meatpacking plants to reopen, but it didn't include protections for workers. By May 2020, infection rates in rural counties surrounding meatpacking plants were "five times higher on average" than the rates in other rural areas. Ten of the fourteen rural counties with the highest COVID infection rates in the country were home to major meatpacking plants that had outbreaks.[4]

Indeed, at the time, proximity to a meatpacking plant was the greatest predictor of a community's increased likelihood of COVID infection, illness, and death. Research published in July 2020 found that communities near meatpacking plants had more COVID deaths than would be expected by the baseline, in the range of 4,300 to 5,200 excess deaths, representing an elevation of between 37 and 50 percent above the baseline rate. The researchers also reported that these impacts were lessened in communities where the meatpacking plants chose to shut down. Yet most didn't, and those that did close reopened within an average of nine days.[5]

In response to the research, leader of United Food and Commercial Workers Kim Cordova said, "This needs to go down in the history books as one of the biggest failures to the working man or woman that this country has ever seen."[6]

Culling the Herd

The justification for putting workers' lives on the line was the looming specter of an alleged meat shortage. At a time of great uncertainty, many Americans readily accepted this argument. The former president's executive order in late April was to ensure "America's meat and poultry processors . . . continue operations."[7] To legitimize this request, Trump evoked powers under section 101(b) of the 1950 Defense Production Act to prioritize products that were deemed "scarce and critical material essential to the national defense." While the legal standing of the executive order was questionable, it gave the meat-packers ample cover to order their workers back into the plants.[8]

The meat shortage fears stirred up prior to the executive order initially derived not from the public but from a PR campaign spearheaded by the meat-packers. "The food supply chain is breaking," former Tyson CEO John Tyson wrote in a full-page advertisement that major U.S. publications ran in April 2020. "This is a challenge that should not be ignored," he continued. "Our plants must remain operational so that we can supply food to our families in America."[9]

Striking a similar chord, Smithfield CEO Kenneth Sullivan was outspoken against his company's Sioux Falls factory closure, writing in a press release that it would "push our country perilously close to the edge in terms of our meat supply. . . . It is our obligation to help feed the country, now more than ever."[10]

But was the country's meat supply in such profound peril? Were pork, beef, and chicken "scarce and critical materials essential to the national defense," as proffered by Trump's executive order? The power of hindsight, as well as simple common sense, shows us that while the concentrated meat supply exposed the weak links in the vertically integrated supply chain, processors had enough meat to feed Americans—albeit with the possibility that prolonged closures would cause extended price increases, limited variety, and wasted products.

In reality, it was a booming time for the meat-packers. In April 2020 the pork industry, led by Smithfield and Tyson, exported a record-setting amount of pork to China, reflecting a general internationalized trend line wherein the industry exports the meat and imports the pollution.[11] The industry produces at least 25 percent more pork than needed for domestic consumption, and government data reveals that in the spring of 2020, Smithfield had "hundreds of millions of pounds" of meat in cold storage, or enough to feed the entire country for several months even in the theoretical complete absence of more production.[12] In fact, COVID struck when capacity in the hog market was at an all-time high: 2019 was a record year for U.S. hog production, and many of those hogs were marketed in 2020.[13]

The consequences of the plant closures were not trivial, but the problem wasn't the threat of a true meat shortage. Rather, with so few plants processing a large proportion of the market—and with individual contract growers supplying animals by the thousands—temporary disturbances easily triggered price spikes, layoffs, and other downstream economic impacts.

And then there was the matter of the excess animals. In the pre-CAFO days, when livestock was dispersed among tens of thousands of small farms, a halt in production meant farms were dealing with forty, eighty, or at the top maybe hundreds of animals with nowhere to go. Facing such a logistical puzzle, some farmers would resort to killing the animals, or "depopulating" them, as the industry calls it. But other farmers would successfully find creative ways to distribute the meat in local marketplaces.

Not so today. Contract growers board thousands, even tens of thousands of animals—all bound to a single buyer. When the plants closed, contract growers were in the unsavory position of dealing with, and paying for, depopulating their facilities. Their contracts with the integrators left them few options. Integrators are shielded from many of the costs associated with unexpected herd deaths: the fine print often includes a clause stating that growers are responsible for losses associated with unexpected disturbances such as swine disease outbreaks, weather events, and other "factors beyond control."

The Big Pig Pyramid ensures that the risks associated with factors beyond control fall disproportionately on contract growers at the bottom of the pyramid, not on the meatpacking conglomerates at the top or upon the middle-tier integrators. With each animal that was killed, part of the contract grower's paycheck evaporated. Unable to deliver market-ready hogs for processing—the triggering mechanism for payment—many contract growers were responsible for the cost of killing the animals in the same time frame that their paychecks disappeared.

Officials estimated that during plant closures in April 2020, about seven hundred thousand pigs across the nation could not be processed each week and had to be euthanized.[14] Culling techniques recommended by the American Veterinary Medical Association (AVMA) include gunshot, nonpenetrating captive bolt, electrocution, and blunt force head trauma. Some of these methods are susceptible to failure. In the words of the AVMA, "Not all methods will induce death in a manner that is consistent with euthanasia."[15]

Many CAFO operators resorted to depopulation methods that the AVMA classifies as "not recommended" but "permitted in constrained circumstances."[16] Ventilation shutdown was a common procedure during the 2020 factory closures.[17] Contract growers shut off the ventilation fans inside the CAFOs, closed the vents, turned up the heat, and piped a cocktail of carbon dioxide and steam into the barns. The animals died from overheating, suffocation, and poisoning. The efficacy of the extermination depends on the specifics of the facility and the choices of the individual CAFO operators and consulting veterinarians. Some don't turn the heat up enough; some don't use carbon dioxide at all.[18]

In Iowa in May 2020, a whistleblower employee at Iowa Select Farms, the state's largest pork producer, informed the animal rights group Direct Action Everywhere (DxE) when such an extermination would be taking place. DxE installed a hidden camera. The footage captured the sounds of hogs crying out in agonizing pain and distress for hours. When employees arrived the next morning, some of the hogs were still alive. Workers killed them with bolt guns.[19]

After it learned about the footage, Iowa Select chose to publicly "disclose that it had 'been forced to make this heartbreaking decision' to depopulate its herd."[20]

The whistleblower was a longtime industry employee who became increasingly disillusioned with the treatment of CAFO hogs even prior to the circumstances of 2020. In 2019 the meat-packers, anticipating increased demand for pork in China, glutted the market with a record-breaking number of hogs, pushing their sows and their facilities to the brink. Reportedly, facilities that were already designed to provide hogs with barely enough room to turn around were packed to as much as double their permitted capacity.[21]

Initially the whistleblower was determined to use their own name in the media but later changed their mind. This decision was under-standable. Speaking out publicly against Big Ag is a ticket to permanent ostracization in farm country. "Everything around here is based off this very industry," the whistleblower told a reporter at *The Intercept*, "and with that, it's seeing friends, friends' parents and kids, all seeing you as the bad guy. This industry has done a very good job with its PR campaign: No matter what, before anything is said, you're going to be the bad guy."[22]

The depopulations caused psychological trauma to facility employees and contract growers, some of whom attempted to find creative ways to avoid it, including injecting pregnant sows to induce miscarriages and altering the animals' diets to slow their growth.[23] These efforts were impotent in the face of a monopolized livestock market where only a handful of facilities process meat and the infrastructure for local distribution has all but disappeared. The spiritual and ethical waste of this system was abundantly clear in 2020, when folks around the country were standing in lines at food banks while livestock was being killed and left in piles to decompose.

Tom Butler, a North Carolina hog contract grower with about 7,500 to 8,000 hogs, told his integrator, Prestage Farms, that he would insist on sending his hogs to local butchers and distribute the meat to the hungry. His pitch was unsuccessful, and there was absolutely nothing Butler could do about it. Prestage owned the pigs.[24]

Butler had made a name for himself a couple of years earlier by tes-tifying against Smithfield Foods in the blockbuster North Carolinian nuisance trial that Smithfield ultimately lost and was ordered to pay nearly $550 million in damages. (The amount was later knocked down to $98 million in accordance with a new state law limiting punitive damages.) He is known for his rare willingness to speak against the industry even while continuing to be shackled by his contract with the integrator.

Compared to Butler's average annual loss rate of 3–5 percent, death losses on his farm spiked to 9 percent during 2020. He estimates that at least eight hundred hogs died on his farm due to reduced capacity at the Smithfield pork processing plant in Tar Heel, North Carolina.[25] Prestage left pigs on Butler's farm an additional three to four weeks, far beyond the thirteen-to-twenty-week period needed to achieve their full market weight of 285 pounds. His hogs were confined in pens designed to hold nineteen to twenty-one pigs weighing 265 pounds each. He watched apprehensively as they continued to grow to 325 pounds, which was a formula for disaster, given that pigs are known to attack and kill one another in tight spaces. The overgrown hogs also did damage to penning, feeders, and watering equipment.

Butler estimates that he lost over $30,000, a significant amount in an industry where contract growers are perpetually operating at the brink of loss. Moreover, as with many contract growers, he hasn't had any kind of monetary contract increase in decades.

When Butler's integrator announced tentative plans to come to his farm and kill thousands of healthy adult hogs, he continued his plea to send the hogs to local butchers or just give them away to the community. Butler lives in a rural community where most residents know how to slaughter, preserve, and save pork. Finally, the integrator agreed to remove the overweight animals and transport them to their own meat processing plant in Wright County, Iowa. While an imperfect solution, it was preferable to the total waste that the industry was promoting.

As the contract growers at the bottom of the pyramid absorbed their losses, the integrators cashed in. The National Pork Producers Council advocated for federal assistance to bail out those hog integrators who were unable to get their animals to market. Rich with political connections and financial resources, the NPPC pushed to reimburse the integrators for the depopulation and disposal of their dead hogs due to the supply chain bottlenecks.

A closer look at the distribution of federal bailouts in Minnesota shows that the largest integrators benefited disproportionately from funding that derived from the federal Coronavirus Aid, Relief, and Economic Security (CARES) Act. The Minnesota Department of Agriculture distributed the funds through its Hog Depopulation Cost-Share Program, which offered financial assistance to hog owners. It expressly included integrators and independent farmers but notably *not* contract growers.[26]

My data request with the MDA revealed that most of the program's aid relief was directed to the state's largest corporate integrators:

1. Pipestone System, $841,237.50
2. Christensen Farms, $783,960
3. Schwartz Farms, Inc., $731,340
4. Wakefield Pork, Inc., $536,085

These four corporate integrators received 69 percent of the $4.175 million in program payments. The government funding was advertised as a support system for small family farmers impacted by the pandemic, yet in reality, only thirty-plus organizations applied for payments for euthanizing 311,242 hogs.[27]

A similar situation unfolded in Iowa, where Christensen Farms *alone* received 72 percent of the first round of pandemic relief payments via the Iowa Disposal Assistance Program. The award drew criticism, particularly in light of an unusual $25,000 donation that Christensen Farms made to the campaign of Iowa governor Kim Reynolds. It was one of the governor's largest campaign contributions in 2020.[28]

Corporate pigs ate at the public trough, while the contract growers cut their losses.

Tom Butler and other critics of how the integrators and meat-packers profited from the events of 2020 maintain that the pandemic presented an opportunity for the industry to reduce the market glut of hogs and increase the price of pork products, which the industry had been trying to accomplish for years. There was a reason that Smithfield had hundreds of millions of pounds of pork sitting in freezers when the pandemic hit. In 2020 Smithfield, Hormel, and several other meat-packers were battling the first volley in a series of class-action lawsuits alleging the corporate giants had conspired to fix prices by artificially constricting the supply of pork products beginning in 2009.[29] As of 2022, Smithfield has paid $200 million in antitrust settlements.[30]

The pandemic revealed not only the boundless greed of the meat-packers but also the fragility of the vertically integrated supply chain. With few mechanisms in place for mitigating even very short-term production pauses, the system promptly collapsed under the weight of the virus, and the losses fell squarely on the meatpacking employees, the workers who labor invisibly inside the CAFOs, the contract growers, and the American consumers.

Yet the meat-packers puffed their chests and gloated, not admitting an ounce of self-reflection or shame as their workers died from COVID. In his plea to reopen Tyson plants in April 2020, John Tyson wrote, "We have a responsibility to feed our country. It is as essential as healthcare."[31]

The claim that eating chicken is equal to receiving health care was an odd stance at a time when hospitals were overcrowded, and refrigerated semitrucks served as overload morgues in hospital alleyways. But as noted earlier, the public bought the argument. Within two days of Tyson's publishing his message, Trump signed the executive order to reopen the plants. The message landed so effectively and effortlessly because by 2020, the meat-packers had spent two decades perfecting their corporate message, convincing consumers that CAFO-style "modern" agriculture is the only way to feed the world.

Feed the World Propaganda

One phrase you'll hear most often from Big Ag cheerleaders is "feed the world." America's network of livestock contract growers and feed suppliers are told, on perpetual repeat, that they are feeding the world. Without them and their specific brand of so-called modern agriculture, the world would go hungry. This is why they must continuously expand operations and cram more animals into ever-smaller spaces.

It's why slaughterhouse processing speeds should have no upper limit regardless of the suffering it causes workers and the increased risk of contaminated meat. If speeds slowed, the world wouldn't be fed.

It's why anyone opposed to a CAFO expansion is considered an ignoramus who doesn't understand the unique role that this modern agriculture plays in feeding the world.

And it's why CAFO operators shouldn't feel badly for putting small-scale, independent farmers out of business. Those smaller operations couldn't have fed the world.

While it's true that feeding the world's growing population is an incredibly important challenge, CAFO-style agriculture (for livestock), or corporate-style monoculture, is not the *only* way or even the best way to do it. Ultimately the solution will require an assortment of methodologies with large-scale monoculture perhaps playing a role. Experts increasingly believe that improving the yields of small farms, restoring soil health, supporting local farmers to feed local populations, and adopting various forms of polyculture farming are needed to sustainably and reliably feed the world's population, which stands at eight billion and counting.[32]

In 2015 José Graziano da Silva, the director general of the Food and Agriculture Organization for the United Nations (UN), announced that the UN would increase support for community-based, sustainable agriculture while implementing programs to lessen the environmental, ecological, and economic risks associated with corporatized modern agriculture. Graziano da Silva noted that the world currently produces more than enough food for everyone, yet much of it is wasted even as 805 million global citizens go hungry. Meeting production goalposts is not the sole solution to world hunger. Poverty, war, conflict, the refugee crisis, and climate change are among the major contributors to food insecurity, and a corporatized, bottlenecked global supply chain will always pose a major threat to food security. Local, sustainable agriculture instead will feed the world.

"We need a paradigm shift," Graziano da Silva concluded. "Food systems need to be more sustainable, inclusive, and resilient."[33]

The UN predicts that global food production must increase between 60 and 100 percent by 2050 to feed the projected global population.[34] The Big Ag corporations repeatedly cite this statistic, then each asserts that its specific corporation has a duty—a moral imperative even—to double its own production by 2050.

In reality, if these corporations doubled production, then mostly wealthy nations would be fed, along with the corporations' profits. In 2015, 86 percent of U.S. agricultural exports went to twenty of the world's wealthiest export destinations, while only *0.5 percent* of U.S. agricultural exports went to a group of nineteen countries where hunger is chronic, including Haiti, Yemen, and Ethiopia.[35] According to the UN's Food and Agriculture Organization, the populations of these latter nations experience high or very high levels of undernourishment.

Looking specifically at livestock production, most meat produced in the United States is consumed in the United States, and an ever-growing proportion is exported to Japan, South Korea, Mexico, Canada, and China. The United States and China actually have a serious problem with meat overconsumption, with most Americans eating "more than 1.5 times the average daily protein requirement."[36] Eating more meat than recommended by nutritional guidelines increases the risk of obesity, certain cancers, diabetes, and premature death. Researchers at the University of Oxford estimate that if people cut their meat consumption down to expert-recommended amounts, the world could save a collective $730 billion in health care costs.[37]

Tyson and Smithfield aren't feeding the world; mostly they're feeding people who are already eating too much meat.

This truth doesn't stop Big Ag proponents from claiming that critics of specific aspects and practices of corporate agriculture will prevent the world from being fed. During a speech in Minnesota in June 2022, Terry Wolters, president of the National Pork Producers Council, criticized a new regulation in California that increases the space requirement for sows to twenty-four square feet of space—an improvement over the industry's standard gestation crates, which are so small that the sows are unable to turn around or lie down. "You've got a group of society that wants to inflict mandates, and they don't understand modern agriculture," Wolters said. "And we're in a great position to feed not only this country, but the world in a very efficient manner."[38]

The industry habitually uses its "feed the world" claim to dupe the public and justify harmful policies and practices. In 2016 the president of the Iowa Farm Bureau spoke in opposition to the increasing ranks of Iowa citizens pushing for commonsense industry regulation in the state. "If we don't unite and fight for our ability to operate, we won't be successful in meeting our vision of feeding the world," he said.[39] Fed up with the relentless propaganda, the editorial board at the *Des Moines Register* pushed back. "The claim that U.S. agriculture 'feeds the world' is not a harmless myth," they wrote. "It provides a moral justification for continuing practices that have harmed Iowa's environment and led to low prices for farmers."[40]

The feed the world myth is only the tip of the iceberg of Big Ag propaganda. As examined in chapter 17, the industry seeks to indoctrinate schoolchildren, teaching them that corporatized agriculture is the preferred way to farm. To counteract the pervasive Big Ag propaganda machine, grassroots movements must continue to unite and to persevere. And that's exactly what they're doing.

19

On the Front Lines

"No one anywhere should have to live like this, with hog waste sprayed at their homes, unable to go outside and enjoy fresh air and a beautiful day. They are located here because we are the path of least resistance, because we do not have money, and we do not have a voice in the halls of power. They assumed we would not fight back. They were wrong."—ELSIE HERRING, speaking before the U.S. House, 2019

The front line has been waging the fight against factory farming as long as factory farming has existed, yet it took many years for a national movement to coalesce. The popular front in the CAFO wars was dispersed and underfunded while standing against monied corporations, industry titans, and the politicians supporting them.

It has been a story of taking one step forward, three steps back. Individual townships and counties do prevail on occasion—for example, in blocking a single feedlot—yet the developers simply relocate their operation to another vulnerable rural outpost. Today, the profits of the meat-packers continue to grow as the regulatory environment remains impotent and as the courts oftentimes favor corporations and roll back antitrust enforcement. Meanwhile, the unified and extremely well-financed American Farm Bureau Federation and its industry allies stoke America's partisan divides. Big Ag's encroachment in rural farm country has been an underappreciated factor contributing to the growth of a new political alignment in rural America—one that relies on the politics of grievance and anger to win votes.

The strategic corporate takeover of rural America contrasts with the uncoordinated opposition to corporate farming: local citizens groups, animal welfare groups, anti-monopolists, environmental groups, and isolated farmers and ranchers trying to defend their communities. It's akin to bows and arrows attempting to withstand a heavily armed assault. Handcuffed by a lack of coordination, the scattered, localized efforts have been unable to evict the occupying force.

Yet in my view, the hyper-local organizing that's existed for decades is now bearing fruit, as previously disconnected organizations have begun working together to fuel a larger movement. The drum beats louder as rural citizens build the groundwork for resilience. More are beginning to understand what folks at the front lines have long known: this is not only about factory farms and the fight against corporatism but also about the larger fights for racial, social, economic, environmental, and climate justice that have coalesced in recent years.

In the pork industry, the organized CAFO resistance began mainly in North Carolina, which experienced an absolute explosion of corporatized hog facilities after a 1991 law known as the Murphy Amendment exempted factory farms from many air and water regulations, and a corresponding bill prevented counties from imposing zoning restrictions.[1] The rapid development that followed was concentrated in Duplin and Sampson Counties, rural regions in the eastern part of the state with a dispersed rural population, including many Black communities and poor communities. This area was known as "the hog capital of the world" before Iowa took up the distinction. In Duplin County, hogs outnumbered people by thirty-eight to one in 2019.[2]

Elsie Herring was a resident of Duplin County, where her grandfather was born a slave and later acquired land that his descendants now own. Herring was one of the earliest grassroots organizers in the area. In testimony before a U.S. House committee two years before her death in 2021, Herring spoke about the ag industry's targeting of Duplin County. Citing a 2014 civil rights complaint filed with the EPA, she asserted that CAFO facilities were permitted "to operate with grossly inadequate and outdated systems of controlling animal waste and little provision for government oversight, which has an unjustified disproportionate impact on the basis of race and national origin against African Americans, Latinos and Native Americans."[3]

Despite the community's lack of financial resources and political influence, Herring and many others in North Carolina's hog country fought back, eventually scoring major wins, including the successful litigation against Smithfield Foods (see chapter 16). Frontline organizations that Herring was involved with—and are still going strong today—include the North Carolina Environmental Justice Network and the Rural Empowerment Association for Community Help.

Another early organizer in North Carolina was Don Webb, a former swine CAFO operator in Duplin County who shut down his barns and moved away after friends and neighbors confided that his facility was "making their lives miserable."[4] Webb later moved back to Duplin County and became a full-time organizer upon observing how dramatically the situation in the county had worsened. He founded the Alliance for a Responsible Swine Industry, which later became Coastal Carolina Riverwatch. Today many of the organizations in North Carolina have evolved into or have partnered with nationally active groups such as the Waterkeeper Alliance, the Environmental Working Group, and Earth Justice to pursue industry reforms.

When North Carolina banned new CAFO development in 1997, the corporate swine industry pursued dominance in Iowa, Missouri, Minnesota, and Illinois. More recently, the industry has commenced a full-court press to expand operations in the Dakotas and Wisconsin.[5] People in these states have responded with highly localized strategies as the laws governing feedlots are so different depending on locality. Robust community organizations have risen to the challenge: the Land Stewardship Project in Minnesota, the Sustain Rural Wisconsin Network, the Dakota Resource Council, the Iowa CCI (Citizens for Community Improvement), the Iowa Alliance for Responsible Agriculture, the Citizens Legal Environmental Action Network, and the Illinois Citizens for Clean Air and Water. This only scratches the surface; the list goes on.

North Carolina wasn't the only state mired in conflict during the early CAFO battles of the 1990s. An interesting story of early resistance took place in Missouri, when a shocked community attempted to resist what was, at the time, one of the largest factory farms in the Midwest.

"We Got It Done under the Radar"

The tale of how Premium Standard Farms infiltrated Missouri—an appalling metonym, a stand-in for the larger story—tells you everything you need to know about corporate Big Ag. It began in 1986 with Tad Gordon, a Wall Street stocks and bonds trader in his early thirties who, by his own account, knew nothing about hogs. While reading about how banks and insurers were buying up midwestern farmland as farmers defaulted during the farm debt crisis of the 1980s, he wondered how he could profit from this. After looking into the matter, he decided to invest $5 million in hog barns in Iowa.[6]

Gordon incorporated Premium Standard and arrived in Ames, Iowa, in 1988 to build the first barn. "This is the first time I have stepped foot in Iowa, so I have no idea what I'm doing," he revealed in a 2018 interview with *Successful Farming* magazine. Iowa's laws at the time protected farmland and farmers from corporate buyouts, and Gordon's permit was pulled. Undeterred, he moved the operation to Missouri, where state law at the time limited corporate farmland ownership to 2,500 acres.

"We knew we had to change some laws if we wanted to stay there," Gordon recounted. He and his business partner arranged a meeting with John Ashcroft, then the governor of Missouri. Ashcroft supported their vision and assisted in contacting state representatives to adopt new pro-corporate farm laws.[7]

"A couple of local representatives and a senator snuck it in a bill," Gordon said. "We got it done under the radar."

After securing an $800 million loan from Morgan Stanley, Premium Standard bought out small farmers, hoarded Missouri farmland, and built massive hog confinements, many with outdoor manure storage lagoons based on the North Carolina model. Gordon characterized the bank's loan as "too much too fast. We just went crazy." Manure management was their "big problem" because they needed large holdings of adjoining acreage to spread the waste. According to Gordon, they "did everything on the lowdown" as they convinced small independent farmers to sell their land.[8]

By 1994 Premium Standard was operating multiple massive CAFO complexes housing upward of one hundred thousand hogs apiece and was cobbling together manure management plans as it went along. By 1996 the company filed for bankruptcy and restructured. By 1998 the company was producing six hundred million gallons of manure annually and was responsible for multiple manure spills and large-scale fish kills, with far-reaching impacts on the local economy.[9] In 2006 Premium Standard was acquired by Smithfield Foods, which deemed one of Premium Standard's Missouri operations "the worst hog farm in America," citing its manure management, labor, and hog health problems.[10]

Tad Gordon cashed out and today serves as the CEO of his pet project, a movie theater company.[11] Meanwhile, the number of hog farmers in Missouri decreased by 90 percent between 1985 and 2004.[12]

One victim of the Premium Standards takeover was Scott Dye, who grew up in Lincoln Township, Putnam County, in northern Missouri on a 340-acre family farm founded by his grandfather in 1885. During the summer of 1994, Dye learned that an adjacent farm sold to Premium Standard and would soon host seventy-two separate hog confinements, with each holding upward of 1,100 animals, or nearly 80,000 hogs.[13] Dye started writing opinion pieces in opposition to the coming facility that were published in the *St. Louis Post* and the *Kansas City Star*. At the time, he worked third shift as a computer specialist for the Missouri Farmers Association (MFA), a farm co-op. (After undergoing various mergers, today the MFA Incorporated is a $1.6 billion farm supply business.) Soon enough, Dye was fired.[14]

"I was told that my opinion was detrimental to all agriculture," Dye said. He later learned that the MFA was selling millions of dollars of grain per year to the factory farm facility in question.

Dye and other neighbors joined with the Missouri Rural Crisis Center to resist the facility's permit. Together with Farm Aid, the group organized an event in Putnam County scheduled for April 1, 1995, featuring the iconic musician Willie Nelson. Many locals couldn't believe that Nelson was really coming to little Putnam County. A rumor spread that the event was an April Fools' Day joke.

But Big Ag's local sycophants took it all very seriously. In the week leading up to the event, the local Farm Aid office and individuals on Willie Nelson's tour bus received menacing calls and death threats. "It was very disturbing," Dye recalled. He was tasked with organizing a security detail in response to the unexpected situation. Thinking on his feet, he hired a motorcycle club—bikers who specialized in event security—out of Des Moines. On the day of the concert, Dye and other neighbors cut a doorway out of the corrugated tin building where the event would take place and constructed a tunnel out of plywood and black fabric leading directly to the stage. Feeling the pressure of protecting the country and western legend, Scott rallied the troops, saying, "Let's get Willie back on the road again safely, boys!"

The show was a success. Upon learning that some had deemed it an April Fools' joke, afterward Nelson and his crew drove seven miles to Unionville, the county seat, and parked the tour bus in the middle of town for two hours—just to make a statement.

Ultimately the factory farm moved forward and began operations, with predictable consequences for the health of neighboring residents and for the area's air and water quality. Dye still owns his family's farm, Willow Branch Farm, but he and his wife now live in Columbia, Missouri, unable to raise their family next door to eighty thousand hogs. Big Ag continues to erase farm families from the land.

Determined to ensure that other communities didn't endure the same fate, Dye dedicated his career to fighting the installation of corporate factory farms. For fifteen years, he worked for the Sierra Club and later for the Socially Responsible Agriculture Project.

Along with nearly three hundred neighbors, Dye was one of the plaintiffs in a nuisance lawsuit against Smithfield initiated in 1999. The neighbors won that suit in 2012 after a long legal battle.[15] A contemporaneous federal citizens-action lawsuit filed against Premium Standard alleged improper manure waste disposal and resulted in a 2002 federal consent decree requiring Premium, and then Smithfield, to improve its manure disposal methods. Ultimately, after another protracted legal battle, negotiations are ongoing, and the decree has not yet been fully enforced.[16]

Similar to Minnesota, Missouri is a state where—until recently—counties retained local control over factory farm permitting and regulation. Premium Standard managed to force through the initial wave of CAFOs by evading local oversight, entering into secret land buyouts, scheming with the governor, and preventing coverage in the local press. But for some time after the secretive takeover, county officials and voters in Missouri took advantage of local democratic pathways and chose to prevent new CAFOs from entering their backyard. They also passed ordinances to regulate the existing CAFOs, with at least twenty counties in Missouri approving health and zoning ordinances that were stricter than those of the state.[17] As a result, CAFO expansions in Missouri became relatively limited as the industry busied itself expanding in Iowa, Illinois, and Minnesota.

But the nuisance lawsuits, along with creeping CAFO oversaturation and swine disease outbreaks in neighboring states, brought the industry's attention back to Missouri. In 2011 in response to the pending nuisance lawsuits, pro-industry players in the Missouri legislature passed a law capping nuisance payouts.[18] In 2019, after years of fierce resistance from rural residents, Missouri lawmakers passed new laws barring counties from approving feedlot ordinances that are more rigorous than those of the state.[19]

Industry-aligned lawmakers had been pursuing this legislation for years in Missouri. They finally got their way. Rural health advocates fear the new laws will allow Missouri to become the next Iowa, where independent farmers have all but disappeared.

It's a sad irony that Iowa became the cautionary tale, because in the very early years of the CAFO expansions, state laws protected farmland from corporate investors. That changed dramatically in 1994. The owners of Iowa Select Farms, the state's largest hog operation, joined with other industry leaders to leverage political connections, roll back industry regulation, and craft new laws enabling a full-throttle takeover of livestock agriculture in Iowa. A new industry group, the Iowa Pork Alliance, deployed a public relations campaign highlighting the importance of hogs to the state's economy. Iowa Select and others donated to the campaign to reelect the governor, Terry Branstad. Iowa Select even hired Branstad's former chief of staff as its lobbyist.[20] The following year, in 1995, Branstad signed House File 519, which permanently changed agriculture in the state by removing all local control of feedlot permitting.

Despite this loss, for many years independent farmers and local residents fought hard to save their family farms. For every new corporate feedlot, there was a local county or township that didn't want it.[21] A 1995 *Wall Street Journal* article about the feedlot battles embroiling rural Iowa described one county where a panic button had been installed at the board of supervisors' meetings. The dean of Iowa State's Agriculture Department said at the time he was worried "about towns getting torn apart."[22]

The resistance continued, but the laws—and, increasingly, the politicians—favored the corporations. Feedlots are permitted and regulated by Iowa's Department of Natural Resources and the Iowa Environmental Protection Commission, two critically underfunded agencies that rubberstamp CAFOs and don't respond to the vast majority of citizens' complaints. Iowa now produces more manure waste than any other state, by far: its annual manure output is equivalent to that of Bangladesh, a country with 165 million people. Over the past two decades, nitrogen pollution flowing from the Iowa River and ultimately into the Gulf of Mexico increased by 50 percent, making the state of Iowa the largest contributor to the Gulf's dead zone.[23]

The majority of voters in Iowa, including the majority of Republican voters, favor a statewide CAFO moratorium, and 75 percent favor stricter permitting requirements.[24] For six consecutive years—annually since 2018—members of the legislature introduced a bill cosigned by dozens of local organizations to enact a CAFO moratorium in Iowa and to tighten the regulation of existing facilities. Yet nothing happens. The state's legislature won't even bring the bill to the floor.

20

Expanding the Corporate Empire

"Now more than ever we must stand up for agriculture on behalf of all North Dakotans and all Americans. We have to ensure elitist activists do not continue to erode our property rights based on false climate change claims and fake fixes to such claims. Do you want to be told what you are doing incorrectly, or do you want to share what you are doing to better your country?"—DERYL LIES, North Dakota Farm Bureau president, 2022

In states where counties retain some local control over permitting and regulation, it's been interesting to see how Big Ag deploys a hodgepodge of tactics to circumvent local decisions. Ongoing conflicts in Minnesota, Wisconsin, and North Dakota highlight the necessity of reform to counter the systematic corporate exploitation of rural places and people. In the absence of a functioning federal regulatory infrastructure, local feedlot disputes are operating in a Wild West, with residents duking it out over ambiguous and sometimes entirely lacking local ordinances or state laws. Particularly in the days since Trumpian politics took hold of many farm communities, the localized feedlot battles assumed a darker tenor. Legalistic disagreements over land use policies and nuisance laws now mingle with increasingly demagogic rhetoric coming from contract growers and the Farm Bureaus.

Farm families and rural residents in Minnesota have courageously engaged in isolated battles across the state for many years, including in the counties of Freeborn, McLeod, Rock, and Todd.[1] Locals pay expensive legal fees out of their own pockets while industry giants and their factory farm operators enjoy ready access to industry funding, creating further animosity among neighbors in rural areas.

A particularly complicated legal battle has unfolded in Becker County in the Lake Country region of northern Minnesota. (Readers might recall the story in chapter 13 of Mariann Guentzel from another county in Lake Country.) Swine disease outbreaks and land use conflicts are hampering factory farm development in southern Minnesota, so the industry is venturing north into previously unsullied areas used heavily for fishing and recreation. The folks up north, seeing what happened downstate, are wise to what's happening.

In 2022 Erica and Eric Zurn applied for a permit for three CAFOS housing a total of three thousand pigs in Becker County. The operation's "majority investor" is reportedly a farmer who lives hours away and remains anonymous. Conveniently, the application claimed the facilities would hold exactly 999 animal units—1 short of the number that could have triggered a detailed environmental review.[2]

The applicants knew what they were doing. Eric Zurn is the son of Karolyn and Bill Zurn, soybean producers and active Farm Bureau members who serve many industry advocacy roles, including for Ag in the Classroom.[3] Bill Zurn acknowledged that the family's interest in his son's swine CAFO in Becker County is primarily the manure— that is, the 2.8 million gallons of manure that the Zurns intend to use on the family's crop production acreage.[4]

In other words, the siting of the CAFO was decided according to the Zurn family's peripheral financial interests rather than on the best location to mitigate health, environmental, and other nuisance impacts. County boards are required to consider the latter, not the former, when approving feedlots. The Becker County Board nevertheless approved the operation, though it did express concern about the issues raised during the public hearing. The Zurn application for a factory farm permit was "the most controversial issue ever brought in front of the county board," according to an anonymous Becker County resident.[5]

The Becker County Board, having approved the conditional use permit, also placed a one-year moratorium on future feedlot applications. This move provided false cover, a misleading assurance to the area's residents that the board intended to take further action to limit the future development of factory farms. Sadly, residents discovered that the moratorium was simply a delay tactic, as it was rescinded a few months later.

Meanwhile, public officials in Spring Creek Township, where the proposed CAFO is sited, openly opposed the feedlot. As of this writing, township officials are moving forward with plans to adopt local planning and zoning to protect the community and halt the encroachment of factory farms in the township. Other townships in Becker County are similarly working on the process to adopt local planning and zoning.

With the outcome of the Zurn operation uncertain, a third player entered the scene—White Earth Nation, a Chippewa Indian community whose reservation encompasses the proposed feedlot site. Legal counsel for the White Earth Legal Department attended a feedlot hearing and argued that in accordance with federal law, White Earth should have been involved with the permitting process from the get-go. White Earth residents were concerned about the possible contamination of the hundreds of nearby lakes, rivers, and streams that would pose health risks and threaten tribal food products such as wild rice, mussels, and fish. The tribe placed a two-year moratorium on feedlot applications within White Earth's boundaries.[6] As of this writing, the developers intend to move forward with the project at an alternate location just outside the White Earth Reservation's boundaries.[7]

This legal wrangling between the developers, the county, the township, and White Earth Nation shows the uncertainty and drama shouldered at the local level when commonsense state and federal regulations are absent.

Elsewhere in Minnesota, a similarly labyrinthine legal contest is taking place in Winona County in the southeastern corner of the state. Winona County's story stands out because it adopted responsible CAFO regulations at the county level, including a cap of 1,500 AUs per feedlot.[8] In 2018 the county's largest dairy, Daley Farms, submitted an application known as a variance request to expand the existing operation to 5,968 AUs.[9]

After considerable public outcry over this attempt to circumvent the county ordinance, the Minnesota Pollution Control Agency agreed to extend the public comment period by fifteen days, allowing more time for constituents to review the environmental assessment worksheet.

Enraged by the MPCA's rare acquiescence to factory farm opponents, Daley Farms and an array of industry and lobbyist groups together sued the agency for the frankly comical grievance of its having allowed two weeks' extra time for environmental review. Plaintiffs in the lawsuit included Daley Farms, the Minnesota Milk Producers Association, the Minnesota Farm Bureau Federation, and the Minnesota Pork Producers Association.[10] The plaintiffs lost that suit, and in 2019 the Winona County Board rejected the variance request.

Undeterred, Daley Farms sued Winona County, accusing the county board of bias because some members had spoken positively about the Land Stewardship Project, a nonprofit group that supports independent farmers.[11] The district court agreed. (I can't help but notice that the courts don't mind the egregious pro-industry bias of county board members, including when members have a financial stake in the project they're approving. But in this case, the court recognized the bias when it was allegedly anti-industry.)

The Minnesota Court of Appeals later rejected Daley's request to grant approval of the feedlot application directly through the court, sending the decision back to Winona County for reconsideration. In 2021 the Winona County Board—staffed with new members to satisfy the court's order against bias—again rejected the variance request.

That should have been the end of it, particularly because from the outset, the variance request clearly ran afoul of the county's 1,500-AU cap. The problem is, at a fundamental level, the industry doesn't believe it should be regulated, having become accustomed to its relative free rein under federal and state law. Heck, the industry crafted the pro-corporate laws itself. When counties and townships exercise their legal authority to administer local planning and zoning regulations, industry players see it as an inconceivable affront.

One additional case is currently pending in Winona County courts: Daley Farms is appealing (again) the county's denial of its variance request. In a second action, Daley Farms waged a bizarre action against individual members of the Land Stewardship Project and the county board, alleging they conspired to stack the vote. Lawyers refer to this type of lawsuit as a SLAPP (strategic lawsuit against public participation) suit. They're uncommon, typically used as a strategy to bully and intimidate, and often quickly dismissed. In a *Star Tribune* article, LSP spokesperson Sean Carroll described the suit as a "bullying tactic, designed to threaten anyone else from speaking out against the expansion."[12] Within days following the piece, Daley Farms dismissed the action.

It appears that Winona County will successfully stave off the feedlot despite the industry's efforts to supersede the local law and the democratic process. The citizens prevailed.[13]

Farm Bureau Country

I've learned over the years that when a feedlot is proposed on a site that poses obvious environmental risks, an influential Farm Bureau member is likely behind it. This was the case recently in Fillmore County in southeastern Minnesota, where prominent Farm Bureau member Al Hein proposed a large swine farrowing facility.[14] Hein was the past director of the Fillmore County Farm Bureau and a delegate to the state Republican convention.

When the township moved to adopt a one-year feedlot moratorium, Hein sued. When the MPCA took the rare step of denying the permit, citing groundwater contamination risks, he reapplied. Ultimately, in February 2019, he withdrew the application, admitting defeat.[15]

Hein's effort to place a large facility over sensitive karst topography, especially in a county where nitrate contamination was already a major problem, didn't make sense. "This is one of the most sensitive areas of the state from a groundwater contamination point of view," MPCA commissioner John Linc Stine said at the time.[16] Hein attempted to move forward with his project anyway, knowing that the vast majority of industrialized feedlots are approved.

This might be changing.

Feedlot fights in Minnesota have tested whether local laws and ordinances can effectively blockade new CAFO development and regulate existing feedlots. As the industry moves aggressively into Wisconsin and North Dakota—states where local control is uncertain, with gray areas in the law—the Minnesota experience is instructive. Will these states become the next Iowa, or will local officials retain some latitude over permitting and regulation?

In 2018 in North Dakota, Taylor Aasmundstad, the twenty-three-year-old son of the former president of the North Dakota Farm Bureau, submitted a permit application to build a factory farm that would supply up to forty-four thousand piglets annually to large farrowing operations. Aasmundstad and his buddy from college would co-own the facility, which they would operate as a company called Grand Prairie Agriculture.[17] Conveniently, the permit application claimed the facilities would hold 999.6 animal units.[18]

Grand Prairie's proposed site is surrounded by wetlands that drain into Devil's Lake, only a half a mile away. Floods are common in the area. The local economy relies heavily on the region's walleye fishing and other recreational industries, and a Native American tribe living in the nearby Spirit Lake Nation views Devil's Lake as an important spiritual site and a cornerstone of the tribe's culture and economy. As for the lake itself, it's a closed basin, fed only by precipitation and runoff.[19]

What could go wrong?

Pelican Township, where the project was sited, denied Grand Prairie's application, citing numerous zoning regulations that ran afoul of the proposal. The developer appealed this decision to the district court, which upheld the township's decision. Following the industry playbook, the developers appealed again. In 2021 the state's supreme court overturned the district court's decision, and the project moved forward. One of the developers credited the North Dakota Farm Bureau for keeping the development alive in the face of the community's resistance. "They're the reason we're still standing," he said.[20]

A similar situation unfolded near tiny Buffalo Township in Cass County, North Dakota, when residents sued the North Dakota Department of Health after it approved the permit for a nine-thousand-head swine factory farm. An agricultural economist at North Dakota State University, Randy Coon, was among the experts who warned about the environmental impacts of the operation. Coon calculated that the facility would produce two million gallons of manure in excess of the acreage that the developers stated they had available for manure spreading.[21] But this CAFO, as with the one near Devil's Lake, was allowed to move forward.

The trend lines in North Dakota are worrisome. State law once protected independent farmers and rural residents, but that's been changing. Legislators passed a bill in 2015 weakening existing regulations of corporate farmland buyouts. In 2023 Governor Burgum signed into law House Bill 1371, allowing corporations and corporate meat-packers to own farmland and operate cattle, hog, poultry, and dairy CAFOs in the state.

The law, however, overrides the will of the people. In 2016 the same matter was on the ballot in a statewide referendum; 76 percent of the voters rejected the proposed pro-corporate rule.[22]

In Wisconsin, residents likewise face industry backlash when townships or counties regulate feedlots or deny permits. Folks have been on the offensive with the new hog feedlots because of Wisconsin's preexisting dairy CAFO problem; the facilities have caused nitrate and bacterial contamination in private wells and impaired lakes, rivers, and streams. In 2016 health officials and lawmakers deemed bacterial contamination of private and public water supplies in Wisconsin a "public health crisis."[23]

With the hog industry now moving in as well, counties and townships across the state have enacted moratoriums and begun developing commonsense regulations. Polk and Burnett Counties in northwestern Wisconsin, for example, passed moratoriums in 2019 to give local officials more time to study the potential impacts of the largest hog facility ever proposed in northern Wisconsin. Suidae Health and Production, an Iowa-based vet clinic, had partnered with an area farmer, created a shell company called Cumberland LLC, and announced plans for a massive CAFO that would house up to twenty-six thousand pigs at a time.[24]

Waters from the town where the CAFO is proposed, Trade Lake, feed into the federally protected St. Croix National Scenic Riverway.

Wisconsin's Department of Natural Resources rejected the CAFO application based on the insufficient information provided in the environmental review. Additionally, the town of Trade Lake enacted a moratorium, giving officials time to research, develop, and enact an operations ordinance.[25] The cutting-edge ordinance required CAFO operators to detail how they would address water and air pollution, as well as biosecurity, carcass disposal, and other matters.

Trade Lake then partnered with five adjacent towns to conduct research to strengthen the ordinance. Five of the six towns in the partnership adopted similar operations ordinances in 2022, creating a virtual fence of sorts to protect two hundred square miles from factory farm development and prevent corporate intrusion. Predictably, in short order the Wisconsin Chamber of Commerce, in partnership with Farm Bureau industry advocates, sued one of the affected towns, Laketown, claiming it didn't have the authority to pass the ordinance. Local farmer Lisa Doerr, who operates a commercial forage business with her husband, was among the bipartisan community organizers who helped develop the ordinance. Doerr says that the town's ordinances represent "a Jeffersonian approach to community protection that terrifies the industry."[26]

Somewhat unexpectedly, Wisconsin's DNR was also playing hard ball. It asked the developer, Cumberland LLC, several follow-up questions about the next manure management plan it submitted after the DNR rejected the first one. The developer was unable to answer the DNR's questions. The DNR suspected the manure easement agreements that Cumberland claimed were locked in with area farmers didn't exist. Upon further questioning, Cumberland insisted that it intended to haul some of the manure to Minnesota, but the DNR was unable to verify the details of that plan.

The Sustain Rural Wisconsin Network, a citizen's consortium, called for a statewide moratorium on the construction and expansion of CAFOs until state law can effectively regulate them. As the group states, the moratorium should remain in place "until the DNR has the authority to enforce water quality protections, groundwater protection policies are passed, local elected officials have more control to protect lakes, rivers, and groundwater, and all existing CAFOs are brought up to compliance."[27]

To witness the growing resistance to corporate intrusion in neighboring states has been downright inspiring for me. And as the larger national ag reform movement builds momentum, its aims have matured and evolved. Let's take a look.

21

A New Vision for Farm Country

"What we do to the soil, we do unto ourselves. Soil, its health, or lack of it, its loss or regeneration, as in the past, is again at the center of global mass migrations, hunger, malnutrition, economic collapse, climate change ... the list goes on."—REGINALDO HASLETT-MARROQUÍN, Regenerative Agriculture Alliance founder

The local resistance to industrialized feedlot development can feel like a frustratingly small-scale approach. Yet in the past several years, I have watched magic occur. Local ag reform groups and leaders are creating new partnerships and networks, learning from one another, and developing new ideas for reclaiming farm country from the corporate colonist. Through the piecemeal approach of supporting democracy at the local level, something wonderful emerged: alliances formed, and the goals shifted from an "either/or" approach to a "yes/and" approach, as the interconnectivity of the ag reform movement's goals clarify.

Consortiums composed of many member organizations—such as the Western Organization for Resource Councils, the Waterkeeper Alliance, and the National Sustainable Agriculture Coalition—allow them to partner more easily with national advocacy groups such as Food & Water Watch and Farm Action. Coalitions are better resourced to pursue policy actions at the national level: supporting federal antitrust enforcement, lobbying for environmental regulations, pushing for a national moratorium on concentrated animal feeding operations.

These alliances inform and shape the larger goals. People working at the local level, as I do, tend to focus on blocking factory farm development and advocating for improved feedlot regulations. This work is but one piece of a larger puzzle, one that includes climate policy, immigration reform, land use policy, policy initiatives to support small independent farmers, and the strengthening of local food marketplaces.

I've learned a great deal. My perspective has broadened. I first entered the CAFO wars for relatively narrow reasons: my family's farm was at risk, and my hometown was harmed by Big Ag's takeover. Recognizing the forced silence of many rural residents, standing on the sidelines was no longer an option.

I soon felt a growing determination to do more to support the revitalization of rural America. Folks living in rural farm country are silenced by local Big Ag errand boys, but I wasn't as susceptible to this intimidation. Although born and reared in Dodge County, Douglas and I did not attend church locally, our children did not go to local schools, and our jobs did not rely upon the local economy. We could provide comments at public hearings and criticize the industrial model with fewer consequences. Big Ag's ripple effects go far beyond the shuttering of stores on Main Street and the exodus of small farmers. The environmental consequences are staggering, the health impacts are broader than we previously understood, and corporate food production further harms local economies by systemically excluding communities with less access to political capital, loans, training, and education. As a white farmer living in a state where 99 percent of farmers are also white, I hadn't given enough thought to why other communities have long been shut out. I'm grateful to the people at organizations such as the Midwest Farmers of Color Collective for teaching and inspiring me.

When thinking about alternatives to industrialized farming, I originally envisioned a regression to my childhood experience in the 1970s, when rural farm country comprised small family farms with diversified crops. I now see that as one among many routes to reclaiming and revitalizing independent farming. Thanks to the voices at organizations such as the Regenerative Agriculture Alliance, I've learned more about the Indigenous approaches to agriculture, the centrality of soil health in supporting regenerative ag models, and the integral role that food chain workers and immigrant farm workers play, not only in upholding the food economy, but also in driving the solutions to Big Ag's abuses. Today's ag reform movement is a multiracial, multi-issue, intersectional coalition standing against corporate abuse with ambition and resolve.

"Monitor the Activists All the Time"

To assess the vitality of today's ag reform movement, look no further than the industry's worried reaction to it. Pro-industry advocates and American Farm Bureau Federation leaders are concerned that their unchecked dominance has been challenged. "Anti-CAFO advocates are getting more organized, and their alliances are crossing states lines," warned Howard AV Roth, past president of the NPPC Board of Directors, at the Wisconsin Farm Bureau's annual meeting in 2020.[1]

A growing number of Big Ag advocacy organizations exist primarily to troll the ag reform movement. One such group is the Animal Agriculture Alliance, a Virginia-based nonprofit with a mission to "safeguard the future of animal agriculture" by arming "key food industry stakeholders" with "responses to emerging issues." The alliance pursues this mission by "exposing those who threaten our nation's food security with damaging misinformation."[2]

The alliance's past CEO and president, Kay Johnson-Smith, advised a large gathering of Farm Bureau members in 2020 on how to disarm the "activist, anti-business" groups that supposedly threaten modern agriculture. Correctly asserting that these groups seek to implement regulations at the local level, Johnson-Smith assured the Farm Bureau gathering that these local efforts are usually defeated. She boasted about the state of Georgia's recent success in eliminating county-level authority over CAFO siting, though she cautioned that this change is unpopular "because counties tend to be protective of local control."[3]

Johnson-Smith further advised the group that her organization, the Animal Agriculture Alliance, can "dig up dirt" on local residents that oppose CAFO developments. "You have to monitor the activists all the time," she said. "They are loud, well-funded, and *their goal is to eliminate animal agriculture*. Our Alliance is here to help [emphasis mine]."[4]

These paranoid remarks are a good example of how Big Ag's propaganda machine divides rural communities. Johnson-Smith's "activists" are normal rural residents and neighbors, and while I'd generously concede that perhaps some neighbors are loud, they don't seek to end animal agriculture. That last descriptor is one of the more upsetting falsehoods regularly proffered by Big Ag advocates. In my experience, many who stand against Big Ag's abuses are livestock farmers who are deeply invested in protecting the sustainability of animal agriculture for future generations.

Another propogandist organization is the U.S. Farmers & Ranchers Alliance (USFRA). Launched in 2011 by Big Ag's largest lobbyist groups, including the Farm Bureau and the NPPC, USFRA is funded by a number of chemical corporations, including Monsanto and DuPont. The group uses TV ads, online content, sponsored events, and social media campaigns to "fight the label 'Big Ag'" and to "reshape the dialogue" around the U.S. food supply.[5]

USFRA's founding was the industry's response to the growing popularity of organic and locally produced foods. One of its founding members, the lobbyist group American Meat Institute, stated on its website that too many Americans learn about how their food is produced from "the news media, books, and movies [referring to documentaries]."[6] USFRA hoped to solve this "problem." Better instead to learn about food production from Big Ag's lobbyist groups, apparently.

USFRA is still going strong over a decade later. Its focus has shifted. Its media campaigns now frame Big Ag as a leading champion of the sustainable, organic, locally produced foods that the American consumer desires. Co-opting terms from the sustainable foods and farm-to-table movements, its website is plastered with claims about sustainable farming and investments in clean energy, clean air, and water conservation. Taking notes from the Big Oil lobbyists, Big Ag corporations are fine-tuning their "greenwashing" techniques.[7]

Greenwashing has become a major public relations strategy for Big Ag. The industry implements limited sustainability programs, then sings about them very loudly in the public square. Meanwhile, the livestock industry is the biggest driver of global deforestation, is a leading contributor to greenhouse gas emissions, and may be consuming as much as *half* of the world's carbon budget by 2030.[8]

Some recent sustainability initiatives at major corporations such as McDonald's and Cargill can have positive impacts vis-à-vis their programs' specific goals—for example, limiting emissions at a particular farm—but the meager gains are offset by how these small-scale sustainability programs are used to justify continuing business as usual. In the pork industry, many of the so-called sustainability initiatives exist only to fulfill either government-mandated benchmarks or court-ordered actions to resolve nuisance and class action lawsuits.

The pork producers are talking a big game lately about reducing emissions by converting methane into biogas. This process works by covering up the manure pits and storage lagoons, trapping the methane, converting it into natural gas, and funneling it into a pipeline. The big meat-packers, particularly Smithfield, have launched a number of such pilot projects. Smithfield claims this method will significantly reduce odors and methane emissions.[9]

The state of North Carolina ordered Smithfield to invest in sustainability solutions for manure waste back in the year 2000.[10] Biogas programs provide Smithfield a relatively cheap way to claim the company is fulfilling the state's requests. Unfortunately, biogas carries with it new environmental problems: the methane pipelines are fraught with engineering challenges, carbon dioxide is created when the methane is processed, and existing pipeline projects have been shut down due to biohazard problems and explosion risks.[11] Covering the lagoons also concentrates the nitrogen content in the manure, which is still spread and sprayed as usual. If biogas conversion becomes widespread, water contamination from CAFO manure runoff and application could worsen significantly.[12]

Biogas projects are funded in part by the federal government, including by the USDA. The meat-packers also receive large tax breaks and investments for sustainability programs in general; these programs have become yet another avenue for Big Ag to expand its operations and build new facilities.

Smithfield claims it will reduce its methane footprint, but it doesn't want to be *required*, in any way, to reduce or even merely report its greenhouse gas emissions. In 2022 the National Pork Producers Council successfully lobbied against the EPA's latest attempt to require CAFOs to report emissions under the Clean Air Act.[13] The industry's total exemption under the CAA continues.

True Sustainability Solutions

Better methods for reducing the polluting footprint of factory farms do exist. Agribusiness giants such as Smithfield choose not to adopt them because (1) they're expensive, and (2) in the absence of regulation and emissions reporting requirements, there really isn't an incentive to do so.

As mentioned previously, in the year 2000, Smithfield signed the Smithfield Agreement with the state of North Carolina to fund research, in partnership with state universities, for developing superior waste management and disposal methods. The agreement was prompted by the devastating aftermath of Hurricane Floyd, when several manure lagoons burst and others flooded, causing catastrophic pollution and fish kills. Then-governor Jim Hunt demanded that the lagoons be replaced within ten years.[14] That didn't happen.

The researchers funded by Smithfield ultimately recommended five manure management solutions, including anaerobic digester systems (e.g., biofuel conversion); chemical flushing systems that remove bacteria, nitrogen, and phosphorus from the manure; and an open tank model that could replace the earthen pit lagoons. Smithfield promptly deemed all of them too expensive to fully implement. In the words of Smithfield's director of renewables, the recommendations did not meet "the criteria for operational and economic feasibility."[15]

Smithfield is unwilling to replace its current system, and the government is unwilling to force the issue. Perhaps the time will come when political and consumer pressures force Big Ag to overhaul its manure management system. I'm not holding my breath. Until the government subsidizes small farmers instead of Big Ag, the onus has been placed on everyday farmers and food supply workers to make the improvements on their own.

Today, small farmers across the country, from organic dairy farmers in rural Wisconsin to urban ag enthusiasts in metropolitan centers, practice alternatives to the Big Ag model. Practitioners of regenerative agriculture highlight the importance of promoting soil health through techniques such as detoxification, soil carbon sequestration, rotation-based polyculture, no-till planting, cover crop implementation, agroforestry, and pasture-raised animals. These methods reduce water pollution and air emissions, decrease input costs, and increase yields.[16]

The 2018 Intergovernmental Panel on Climate Change report highlighted methods for removing carbon from the air and returning it to the soil as major strategies for combating climate change. The report concluded that carbon sequestration through simple climate-friendly farming practices is more effective than the high-tech carbon capture solutions that Big Ag and Big Oil tend to support. Soil carbon scientist Keith Paustian argued that restoring soil health is so central to reducing carbon dioxide in the atmosphere that it "should be an urgent, societal mission. A Manhattan project."[17]

Despite this, the massive, lumbering system of federal farm subsidies still upholds the polluting factory farm infrastructure, which depends on the continued dominance of corn monoculture to exist. One of the many ways the U.S. government subsidizes Big Ag is through crop insurance against losses; the USDA pays out billions of dollars per year.[18] As extreme weather drives flooding, heat, and drought, crop insurance is a major safety net for farmers but mostly flows to large agribusiness operations practicing soy and corn monoculture. The safety net not only further subsidizes monoculture farming but also de-incentivizes farmers from adopting the climate-friendly polyculture practices that would mitigate the risks of flood and drought in the long term.

Even within this counterintuitive incentive system, a counterculture of organic farming has grown. Between 2011 and 2016, the number of certified organic farmers in the United States increased by 56 percent.[19] The latest numbers show there are 17,445 organic farmers in the country.[20] Importantly, organic food imports have increased substantially, suggesting consumer demand for organic food is not being met domestically.[21]

New coalitions are sprouting up to support organic farmers and independent farmers by re-creating the local farm-to-table distribution pathways that Big Ag so efficiently destroyed. The Midwest Row Crop Collaborative, for example, partnered with the Missouri Rural Crisis Center to help a group of farmers start the Patchwork Family Farms, a co-op for pasture-raised pork that provides an alternative market for independent hog farmers. The Western Organization of Resource Councils is likewise doing interesting work to bolster new markets, including by supporting small farms sited closer to urban centers.[22]

Small farmers are absolutely brimming with innovative ideas for carbon-friendly practices. One of my favorites locally is David Legvold in nearby Northfield, Minnesota, who operates a strip-tilling machine that he baptized the Soil Warrior. Working his 750 acres, the Soil Warrior has allowed him to keep 9.9 million pounds of carbon in the soil and prevented 16.5 million from being emitted into the air.[23]

Today it's typically easier for a small farmer to start a sustainable farm from scratch than for a conventional farmer to make the switch.[24] It appears, however, the USDA is finally wising up to the huge potential of incentivizing farmers to transition from conventional to organic practices. In 2022 the department announced at $300 million investment in the Organic Transition Initiative, which "will help build new and better markets and streams of income for farmers and producers."[25] This is the type of around-the-margins policy win that Tom Vilsack, USDA secretary under President Biden, has managed to score. But the overall pro-CAFO regulatory and tax infrastructure stands strong.

Most everyone fighting for ag reform agrees that revitalizing antitrust enforcement through the Packers and Stockyards Act and reinstating the Grain Inspection, Packers, and Stockyards Administration as an independent agency are necessary first steps for mitigating Big Ag's harms. In chapter 8, we saw that enforcement under the Packers and Stockyards Administration steadily declined beginning in the 1980s, while GIPSA was effectively neutered under the Obama and Trump administrations.

A ray of hope is the Food and Agribusiness Merger Moratorium and Antitrust Review Act cosponsored by Democratic senators Cory Booker, Jon Tester, Jeff Merkley, and Elizabeth Warren. Booker originally introduced the bill in 2018, and its mounting popularity in Washington is a promising indication that ag reform is at least becoming a higher priority. The bill would place an immediate moratorium on acquisitions and mergers in the food and agriculture sector until Congress passes comprehensive legislation addressing market concentration in the ag sector.

Another bill on the table is the bipartisan Opportunities for Fairness in Farming Act cosponsored by Senator Booker and Republican senator Mike Lee.[26] The bill would bring long-overdue oversight to the federal checkoff program, including enforcement of the rule prohibiting checkoff funds from being used for advocacy (see chapter 17 for checkoff abuses). As one might expect, Big Ag lobbyists fiercely oppose the bill.

The third bill in the ag reform trio that Booker spearheaded is the Farm System Reform Act, which would strengthen the Packers & Stockyards Act, restore country-of-origin labeling requirements, and place a national moratorium on large CAFOs. Booker has reintroduced this bill every year beginning in 2019, along with additional bills that protect farm, meatpacking, and food chain workers.

Freeing Ourselves from Big Ag

On the day of former president Trump's inauguration in 2016, an elated Zippy Duvall, president of the American Farm Bureau, told a reporter, "The farmers and ranchers and the people in the Rust Belt came out and paved the road for President-elect Trump to make it to the White House."[27] Most analysts would agree: white rural residents in the Midwest, many of them farmers, helped bring the former president to power. Rural America increasingly supports conservative politicians who favor pro-corporate policies, while the Democratic Party struggles to recapture the support of working-class rural voters.

Yet most rural Americans understand that federal policy molded and enabled today's harmful Big Ag dominance. In a 2019 *Time* magazine investigation of the decimation of small farmers, reporter Alana Semuels spoke with down-and-out farmers across the country and concluded, "Most family farmers seem to agree on what led to their plight: government policy. The government is on the side of big farms, they say, and is ambivalent about whether small farms can succeed."[28]

Rural residents of all political stripes are suspicious of corporate overreach and support policies that break up the Big Ag giants. This is true on Capitol Hill as well, with some ag reform bills being supported by prominent Republican legislators, including Senators Lee and Grassley. Yet reforms have failed, and a far-right ethos has taken hold of rural America, which is suspicious of any kind of governmental oversight or regulation. The reasons for this are many, but I submit that the anti-science, anti-regulation corporate propaganda that lobbyist groups such as the Farm Bureau have spearheaded for two decades now is part of this picture. Additionally, the simple lack of economic opportunity can beget dangerous forms of so-called populism.

The years leading up to 2016 were particularly devastating for farmers as corporate consolidation reached its apotheosis. The three years before the 2016 election saw "the sharpest decline in farm incomes since the Great Depression," according to Claire Kelloway, ag policy researcher at Open Markets Institute. Kelloway argues that while many pin the growing rural-urban economic divide on globalization and technology, it's also caused by "public policy, embraced by both parties, that enabled predatory monopolies to strip wealth away from farmers and rural communities and transfer it to America's snazziest zip codes."[29]

Economic inequality is the major fallout of unchecked corporate power that Big Ag, Big Tech, Big Oil, and all the rest enjoy today. We're living in an age where antitrust enforcement has been minimal for decades, and thanks to corporate influence, commonsense policies to regulate corporations can't get through legislative hurdles. Wealth inequality has widened, and the era-defining *Citizens United* decision by the U.S. Supreme Court allows unlimited corporate spending in U.S. elections.

Corporate lawlessness has consequences. Today's rural Americans stand among the ashes of hometowns ravaged by corporate giants, crushed by the corporate intruder. Corporate agriculture has not only destroyed the rural spirit and harmony of living as one with the land but of living with one another as well.

As did so many farmers before him, my father, Lowell, dedicated his life to caring for the land. He was appalled as he watched the gloomy shadow of corporate factory farms evaporate friendships, corporatize the food system, annihilate independent farmers, break the animals' connection to the land, and shatter the joys that make up rural life. We mourn what we have lost. But in loss, there is opportunity. Even as Lowell saw the CAFOS encircling our home like an occupying force, he continued to frequently say, "Small farmers will feed this country when it gets into trouble."

I understand now more than ever what he meant. Lowell didn't live to see the collapse of the food chain under COVID, but he saw the trouble brewing in rural America: the ideological divides, the emboldened racism, the hate and rancor. He understood the warnings of the climate scientists, the climate migrations already underway, and the looming disasters that both implicate and threaten modern agriculture.

My father was right. As we continue to make decisions taking us to the brink of disaster, there is hope in this knowledge: local farmers can once again feed local communities. While the majority of today's American farmers are contract growers, fish hooked on a line baited by multinational corporations, this situation defies the ethos of the independent rural resident, the proud American farmer. It's time to bring that spirit of independence back to farm country. It's time to cut bait.

Lowell never seemed to understand his age. As he approached his ninetieth birthday, I recall asking, "Dad, if you didn't know your age, how old are you?" He thought about it for a minute and answered, "Sixty-five." Noting my surprise, he said, "Well, a lot hasn't changed over the years!"

But as he knew well, things do change—sometimes for the better, sometimes not. Like a scene out of a bad western movie, my family witnessed the battles in our hometown, the harassment and intimidation, and the corporate stickup that forced factory farms into Dodge. My dad spent his golden years fighting hog wars. He would have preferred to have been left in peace, picking corn, watching the Weather Channel, and playing with his grandkids. But he had high hopes that resisting the corporatization of Dodge would open a dialogue, one that would bring change not only to his community but to all rural communities.

He continued these efforts to the end of his life. In 2017, at the age of eighty-seven, Lowell joined with the Dodge County Concerned

Citizens and thirty-four other advocacy groups in a petition that Food & Water Watch sent to the EPA challenging factory farm pollution and demanding enforcement of the Clean Water Act. (Five years later, after continuing inaction from the EPA, the Dodge County Concerned Citizens again joined advocacy groups in fifteen states to compel the EPA to address these concerns.)[30] In 2018 Lowell joined another petition against the EPA, this one fighting the Trump administration's move to exempt large CAFOs from reporting under the Emergency Planning and Community Right-to-Know Act, which requires polluting industries to report hazardous and toxic emissions.[31]

In the spring of 2019, Lowell celebrated his ninetieth birthday, a feat not accomplished by any previous family member. Soon thereafter, he suffered from a number of health problems, and in June 2019 he pushed his walker into the nursing home he had advocated for as a Dodge County commissioner. A fighter to the very end, he insisted on staying at the farm and running the combine that fall.

The day of his passing in October 2019 was peaceful.

In a final act of retaliation against the Trom family, local industry operatives spread manure on the land for nearly thirty-six hours the weekend of Lowell's visitation and funeral. They spread it just steps from the funeral home in Blooming Prairie on the day of the visitation. As Brad entered the building, he suffered a bloody nose caused by the raw waste hanging over the area with its noxious and inescapable stench. Spreading continued through the night and the following day. As our family gathered around my father's rural gravesite, several family members had to remain inside their vehicles, unable to bear the foul odor.

Three days after the funeral, I received a call from a real estate agent inquiring on behalf of an anonymous farmer about the possible sale of our farm. Three days—hell, I was surprised the inquiry didn't occur the day of the funeral, knowing what I do about the lack of community spirit among today's corporate farmers. I was prepared for the unwelcome call. I asked the agent to send the following message to all area farmers: "This is a legacy farm. This is a family farm. It is not for sale. It is not for rent. Do not call again!"

I know that my dad rests in peace, confident that his children will continue to do the right thing. My family's fight to save our farm was not unique and perhaps pales in comparison to what other frontline families have faced. What I know for sure is people will continue to resist this unscrupulous, unethical industry. Our rural revolution brings hope of rural rejuvenation. These days, as I speak with public officials about responsible CAFO regulation, respond to emails from people determined to protect their town's waterways, and learn more about sustainable agriculture from independent small farmers, the same thought often crosses my mind: Lowell would be proud.

NOTES

1. Moving to the Country

1. For overviews of the consolidation of livestock agriculture, see Claire Kelloway and Sarah Miller, "Food and Power: Addressing Monopolization in America's Food System," Open Markets Institute, March 27, 2019, updated September 21, 2021. See also U.S. Department of Agriculture (USDA) Economic Research Service, "Consolidation in U.S. Agriculture Continues," 2020; and Mary K. Hendrickson et al., "The Food System: Concentration and Its Impacts: A Special Report to the Family Farm Action Alliance," November 19, 2020.
2. Data from the USDA Economic Research Service, "U.S. Hog Sector Increased Specialization, Production Contract Use, and Farm Size from 1992 to 2015," last updated October 5, 2022, https://www.ers.usda.gov/data-products/chart-gallery/gallery/chart-detail/?chartId=104871.
3. For an interesting analysis of Murphy's rise to power in North Carolina, see Corban Addison, *Wastelands: The True Story of Farm Country on Trial* (New York: Knopf, 2022).
4. Sarah Porter and Craig Cox, "Manure Overload: Manure plus Fertilizer Overwhelms Minnesota's Land and Water" (Washington DC: Environmental Working Group, May 28, 2020).
5. Minnesota State Demographic Center, *Greater Minnesota: Refined & Revisited*, January 2017.
6. Environmental Working Group analysis via data from the Minnesota Pollution Control Agency (MPCA) feedlot database, cited in Porter and Cox, "Manure Overload."
7. Porter and Cox, "Manure Overload."
8. Porter and Cox, "Manure Overload."
9. Food & Water Watch, "The Economic Cost of Food Monopolies: The Hog Bosses," 2022. The report uses data from the U.S. Census of Agriculture, the Iowa Department of Revenue, the U.S. Census Bureau's American Community Survey, and the U.S. Department of Commerce's Bureau of Economic Analysis.
10. Charlie Hope-D'Anieri, "'Towns Just Turned to Dust': How Factory Hog Farms Help Hollow Out Rural Communities," *The Guardian*, May 5, 2022.
11. Food & Water Watch, "Economic Cost."
12. Food & Water Watch, "Economic Cost."

13. "CEO's Total Package at Smithfield Last Year: $37.5M," *Virginian-Pilot*, April 28, 2015, https://www.pilotonline.com/business/article_e693707f-d949-52ca-81ea-f14212d5abc0.html.

14. Natural Resources Defense Council, "Water Pollution: Everything You Need to Know" fact sheet, January 11, 2023, https://www.nrdc.org/stories/water-pollution-everything-you-need-know.

15. Porter and Cox, "Manure Overload."

16. "U.S. Pork Demand Strong, but Trade Disputes Could Hit Exports," Reuters, February 1, 2018.

17. Minnesota Pollution Control Agency Feedlot Program, "2016 Annual County Feedlot Officer Annual Report and Performance Credit Report," revised January 6, 2017, https://www.co.dodge.mn.us/EnvironmentalServices/2016%20Dodge%20County%20%20Feedlot%20Report.pdf, lists 237 registered feedlots in Dodge County. Following Dodge County's withdrawal from the MPCA delegated county program, annual reporting by county officials apparently ceased in the county. According to the MPCA's "County Feedlot Officers," https://www.pca.state.mn.us/business-with-us/county-feedlot-officers, Dodge County had 305 registered feedlots as of April 2022.

18. Minnesota Farm Bureau, "Moving to the Country: What You Should Know about Agriculture in Rural Minnesota," developed in cooperation with the Minnesota Soybean Research and Promotion Council and the Minnesota Realtors Association, along with nine agricultural associations and the Minnesota Department of Agriculture, no date, "Know the Neighborhood" section. Copy from 1990s in author's possession.

19. Minnesota Farm Bureau, "Moving to the Country," "Farm Country" section.

2. Fertile Soil

1. Minnesota Historical Society, "Traverse des Sioux: Learn" fact page, 2024, https://www.mnhs.org/traversedessioux/learn.

2. Kenneth Carley, *The Dakota War of 1862: Minnesota's Other Civil War* (Saint Paul: Minnesota Historical Society Press, 1961), 2.

3. For a detailed accounting of the circumstances surrounding the Treaty of Mendota, the second of the two major treaties referenced, see Alan R. Woolworth, "The Treaty of Mendota" (Saint Paul: Dakota County Historical Society, 2013), 4–12, https://www.dakotahistory.org/images/OvertheYears/OTY-201212-Treaty-of-Mendota.pdf.

4. Carley, *Dakota War of 1862*, 58.

5. Ed Trom, "A Spring River," in author's possession.

3. The Big Pig Pyramid

1. U.S. Securities and Exchange Commission, *Form 10-Q* filed by Hormel Foods Corporation for the quarterly period ended April 29, 2018, 38, https://www

.sec.gov/Archives/edgar/data/48465/000004846518000033/hrl-20180429x10q
.htm.

2. Kelloway and Miller, "Food and Power."

3. Betsy Freese, "Pork Powerhouses 2020: Backing Up," *Successful Farming*, October 7, 2020.

4. See Timothy Langdon et al. v. Holden Farms, Inc., Minnesota District Court (Rice County), Civil File No. 66-CV-14-2123, transcript of proceedings, August 22–26 and March 24, 2017.

5. See Langdon v. Holden Farms, Inc., Civil File No. 66-CV-14-2123, trial exhibit 32, emails to/from Donald Bohn, Sr. Credit Officer, AgQuest Financial Services to Director of Swine Services, Interstate Mills, LLC, dated August 16, 2008.

6. See Langdon v. Holden Farms, Inc., Civil File No. 66-CV-14-2123, trial exhibit 24, "MN Wean to Finish Independent Contractor Agreement," dated June 1, 2008, at paragraph 2, and exhibit A (Grower Payment Schedule).

7. See Langdon v. Holden Farms, Inc., Civil File No. 66-CV-14-2123, transcript at 320.

8. See Wanda Duryea et al. v. Agri Stats, Inc., Clemens Food Group, LLC, Hormel Foods Corporation, Indiana Packers Corporation, JBS USA, Seaboard Foods, LLC, Smithfield Foods, Inc., Triumph Foods, LLC, and Tyson Foods, Inc., U.S. District Court, District of Minnesota, Case 0:18-CV-01776, Class Action Complaint filed June 28, 2018, at paragraph 70, https://www.courthousenews.com/wp-content/uploads/2018/06/PorkAntitrust.pdf.

9. See Langdon v. Holden Farms, Inc., Civil File No. 66-CV-14-2123, complaint date August 8, 2013, and accompanying "MN Wean to Finish Independent Contractor Agreement" between Holden Farms, Inc., a Minnesota corporation, and Timothy and Jennifer Langdon, Growers, June 1, 2008.

10. Hendrickson et al., "Food System," 19.

11. "Making 30 Pigs per Sow per Year Dream Come True," *National Hog Farmer*, January 15, 2009.

12. *Pig Farming VR Experience: See Inside a Real Pig Barn*, Porkcares.org and Pork Checkoff, October 25, 2019, https://youtu.be/cQ-5F-gT-6c.

13. See *Pig Farming VR Experience*.

14. Jeff Tietz, "Boss Hog: The Dark Side of America's Top Pork Producer," *Rolling Stone Magazine*, December 14, 2006.

15. Ted Genoways, "There's a Horrifying Pork Factory Video Going Around. The Story behind It Is Even Worse," *Mother Jones*, November 12, 2015.

16. Ted Nace, *Gangs of America: The Rise of Corporate Power & the Disabling of Democracy* (San Francisco: Berrett-Koehler, 2003), 2.

17. National Archives, Founders Online tool, "Thomas Jefferson to George Logan, 12 November 1816," https://founders.archives.gov/documents/Jefferson/03-10-02-0390.

18. Nace, *Gangs of America*, 5.

4. The Meeting at Lansing Corners

Epigraph: From Madison McVan, "American Farm Bureau Federation Claims It's the 'Voice of Agriculture.' Others Beg to Differ," *Missouri Independent*, February 15, 2022.

1. Karen Jorgenson, "Toquam Family Provides Quality Pork to Consumers," *Steele County (MN) Times*, October 26, 2022.

2. Ted Genoways, *The Chain: Farm, Factory, and the Fate of Our Food* (New York: HarperCollins, 2014), 30. Genoways's reporting on the hog industry includes an account of the trajectory of Hormel Foods during the era of consolidation and integration.

3. Christopher Leonard, *The Meat Racket: The Secret Takeover of America's Food Business* (New York: Simon & Schuster, 2015), 196. Leonard's book provides a thorough examination of the larger market and economic forces impacting the hog market in the 1990s.

4. Leonard, *Meat Racket*, 30, 31.

5. Georgina Gustin, John H. Cushman Jr., and Neela Banerjee, "How the Farm Bureau's Climate Agenda Is Failing Its Farmers," *Inside Climate News*, October 24, 2018.

6. William L. Chenery, "Farmers in the Pit," *The Atlantic*, March 1925, https://www.theatlantic.com/magazine/archive/1925/03/farmers-in-the-pit/648630/.

7. Gustin, Cushman, and Banerjee, "Farm Bureau's Climate Agenda"; Molly Ball, "How Republicans Lost the Farm," *The Atlantic*, January 27, 2014; and McVan, "American Farm Bureau Federation."

8. Ian T. Shearn, "Whose Side Is the American Farm Bureau On?" *The Nation*, July 16, 2012.

9. Sky Chadde, Eli Hoff, and Mark Ossolinski, "The Iowa Farm Bureau Is a Small Nonprofit. It's Sitting on a Huge Business Empire," *Investigate Midwest*, October 7, 2021.

10. Shearn, "Whose Side?"

11. Sam Husseini, "Right-Wing Business in Farmer's Overalls: The American Farm Bureau Federation," FAIR *Magazine*, September 1, 2000.

12. Shearn, "Whose Side?"

13. Shearn, "Whose Side?"

14. Sky Chadde and Mark Ossolinski, "The Iowa Farm Bureau Is a Small Nonprofit. It's Sitting on a Huge Business Empire," *Investigate Midwest*, October 7, 2021.

15. Terje Mikael Hasle Jorangler, "The Migration of Tradition: Land Tenure and Culture in the U.S. Upper Mid-West," *European Journal of American Studies*, August 2008, para. 20, https://journals.openedition.org/ejas/3252?lang#toctoln7.

16. Constitution of the State of Minnesota, Article 1, section 15, adopted October 13, 1857, https://www.revisor.mn.gov/constitution/#article_1.

5. Get Big or Get Out

1. Hendrickson et al., "Food System."
2. "Birth to bacon" and "squeal to meal" terminology borrowed from David Barboza, "Goliath of the Hog World; Fast Rise of Smithfield Foods Makes Regulators Wary," *New York Times*, April 7, 2000.
3. Hendrickson et al., "Food System."
4. John D. Lawrence, "Hog Marketing Practices and Competition Questions," *Choices* (a publication of the Agricultural & Applied Economics Association), 2010, https://dr.lib.iastate.edu/server/api/core/bitstreams/79170c14-1af0-4495 -a3c1-7fa4aad0813e/content. Lawrence provides an excellent overview of how the hog market changed beginning in the early 1990s and how marketing and production contracts function in today's hog market.
5. Barboza, "Goliath of the Hog World."
6. See Langdon v. Holden Farms, Inc., Civil File No. 66-CV-14-2123, transcript of proceedings at 168.
7. Minnesota Pollution Control Agency, Permit Application for an Animal Feedlot or Manure Storage Area, submitted by Mark Finstuen, September 3, 2002.
8. "Springs, Springsheds, and Karst," Minnesota Department of Natural Resources, 2024, https://www.dnr.state.mn.us/waters/groundwater_section /mapping/springs.html.
9. Kay Fate, "Dodge County Board Denies Request for EIS," *Owatonna (MN) People's Press* (Adams Publishing Group Media of Southern Minnesota), June 25, 2003, https://www.southernminn.com/owatonna_peoples_press/archives /dodge-county-board-denies-request-for-eis/article_0f853d86-7d3c-58b9 -ad4e-f66196bc148c.html.
10. *Dodge County Water Monitoring Update—2017*, https://slideplayer.com/slide /12076851/.
11. Minutes, Dodge County Planning Commission, July 3, 2002. Dodge County Planning Commission minutes are searchable at https://dodgecountymn .iqm2.com/Citizens/Calendar.aspx#.
12. See Berne Area Alliance for Quality Living et al. v. Mark Finstuen et al., State of Minnesota, County of Dodge (Court File No. 20-C6-02-000653).
13. According to the Dodge County website, https://www.co.dodge.mn.us, the Dodge County Planning Commission did not meet during the month of January 2003: "No meeting was held in January 2003. NOTE: Planning Commission Members were re-appointed by Commissioners. Richard Murray, Ken Folie and Kerry Glarner are no longer on. Rhonda Toquam, Barb Erler and Galen Johnson will be the new members."
14. Request for Public Hearing, Dodge County, March 10, 2003.
15. This is the recollection of an anonymous Berne Area Alliance member who was present at this meeting. Meeting minutes were not kept.

16. For a full discussion of the environmental impact statement review and the debatable applicability of the proposed feedlot under Minn. Stat. § 116D.04, subd. 2a (2004), see Berne Area Alliance for Quality Living v. Dodge County Commissioners et al., 694 N.W.2d 577 (Minn. Ct. App. 2005); and access discussion of the EIS review at https://casetext.com/case/berne-area-alliance-v -dodge-county-comrs.

17. Minutes, Dodge County Planning Commission, April 2, 2003.

18. Minutes, Dodge County Planning Commission, May 7, 2003.

19. See Berne Area Alliance for Quality Living et al. v. Dodge County Board of Commissioners et al., State of Minnesota, County of Dodge (Court File No. 20-C6-03-000453).

20. See Berne Area Alliance v. Dodge County Board of Commissioners et al., 694 N.W.2d 577, for full text of appeals court decision.

21. See Berne Area Alliance v. Dodge County Board of Commissioners et al., 694 N.W.2d 577.

22. Minutes, Dodge County Planning Commission, July 6, 2005.

23. This information was relayed in an author interview with Theresa Benda, October 4, 2022, and October 10, 2022.

24. I spoke with several Berne Area Alliance members who confirmed and corroborated key details for this chapter. Only one alliance member, Theresa Benda, consented to my using her name.

25. Again, several Berne Area Alliance members confirmed and corroborated key details for this chapter. I include direct quotes from two members who requested anonymity.

6. The Battle in Ripley Township

1. Leonard, *Meat Racket*.

2. Leonard, *Meat Racket*, 196.

3. Minnesota Farm Bureau Foundation, "When an Activist Group Comes to Town: Protecting Your Community from Unwanted Division" (Eagon: Minnesota Farm Bureau Foundation, 2003), 3. The guidebook's title page says it was "written and produced by a partnership of concerned individuals and organizations involved in production agriculture of all shapes and sizes."

4. Minnesota Farm Bureau Foundation, "When an Activist," 16.

5. Josephine Marcotty, "Appeals Court to Decide Dodge County Hog Farm Lawsuit Pitting Pollution vs. Water," *Star Tribune* (Minneapolis), February 11, 2017.

6. Land Stewardship Project, "When a Factory Farm Comes to Town: Protecting Your Township from Unwanted Development," 3rd ed. (Minneapolis: LSP, September 2018), https://landstewardshipproject.org/repository/1/2682/when _a_factory_farm_comes_to_town_final_9_15_18.pdf.

7. Minnesota Farm Bureau Foundation, "When an Activist," 12.

8. Minutes, Dodge County Planning Commission, November 5, 2003. The quotation is attributable to then planning director Duane Johnson.

9. Minutes, Dodge County Planning Commission, December 2003. The commissioner mentioned in the text is Galen Johnson. See also minutes, Dodge County Planning Commission, April 14, 2004; and minutes, Dodge County Planning Commission, April 6, 2005.

10. "2,115-Cow Dairy to Be Subject of Jan. 20 Meeting," *Rochester (MN) Post Bulletin*, January 11, 2005.

11. "Iowa City of 5,000 Faces a Hog Confinement Planned Nearby," *Des Moines Register*, October 23, 2020.

12. C. Nicholas Cronauer, "Flushing Out the Illinois Livestock Management Facilities Act," *Valparaiso University Law Review* 45, no. 2 (2011).

13. David Jackson and Gary Marx, "The Price of Pork: Cheap Meat Comes at High Cost in Illinois," *Chicago Tribune*, a four-part investigation, August 2016.

14. Minutes, Dodge County Planning Commission, July 2, 2003.

15. The dairy was proposed by Bill Rowekamp, and his primary investor was New York businessman Ben Zaitz. The person referred to as "Sarah" asked me to use a pseudonym; author's interview with "Sarah," October 6, 2022. Her account of these events was confirmed by the author via multiple interviews and cross-referencing with press reports and other sources.

16. Minutes, Dodge County Planning Commission, October 6, 2003.

17. Adam Warthesen, "When Democracy Comes Home to Stay," *The Land Stewardship Letter* 21, no. 4 (October/November 2003): 5.

18. The number of registered voters from "Feedlot Fight: Sign of the Times," *Rochester (MN) Post Bulletin*, February 23, 2004.

19. Warthesen, "When Democracy Comes Home."

20. The meeting attendant who was accosted asked for anonymity. Warthesen, "When Democracy Comes Home."

21. Minutes, Dodge County Planning Commission, April 6, 2005: "Ripley Township held a special meeting last Thursday. There have been changes in Township Supervisors and with that they are now considering a moratorium and having their own ordinance which would have an impact on the dairy project. . . . The County is not sure of the implications yet but is aware it could very well turn into a legal issue."

22. See Ripley Dairy, LLP v. Ripley Township, State of Minnesota, County of Dodge (Court File No. 20-CV-05-385). Summons and complaint filed May 5, 2005.

23. Minutes, Dodge County Planning Commission, June 8, 2005.

24. Ripley Township Land Use Ordinance, adopted December 5, 2005, 2.

25. Sea Stachura, "The Fight over Ripley Dairy," *Minnesota Public Radio (MPR) News*, February 9, 2006. See also Robert Franklin, "Dairy Spurned by

Township May Get Pulled into the City," *Star Tribune* (Minneapolis), April 25, 2006.

26. Franklin, "Dairy Spurned."

27. Stachura, "Fight over Ripley Dairy."

28. See Ripley Township, LLP v. Ripley Township, State of Minnesota, County of Dodge (Court File No. 20-CV-06-114). Order for judgment dated August 9, 2006.

29. Jason Kroeker, "Ripley Dairy Withdraws Claremont Annexation Plans," *Owatonna (MN) People's Press*, September 13, 2006.

30. Heather Carlson, "Neighbors Happy with Dairy's Demise," *Rochester (MN) Post-Bulletin*, December 22, 2006.

31. The Land Stewardship Project was instrumental in organizing the neighborhood during the fight against Ripley Dairy. Bobby King and Adam Warthesen worked tirelessly. Truly, but for the LSP's assistance, the dairy would be standing today. The LSP continues to be active in Minnesota, now under the leadership of Sean Carroll, Matthew Sheets, and others.

32. Dodge County Zoning Ordinance, chapter 8: "Agricultural District," section 8.2, 2005, https://cms4files.revize.com/dodgecountymn/Ag%20Covenant %20recording%202023.pdf.

33. Dodge County Zoning Ordinance, chap. 8, section 8.1.

34. Author's interview with Dodge County resident Darin Johnson, August 25, 2023. Darin Johnson is a pseudonym.

35. Terence J. Centner, "Nuisances from Animal Feeding Operations: Reconciling Agricultural Production and Neighboring Property Rights," *Drake Journal of Agricultural Law* 11, no. 1 (2006).

36. Minutes, Dodge County Planning Commission Meeting, December 7, 2005.

7. Economics of the Great Pig Explosion

1. The Minnesota legislature amended Minn. Stat. 116D.04, subd. 2a, https:// www.revisor.mn.gov/statutes/cite/116D.04, to exempt feedlots of less than a thousand animal units from the environmental impact review process.

2. See Minnesota Pollution Control Agency, "Feedlots," https://www.pca.state .mn.us/business-with-us/feedlots; and Minnesota Pollution Control Agency, "County Feedlots Officers," https://www.pca.state.mn.us/business-with-us /county-feedlot-officers.

3. Minutes, Dodge County Planning Commission, March 1, 2006.

4. Minutes, Dodge County Planning Commission, April 5, 2006.

5. Minutes, Dodge County Planning Commission, May 3, 2006.

6. Minutes, Dodge County Planning Commission, May 3, 2006.

7. Minutes, Dodge County Planning Commission, May 3, 2006.

8. Minutes, Dodge County Planning Commission, April 2, 2008. The planning commission member referenced in the text is Richard Wolf.

9. Minutes, Dodge County Planning Commission, August 6, 2008.

10. D. Lee Miller and Gregory Muren, "CAFOs: What We Don't Know Is Hurting Us," National Resources Defense Council in partnership with the Yale Environmental Protection Clinic, September 2019. This indispensable report provides an overview of EPA and state environmental agency oversight of CAFOs, including a history and description of the litigation and the court decisions that revoked the EPA's ability to regulate CAFOs.

11. Environmental Working Group, "EWG Study and Mapping Show Large CAFOs in Iowa up Fivefold since 1990," January 21, 2020.

12. Kelloway and Miller, "Food and Power."

13. Data from the USDA's Economic Research Service.

14. Alana Semuels, "'They're Trying to Wipe Us off the Map.' Small American Farmers Are Nearing Extinction," *Time*, November 27, 2019.

15. Tietz, "Boss Hog."

16. Semuels, "'They're Trying.'"

17. Semuels, "'They're Trying.'"

18. Food & Water Watch, "Economic Cost." Its analysis uses data from the USDA Census of Agriculture, the Iowa Department of Revenue, the U.S. Census Bureau's American Community Survey, and the U.S. Department of Commerce's Bureau of Economic Analysis.

19. James Merchant and David Osterberg, "Impacts of the CAFO Explosion on Water Quality and Public Health," *Des Moines Register*, January 24, 2018.

20. Charlie Mitchell and Austin Frerick, "The Hog Barons," *Vox*, April 19, 2021. This investigation tells the story of how Iowa Select Farms came to dominate the state, with far-reaching consequences.

21. Austin Frerick, "To Revive Rural America, We Must Fix Our Broken Food System," *American Conservative*, February 27, 2019.

22. Christine Ball-Blakely, "CAFOs: Plaguing North Carolina Communities of Color," *Sustainable Development Law and Policy* 18, no. 1 (2018). For information about the disproportionate impact of CAFOs on communities of color and poor communities, see also Earthjustice, Complaint under Title VI of the Civil Rights Act of 1964, 42 U.S.C. § 2000d, 40 C.F.R. Part 7, https://earthjustice.org/case/petitioning-epa-on-civil-rights-violations.

23. Kelly Leidig, "The Effect of CAFOs on Neighboring House and Land Values," Midwest Environmental Advocates, Spring 2020.

24. Linda Lobao and Curtis W. Stofferahn, "The Community Effects of Industrialized Farming: Social Science Research and Challenges to Corporate Farming Laws," *Agriculture and Human Values* 25, no. 2 (2008): 219–40.

25. Minnesota State Demographic Center, *Greater Minnesota*.

26. Minnesota State Demographic Center, *Greater Minnesota*, 66–67.

27. Janet Adamy and Paul Overberg, "Rural America Is the New 'Inner City,'" *Wall Street Journal*, May 26, 2017.

28. Claire Kelloway, "How to Close the Democrats' Rural Gap," *Washington Monthly*, January 13, 2019.

29. Community and Economic Development Associates, *2018 Comprehensive Plan, Dodge County, MN*, December 12, 2018, 5.

30. Associated Press, "MN Town Offers Free Land, Finds No Takers," KARE 11 News, December 23, 2014.

31. National Center for Education Statistics cited in Semuels, "'They're Trying.'"

32. Hendrickson et al., "Food System."

33. Angela Stuesse and Nathan T. Dollar, "Who Are America's Meat and Poultry Workers?" Economic Policy Institute, September 24, 2020.

34. Leonard, *Meat Racket*.

35. Siena Chrisman, "Long-Delayed Rules to Protect Small Farmers Might Be Too Little Too Late," *Civil Eats*, January 11, 2017. See also Isaac Arnsdorf, "How a Top Chicken Company Cut Off Black Farmers, One by One," *ProPublica*, June 26, 2019.

36. Linda Ray, "Demographics of the Meat Industry," Chron.com, accessed December 2, 2022, https://smallbusiness.chron.com/demographics-meat-industry-24333.html.

37. Stuesse and Dollar, "Who Are America's Meat and Poultry Workers?"; and Eunice Kim, Erika Lee, and Lei Zhang, eds., *Labor & the Economy*, annotated bibliography for University of Minnesota's "Immigrants in Covid America" project, accessed December 4, 2022, https://immigrantcovid.umn.edu/labor-the-economy.

38. Eric Schlosser, "The Chain Never Stops," *Mother Jones*, July–August 2001.

39. Hannah Dreier, "The Kids on the Night Shift," *New York Times Magazine*, September 18, 2023.

40. Minnesota Department of Health, "Free and Reduced Price Lunch Eligibility," accessed August 28, 2019, https://data.web.health.state.mn.us/free-reduced-lunch. (Excluded from this analysis is Mahnomen County, number 1 in terms of the percentage of schoolchildren qualifying for free or reduced lunch. This county is part of the White Earth Indian Reservation and is the only county in Minnesota that is entirely within an Indian reservation.)

41. Minnesota Department of Health, "Free and Reduced Price Lunch (FRPL) Map," accessed August 28, 2019, https://mndatamaps.web.health.state.mn.us/interactive/frpl.html.

42. Warren Fiske, "Fact-Check: Are Meatpacking Companies Making Record Profits?" *Austin (TX) American-Statesman*, July 5, 2022.

43. Brian Deese, Sameera Fazili, and Bharat Ramamurti, "Recent Data Show Dominant Meat Processing Companies Are Taking Advantage of Market Power to Raise Prices and Grow Profit Margins," White House Briefing Room, December 10, 2021.

44. Reuters, "Beef Giant JBS to Pay $52.5 Million to Settle Price-Fixing Lawsuit," *Des Moines Register*, February 4, 2022.
45. "Smithfield Reached $75M Settlement in Pork Price-Fixing Lawsuit," *Feedstuffs*, September 28, 2022.

8. In the Tank for Big Ag

Epigraph: Joe Vansickle, "NPPC Charges GIPSA Lacks Authority for Rule," *National Hog Farmer*, November 22, 2010.
1. Chrisman, "Long-Delayed Rules."
2. Leonard, *Meat Racket*, 36.
3. Food & Water Watch, "Economic Cost."
4. Kelloway, "How to Close."
5. Lina Khan, "Obama's Game of Chicken," *Washington Monthly*, November 9, 2012.
6. Khan, "Obama's Game of Chicken."
7. "PAC Profile: National Pork Producers Council," OpenSecrets.org, based on Federal Elections Commission data, accessed December 12, 2022, https:// www.opensecrets.org/political-action-committees-pacs/national-pork -producers-council/c00201871/summary/2022.
8. Chrisman, "Long-Delayed Rules."
9. Organization for Competitive Markets, "Captured: How Agribusiness Controls Regulatory Agencies and Harms Producers and Consumers," August 24, 2020.
10. Claire Kelloway, "What Biden's Antitrust Order Does for Farmers," *Washington Monthly*, July 15, 2021.
11. Farm Credit Administration, "About Us," accessed December 12, 2022, https:// www.fca.gov/about/about-fca.
12. Loka Ashwood et al., "From Big Ag to Big Finance: A Market Network Approach to Power in Agriculture," *Agriculture and Human Values* 39, no. 4 (2022): 1421–34.
13. Ashwood et al., "From Big Ag to Big Finance."
14. Bert Ely, "In 2015, Almost Half of FCS Lending Goes to Just 4,458 Borrowers," *ABA Banking Journal*, a publication of the American Bankers Association, April 5, 2016.
15. See AgQuest Financial Services, "Ag Financing," accessed December 18, 2022, https//agquest.biz/loan-products.
16. See Langdon v. Holden Farms, Inc., Civil File No. 66-CV-14-2123, transcript at 11.
17. As part of the question-and-answer session following the annual meeting of the Central Farm Service on January 7, 2020, Vice President of Risk and Business Development Rodney Balvitsch publicly disclosed that AgriBank serves as the funding source for AgQuest Financial Services.

18. Farmward Cooperative, *Annual Report 2018: Advancing with Purpose, Vision and Strategy*, 2018, 25n10, https://inetsgi.com/customer/608/a00060fd.pdf.

19. CFS, 2018 Annual Report, Consolidated Financial Statements, August 31, 2018, note 19, which states that the loan guarantee pool is $6 million.

20. See Langdon v. Holden Farms, Inc., Civil File No. 66-CV-14-2123, trial exhibit 32.

21. I worked with a title company to obtain documents pertaining to feed-lot loans that were filed with the Office of the County Recorder in Dodge County.

22. Ashwood et al., "From Big Ag to Big Finance."

9. Getting to Know Your Neighbors

1. Minutes, Dodge County Planning Commission, March 5, 2014.

2. Minutes, Dodge County Board of Commissioners, April 22, 2014. "Ms. DeVetter informed the Board that Jessica Masching purchased a residence outside of Dodge County and cannot serve on the Planning Commission. As a result, the vacancy on the Planning Commission needs to be filled by a citizen of Ripley or Westfield Township. Commissioner Erickson has asked Joshua Toquam if he would be willing to serve on the Planning Commission and Mr. Toquam has indicated that he would."

3. Summary of registered feedlots, Dodge County, Minnesota, information supplied by the Dodge County Feedlot officer. See correspondence of Sonja Trom Eayrs on behalf of Dodge County Concerned Citizens to Melissa DeVetter, Zoning Administrator, Dodge County Planning Commission and Dodge County Environmental Services, December 10, 2014, in Administrative Record, AR-308 to AR-320.

4. See Real Estate Mortgage, A 192161, Certified, filed and recorded on June 20, 2011, Office of the County Recorder, Dodge County, Minnesota, in the amount of $600,000.

5. See Real Estate Mortgage, A 209498, Certified, filed and recorded on January 22, 2015, Office of the County Recorder, Dodge County, Minnesota, in the amount of $778,000.

6. My father had to take my mother to a medical appointment before the meeting. Having only a few days' notice of the public hearing, he was unable to reschedule her appointment, which had been scheduled for weeks.

7. Minutes, Dodge County Planning Commission, April 2, 2014.

8. Correspondence of James P. Peters to Dodge County Board of Commissioners, Dodge County Attorney, and Melissa DeVetter, Zoning Administrator re: Conditional Use Permit Application of Nick Masching and Roger Toquam, section 5, Westfield Township, Dodge County, dated April 8, 2014.

9. Correspondence of James P. Peters to Dodge County Board of Commissioners et al.

10. Minutes, Dodge County Board of Commissioners, April 8, 2014.

11. See Lowell Trom and Evelyn Trom v. County of Dodge, Dodge County Board of Commissioners, Nick Masching, and Roger Toquam, State of Minnesota, County of Dodge (Court File No. 20-CV-14-293).

12. See Trom et al. v. County of Dodge et al. (Court File No. 20-CV-14-293).

10. Industry Watchdogs

1. "Manure Agreements Cover Buyers, Sellers," *National Hog Farmer*, March 15, 2009.

2. Jeff Beach, "Land, Feed, and Demand for Manure Could Spur Animal Agriculture in North Dakota," *Inforum*, a news outlet of Forum Communications Network, October 10, 2022.

3. Dodge County Zoning Ordinance 18.7.2.

4. See Spreading and Manure Easement Agreement between [redacted] and James George Masching and Rebecca Jane Masching, dated April 12, 2014, certified filed and recorded with the Dodge County Recorder's Office, April 21, 2014 (A 205532); Spreading and Manure Easement Agreement between [redacted] and James George Masching and Rebecca Jane Masching, dated April 12, 2014, certified filed and recorded with the Dodge County Recorder's Office, April 21, 2014 (A 205534); and Spreading and Manure Easement Agreement between [redacted] and James George Masching and Rebecca Jane Masching, dated April 12, 2014, certified filed and recorded with Dodge County Recorder's Office, April 21, 2014 (A 205533).

5. See Lowell Trom and Evelyn Trom v. County of Dodge, Dodge County Board of Commissioners and Masching Swine Farms, LLC, State of Minnesota, County of Dodge (Court File No. 20-CV-15-17), AR-466.

6. See Trom et al. v. County of Dodge et al. (Court File No. 20-CV-15-17), AR-591.

7. Leah Douglas, "A Battle Brews in Rural Wisconsin over Factory Farms," *Daily Yonder* (Whitesburg KY), December 12, 2019.

8. Correspondence of Andrew L. Marshall, Esq., Bassford Remele, Minneapolis, Minnesota, to James Jay Rennicke, Burnett County District Attorney, Siren, Wisconsin, dated April 29, 2021.

9. See Trom et al. v. County of Dodge et al. (Court File No. 20-CV-14-293) and Order and Judgment Vacating Conditional Use Permit, dated November 18, 2014.

11. Risk of Pollution

1. "Two Men Died after Falling into a Manure Pit," Nexstar Media/WWLP.com and Associated Press reporting, July 3, 2015.

2. "Iowa Father, Son Die from Manure Pit Fumes," *Des Moines Register*, July 28, 2015.

3. Kelley J. Donham et al., "Community Health and Socioeconomic Issues Surrounding Concentrated Animal Feeding Operations," *Environmental Health Perspectives* 115, no. 2 (February 2007): 317–20.

4. The Humane Society of the United States et al. v. E. Scott Pruitt, in his official capacity, Administrator, United States Environmental Protection Agency, Complaint for Declaratory and Injunctive Relief at ℙ 69, United States District Court for the District of Columbia, filed August 23, 2017 (Civil Action No. 17-1719).

5. The World Banks' Climate-Smart Agriculture informational page, last updated December 1, 2023, https://www.worldbank.org/en/topic/climate -smart-agriculture.

6. Carrie Hribar, "Understanding Concentrated Animal Feeding Operations and Their Impact on Communities" (Bowling Green OH: National Association of Local Boards of Health, 2010).

7. Hribar, "Understanding Concentrated."

8. Robert B. Hamanaka and Gökhan Mutlu, "Particulate Matter Air Pollution: Effects on the Cardiovascular System," *Frontiers in Endocrinology* 9 (November 16, 2018): 680.

9. Ball-Blakely, "CAFOs."

10. California Air Resource Board, "A Preliminary Assessment of Air Emissions from Dairy Operations in the San Joaquin Valley," November 15, 2000.

11. California Air Resource Board, "A Preliminary Assessment"; and Renee Sharp and Bill Walker, "Particle Civics: How Cleaner Air in California Will Save Lives and Save Money" (Washington DC: Environmental Working Group, 2002).

12. Susanne E. Bauer, Kostas Tsigaridis, and Ron Miller, "Significant Atmospheric Aerosol Pollution Caused by World Food Cultivation," *Geophysical Research Letters* 42, no. 10 (May 16, 2016).

13. Nina G. G. Domingo et al., "Air Quality–Related Health Damages of Food," *Proceedings of the National Academy of Sciences* 118, no. 20 (May 18, 2021).

14. Miller and Muren, "CAFOs."

15. See "Emergency Release Notification Regulations on Reporting Exemption for Air Emissions from Animal Waste at Farms; Emergency Planning and Community Right-to-Know Act," *Federal Register* 83, no. 220 (November 14, 2018): 56791–97.

16. Leah Douglas, "A Breathtaking Lack of Oversight for Air Emissions from Animal Farms," Food & Environment Reporting Network, December 20, 2019.

17. Jason Foscolo and Michael Zimmerman, "Alternative Growth: Forsaking the False Economies of Industrial Agriculture," *Fordham Environmental Law Review* 25, no. 2 (2014).

18. Environmental Integrity Project, "Raising a Stink: Air Emissions from Factory Farms," accessed January 19, 2023, http://environmentalintegrity.org/pdf/publications/CAFOAirEmissions_white_paper.pdf.

19. Environmental Protection Agency, "Regulatory Definitions of Large CAFOS, Medium CAFO, and Small CAFOS," accessed January 14, 2023, https://www3.epa.gov/npdes/pubs/sector_table.pdf.

20. Miller and Muren, "CAFOS."

21. Miller and Muren, "CAFOS," 5.

22. Madison McVan, "Large CAFOS Are Known Polluters. Here's Why EPA Permits Only Cover One-Third," *Missouri Independent*, November 21, 2022.

23. Christopher Collins, "Something in the Air," *Texas Observer*, February 3, 2020. The *Observer* conducted this investigative report in partnership with the Food & Environment Reporting Network and the Midwest Center for Investigative Reporting.

24. Application form dated November 20, 2014; see Trom et al. v. County of Dodge et al. (Court File No. 20-CV-15-17), at paragraph 40, first amended complaint dated April 2, 2015.

25. See Trom et al. v. County of Dodge et al. (Court File No. 20-CV-15-17), at paragraph 46, first amended complaint dated April 2, 2015.

26. Dodge County Planning Office Findings of Facts & Recommendations, Masching Swine Farms, LLC—December 11, 2014, Special Meeting.

27. Dodge County Planning Office Findings of Facts & Recommendations, Masching Swine Farms, LLC—December 11, 2014, Special Meeting.

28. Land Application Agreement for Receiving Manure on Cropland, August 15, 2014, included in agenda packet, Special Meeting, Dodge County Planning Commission, December 11, 2014.

29. "Planning Commission Oks Feedlot Ordinance Changes," *Dodge County Independent*, February 11, 2015. See also Elizabeth Baier, "Big Feedlots Feed Big Worries in Southern Minnesota," *MPR News*, April 6, 2015; and Matt Hudson, "Dodge County Commission Votes to Amend Feedlot Ordinance," *Owatonna (MN) People's Press* (Owatonna.com), February 4, 2015.

30. See Trom et al. v. County of Dodge et al. (Court File No. 20-CV-14-293).

31. Minutes, Dodge County Board of Commissioners, February 10, 2015.

32. Minnesota Administrative Rules, chapter 7020, "Registration Requirements for Animal Feedlots and Manure Storage Areas"; Minn. Stat. 116D.04, subd. 2a; and Minn. R. 7020.1600, subd. 4a (2020).

33. Minnesota Feedlot Program Rules, Minn. R. 7020.0505 (2020).

12. Don't Drink the Water

Epigraph: National Pork Producers Council, "Trump Repeals Waters of the U.S. Rule," February 28, 2017.

1. Kate Prengaman, "Groundwater War Pits Wisconsin Farmers against Fish," *Investigate Midwest* in collaboration with the Wisconsin Center for Investigative Journalism, July 23, 2013.

2. Johnathan Hettinger, "Lack of Irrigation Reporting Leaves Uncertain Future for Illinois Groundwater," *Investigate Midwest*, June 20, 2017.

3. DNR, Update for Bonanza Valley GWMA [Groundwater Management Area] Project, accessed February 4, 2023, https://content.govdelivery.com/accounts /MNDNR/bulletins/a3edba.

4. Tony Kennedy, "Compliance Sweep Targets Farm Wells in Southern Minnesota," *Star Tribune* (Minneapolis), March 13, 2015.

5. Eugene Nilsen is a pseudonym.

6. Minnesota DNR, 2018 Minnesota DNR water use permits. (Of note, in Nick Masching's conditional use permit application, he wrote that each hog would require 4 gallons of water per day. At that rate, 2,400 hogs would need 9,600 gallons per day, or an estimated 3.5 million gallons of water per year, for a single industrial swine factory farm.)

7. Minnesota Pollution Control Agency, "Land Application of Manure: Minimum State Requirements" fact sheet, February 2011, 1.

8. Olmsted County Department of Environmental Services, Test Results, April 4, 2017.

9. American Health Association, "Precautionary Moratorium on New and Expanding Concentrated Animal Feeding Operations," November 5, 2019.

10. Hribar, "Understanding Concentrated."

11. Jackie Wang, Nicole Tyau, and Chelsea Rae Ybanez, "Farming Activity Contaminates Water despite Best Practices," *The Californian*, August 15, 2017, cited in Miller and Muren, "CAFOS."

12. Miller and Muren, "CAFOS." See also Michele M. Merkel, "EPA and State Failures to Regulate CAFOS under Federal Environmental Laws," remarks prepared for the National Commission on Industrial Farm Animal Production Meeting, September 11, 2006.

13. "Bacteria Contamination," *Dodge County Water Monitoring Update—2017*, 5.

14. Community and Economic Development Associates, "Land Use and Water Quality," *2018 Comprehensive Plan, Dodge County, MN*, adopted September 10, 2019, 48. See also Dodge County Environmental Services, *Nitrogen in Dodge County Ground and Surface Waters* (PowerPoint presentation), April 2015.

15. Community and Economic Development Associates, *2018 Comprehensive Plan*, 48; and Dodge County Environmental Services, *Nitrogen in Dodge County*.

16. Keith Schneider, "In Minnesota, Families Blame Farm Nutrient Contamination on Heavy Cancer Toll," Circle of Blue, September 19, 2023, https:// www.circleofblue.org/2023/world/in-minnesota-families-blame-farm -nutrient-contamination-on-heavy-cancer-toll/#:~:text=Menu%20Menu

-,In%20Minnesota%2C%20Families%20Blame%20Farm%20Nutrient
%20Contamination%20On%20Heavy%20Cancer,editor%20of%20The
%20New%20Lede.

17. Sarah Porter and Anne Weir Schechinger, "Tap Water for 500,000 Minnesotans Contaminated with Elevated Levels of Nitrate" (Washington DC: Environmental Working Group, January 2020).

18. Environmental Protection Agency Office of Water, "National Rivers and
Streams Assessment, 2018–19: The Third Collaborative Survey" (Washington
DC: EPA, last updated December 19, 2023), https://riverstreamassessment.epa
.gov/webreport.

19. Iowa Department of Natural Resources, "Impaired Waters Listings,"
2020, www.iowadnr.gov/Environmental-Protection/Water-Quality/Water
-Monitoring/Impaired-Waters. See also Siena Chrisman, "The FoodPrint
of Pork," FoodPrint, a project of the GRACE Communications Foundation,
October 30, 2020, last updated June 6, 2023.

20. Andrea Plevan et al., "Minnesota River *E. coli* Total Maximum Daily Load
and Implementation Strategies" (Saint Paul: Minnesota Pollution Control
Agency, May 2019). See also Ron Way, "From Superstar to Sewer: The Path of
the Minnesota River," *Star Tribune* (Minneapolis), May 3, 2019.

21. Plevan et al., "Minnesota River *E. coli*"; and Way, "From Superstar to Sewer,"
30.

22. Minnesota Pollution Control Agency, "Swimmable, Fishable, Fixable? What
We've Learned So Far about Minnesota Waters" (Saint Paul: Minnesota Pollution Control Agency, April 2015), 9.

23. American Public Health Association, "New Public Health Policy Statements
Adopted at APHA 2019," press release, November 6, 2019.

24. Miller and Muren, "CAFOS," 6.

25. Miller and Muren, "CAFOS," 4.

26. Local citizens called a special town meeting "on petition of 20 percent of the
electors of the town." See Officer of the Revisor of Statutes, "Special Meeting;
for Any Lawful Purpose," Minn. Stat. § 365.52, subd. 1. The board of supervisors could submit to the legal voters of the town, at an annual or special town
meeting, the question of whether the board shall adopt land use and zoning
regulations and restrictions in the town. Minn. Stat. § 366.10. In Minnesota,
the secretary of state maintains a list of registered voters in the local township.

27. Township Minutes, 2015 Westfield Township Annual Meeting, Dodge County,
Minnesota, March 10, 2015.

28. Howard Lestrud, "Covid-19 Affects Area Hog Producers," *Steele County (MN)
Times*, April 29, 2020. This article refers to the O'Connor swine facilities.

29. Copy of email in author's possession.

30. Township Minutes, Special Meeting, Westfield Township, Dodge County,
Minnesota, March 31, 2015. See also "Westfield Meeting Starts with a Surprise:

Ordinance Is a Big Undertaking, Attorney Warns," *Dodge County Independent*, April 8, 2015.

31. Meeting agenda, Westfield Township, March 31, 2015. Of note, the meeting agenda differed from the public notice published in the local newspaper that read: "Westfield Township Dodge County NOTICE OF A SPECIAL TOWN MEETING, Notice is hereby given that a special town meeting at the Westfield Township electors will be held on March 31, 2015, at 7 p.m. at the Westfield Township Hall for the following purpose: To discuss with electors only, the question of whether the town board, consisting of 3 supervisors, shall, at some time, adopt land use and zoning regulations and restrictions in the township of Westfield. Only township electors are authorized to voice their opinion at the meeting." See Public Notice, *Steele County Times*, March 24, 2015.

32. At the March 2016 annual meeting, Westfield Township supervisors disclosed the amount paid for legal counsel during calendar year 2015. See Westfield Township, Expenditures of 2015, reflecting "Legal and P & Z expenses at taxpayer's cost" totaling $18,719.23.

13. The Corporate Bully

1. Call for Service, Dodge County (MN) Sheriff's Office, Incident #201500005436, June 20, 2015. No case number is listed on the report.
2. A clip of this scene is included in *The Dark Side of the Other White Meat*, directed and filmed by Randy Trom (Dodge County MN, 2015), 19 min.
3. Minnesota Farm Bureau Foundation, "When an Activist," 15–16.
4. Details about this incident are preserved in a police report filed by Mr. Gronseth on January 6, 2004, with the sheriff's department of Swift County, Minnesota.
5. Lynn and Nancy Utesch founded the Kewaunee Citizens Advocating Responsible Environmental Stewardship. With sixteen CAFOs and seventy-six thousand cows in their immediate area, their group continues to fight permitting and CAFO-friendly policies.
6. Brian Bienkowski, "Cheap Bacon and Bigger Barns Turn Iowa Inside Out," *Environmental Health News*, November 13, 2017.
7. Bienkowski, "Cheap Bacon."
8. Bienkowski, "Cheap Bacon."
9. Kathie Dobie, "One Woman Takes a Brave Stand against Factory Farming," *O, the Oprah Magazine*, November 2011. Lynn Henning was one of the founders of Environmentally Concerned Citizens of South Central Michigan. Today she works as a field representative for the Socially Responsible Agriculture Project.
10. Goldman Environmental Prize, Lynn Henning biography page, 2010, https://www.goldmanprize.org/recipient/lynn-henning/#recipient-bio.

11. Eric A. Sterling, "Linkages between Concentrated Animal Feeding Operation (CAFO) Expansion and County Board Politics in Rural Illinois," thesis, Northern Illinois University, 2015, https://huskiecommons.lib.niu.edu/allgraduate-thesesdissertations/3808/.
12. Sterling, "Linkages," 41.
13. Information based on author's interviews with Mariann Guentzel on March 11, 2023, and June 18, 2023; on author's interview with Jason Longhenry on June 1, 2023; on a local press account; and on the author's experiences at a township meeting in Byron Township, Minnesota, on December 8, 2015.
14. Elaine Wiegand, "Letter to the Editor: Hogs, Hogs and More Hogs," *Pilot Independent* (Walker MN), December 18, 2015, https://www.walkermn.com/opinion/letters_to_editor/letter-to-the-editor-hogs-hogs-and-more-hogs/article_d76940aa-a58d-11e5-bf51-17559ee0ef21.html.

14. In the Trenches

1. The accounting of this meeting is based on the author's interviews with Mariann Guentzel on March 11, 2023, and June 18, 2023; on the author's interviews with other residents; on a local press account; and on the author's experiences at the Byron Township meeting on December 8, 2015.
2. Based on the author's interviews with Mariann Guentzel on March 11, 2023, and June 18, 2023; on the author's interviews with other residents; on a local press account; and on the author's experiences at the Byron Township meeting on December 8, 2015.
3. Wiegand, "Letter to the Editor."
4. Mariann's home was insured by Farm Bureau Insurance, which reportedly only paid her half of the home's value. Mariann was a longtime Farm Bureau member and hadn't realized her annual membership goes to legal fees for CAFO operators and to "support the swine industry" until she found herself involved in the local fight over a CAFO.
5. This account is informed by the author's interviews with Mariann Guentzel on March 11, 2023, and June 18, 2023; and by the author's interviews with other township residents.
6. With the CAFO project unable to proceed on the property originally owned by area resident Charlie Swenson, neighbor Tom Blattner purchased the land.
7. Minnesota Department of Agriculture, Resources, Minnesota Geospatial Commons, "Animal Ordinances Web Map," accessed June 28, 2020, https://gisdata.mn.gov/dataset/env-app-animal-ordinances.
8. Minnesota Department of Agriculture, "Local Ordinances Regulating Livestock in Minnesota," accessed June 28, 2020, https://www.mda.state.mn.us/local-ordinances-regulating-livestock-minnesota.
9. This account is based on the recollections and experiences of the author and those of other event participants.

10. Likewise, this account is based on the recollections and experiences of the author and those of other event participants.

11. Trom et al. v. County of Dodge et al. (Court File No. 20-CV-14-293); and Trom et al. v. County of Dodge et al. (Court File No. 20-CV-15-17).

12. Lowell Trom et al., Appellants v. County of Dodge et al., Respondents, and Masching Swine Farms, LLC, Respondent, No. A16-1099 (Unpublished Minn. Ct. App. April 17, 2017).

13. *Dodge County Zoning Ordinance*, chap. 18.13.8, "Findings and Recommendations," sections A.1 and A.9.

14. Trom et al. v. County of Dodge et al., No. A16-1099 (Unpublished Minn. Ct. App. April 17, 2017), brief amici curiae, Dr. Jillian P. Fry, PhD, MPH; Dr. Robert S. Lawrence, MD; Ms. Claire M. Fitch, MSPH; and Ms. Carolyn R. Hricko, MPH, October 11, 2016.

15. Trom et al. v. County of Dodge et al., No. A16-1099 (Unpublished Minn. Ct. App. April 17, 2017), brief amici curiae, Fry et al.

16. Trom et al. v. County of Dodge et al., No. A16-1099 (Unpublished Minn. Ct. App. April 17, 2017), brief amici curiae, the Humane Society of the United States and Animal Legal Defense Fund, October 10, 2016.

17. Trom et al. v. County of Dodge et al., No. A16-1099 (Unpublished Minn. Ct. App. April 17, 2017), brief amici curiae, the Humane Society and Animal Legal Defense Fund. See also World Health Organization, "Stop Using Antibiotics in Healthy Animals to Prevent the Spread of Antibiotic Resistance," November 7, 2017.

18. Trom et al. v. County of Dodge et al., No. A16-1099 (Unpublished Minn. Ct. App. April 17, 2017), brief amici curiae, the Humane Society and Animal Legal Defense Fund. See also World Health Organization, "Stop Using Antibiotics"; and Jim O'Neill, chair, *Antimicrobial Resistance: Tackling a Crisis for the Health and Wealth of Nations*, a Review on Antimicrobial Resistance, December 2014, 5.

19. D. Wallinga et al., "A Review of the Effectiveness of Current US Policies on Antimicrobial Use in Meat and Poultry Production," *Current Environmental Health Reports* 9, no. 2 (June 2022): 339–54.

20. M. Carrel et al., "Residential Proximity to Large Numbers of Swine in Feeding Operations Is Associated with Increased Risk of Methicillin-Resistant Staphylococcus Aureus Colonization at Time of Hospital Admission in Rural Iowa Veterans," *Infection Control & Hospital Control Epidemiology* 35, no. 2 (February 2014): 190–93.

21. The Humane Society and Animal Legal Defense Fund, brief of amici curiae.

22. Trom et al. v. County of Dodge et al., No. A16-1099 (Unpublished Minn. Ct. App. April 17, 2017), brief amici curiae, Minnesota Center for Environmental Advocacy and Food & Water Watch, October 10, 2014.

23. Trom et al. v. County of Dodge et al., No. A16-1099 (Unpublished Minn. Ct. App. April 17, 2017), brief amici curiae, MCEA and Food & Water Watch, 5.

24. Trom et al. v. County of Dodge et al., No. A16-1099 (Unpublished Minn. Ct. App. April 17, 2017), brief amici curiae, MCEA and Food & Water Watch, 9.

25. See Trom et al. v. County of Dodge et al., No. A16-1099 (Unpublished Minn. Ct. App. April 17, 2017).

15. The Three-Day Stink Out

1. Call for Service, Dodge County (MN) Sheriff's Office, Incident #201700009562, Case #201700000864, November 11, 2017.

2. Call for Service, Dodge County Sheriff's Office, Incident #201700009587, Case #201700000864, November 12, 2017.

3. As noted in chapter 9, Nick Masching purchased six acres within the Toquams' three-hundred-acre plot as the site for his new swine CAFO.

4. Environmental Protection Agency, "Minnesota: Air Emissions Planning," 2017, https://www.epa.gov/sites/default/files/2017-01/documents/c_minnesota _air_emissions_planning.pdf.

5. Email from Lenny Richards, MPCA, to author, June 12, 2023, confirmed the issuance of Roger Toquam's NPDES permit, March 11, 2011.

6. Paul Brietzke, MPCA, notes of a complaint on Roger Toquam, per email from Lenny Richards, MPCA, May 2, 2018.

7. Test results provided by MPCA pursuant to a data practices request and received May 2, 2018. See also Minn. Stat. § 7009.0080, "Minnesota Ambient Air Quality Standards," which provide that hydrogen sulfide shall not exceed 0.03 parts per million (or 42.0 micrograms per cubic meter) by volume over a thirty-minute average more than two times in five consecutive days.

8. Test results provided by MPCA.

9. Test results provided by MPCA.

10. See Occupational Health and Safety Administration, "Hydrogen Sulfide Hazards" fact sheet, accessed March 14, 2023, https://www.osha.gov/hydrogen -sulfide/hazards.

11. Test results provided by MPCA.

12. Author's communication with a reporter at the *Star Tribune* (Minneapolis).

13. Domingo et al., "Air Quality–Related."

16. Corporate Indoctrination

Part epigraph: John Grisham, foreword to *Wastelands: The True Story of Farm Country on Trial*, by Corban Addison (New York: Penguin Random House, 2022), xv.

1. Ivy Pepin, "What Are Ag-Gag Laws and How Many States Have Them?" The Humane League, June 7, 2022.

2. American Farm Bureau Foundation for Agriculture, "Partnering with National Ag in the Classroom," August 11, 2017.

3. National Agriculture in the Classroom, "2021 Annual Report," https://cdn .agclassroom.org/nat/data/affiliates/report_annual.pdf.

4. Minnesota Agriculture in the Classroom, "2021–2022 Annual Report," Saint Paul.

5. Minnesota Agriculture in the Classroom, Curriculum Matrix: Lesson Plan, accessed March 17, 2004, https://minnesota.agclassroom.org/matrix/lesson /273/.

6. Minnesota Agriculture in the Classroom, *AgMag 6*, Fall, 2, accessed March 25, 2024, https://mnagmag.org/ag-mag/ag-mag-6-fall/.

7. Minnesota Agriculture in the Classroom, *AgMag 4*, Spring, 1–3, accessed March 25, 2024, https://mnagmag.org/ag-mag/ag-mag-4-spring/.

8. Tennessee Foundation for Agriculture in the Classroom, "First Grade Curriculum Notebook," 27.

9. Illinois Ag in the Classroom, "Animal Well-Being," with National Agriculture in the Classroom and the University of Arizona Cooperative Extension, 4, accessed December 13, 2018, https://www.agintheclassroom.org/media /ji4j0ntd/pork-reader-pages-updated-2022.pdf.

10. Pork Checkoff, "Producers, Pigs & Pork" (coloring book) (Des Moines: National Pork Board, 2009, 2018, 2021), https://www.mnpork.com/img _0773/.

11. Mitchell and Frerick, "Hog Barons."

12. Kay Fate, "A FAARM for the Future, U Research, Teaching Center Planned for Udolpho Township," *Steele County (MN) Times*, April 26, 2023.

13. Liz Navratil, "University of Minnesota Regents Select Jeff Ettinger to Be Interim President," *Star Tribune* (Minneapolis), May 8, 2023.

14. Liz Navratil and Anthony Lonetree, "University of Minnesota Regents to Finalize Details of Presidential Transition," *Star Tribune* (Minneapolis), June 1, 2023.

15. Chrisman, "FoodPrint of Pork."

16. Kate Cox and H. Claire Brown, "Academics across the Country Say Agribusiness Has Outsize Influence on Their Research," *The Counter*, January 31, 2019. This in-depth reportorial investigation was based on interviews with academics and researchers across the United States.

17. Cox and Brown, "Academics across the Country."

18. Cox and Brown, "Academics across the Country." Reports indicate the pork industry harassed Wing for his complete dataset until his death in 2016.

19. Addison, *Wastelands*, 183.

20. National Pork Producers Council, "Animal Health," 2024, https://nppc.org /pork-industry-issues/animal-health/.

21. "NPPC Beeps Up Lobbying Efforts," *National Hog Farmer*, July 5, 2007.

22. See, for instance, National Pork Producers Council, "NPPC Weighs In: 'Fatigued' Hogs, Traceability, Antibiotics," *2011 Annual Report*, 7, https://nppc .org/wp-content/uploads/2022/04/CPR-2011-successes.pdf. Annual summaries of the NPPC's lobbying efforts and annual reports for the years 2007 to the present are no longer listed at the organization's website; they must be sought individually using a search engine online. Note that the NPPC refers to the Downed Animal and Food Security Protection Act as a prohibition on "fatigued hogs from being processed" (1).
23. Erica Hellerstein, "Hogwashed, Part 1: Hundreds of Poor, Mostly African-American Residents of Eastern North Carolina Say Big Pork Is Making Their Lives Miserable," *Indy Week*, July 12, 2017. *Indy Week* published the three-part investigation of the hog-farming industry by Erica Hellerstein and Ken Fine during the Smithfield Foods trial in North Carolina in 2017.
24. Hellerstein, "Hogwashed, Part 1."

17. The Pork Board

Epigraph: National Pork Producers Council, "Written Testimony of the National Pork Producers Council on Impact of Federal Environmental Regulations and Policies on American Farming and Ranching Communities before the Senate Environment and Public Works Committee," February 7, 2018, 7, https://www.epw.senate.gov/public/_cache/files/2/6/26be4143-e654 -4ac1-9267-817a8f727d26/DC03448AB5E08D6AB40462A9A8969327.hill -testimony-02.07.2018.pdf.

1. Danielle Diamond et al., "Agricultural Exceptionalism, Environmental Injustice, and U.S. Right-to-Farm Laws," *Environmental Law Reporter* 52, no. 9 (September 2022).
2. Diamond et al., "Agricultural Exceptionalism."
3. Mike Mosedale, "Bill to Protect Factory Farms from Lawsuits Stalls," *Minnesota Lawyer*, March 28, 2017.
4. Addison, *Wastelands*, 139.
5. Addison, *Wastelands*, 145–47.
6. "What's behind Big Ag's Move to Change Minnesota's Nuisance Laws—and Why It Matters," *Bluestem Prairie News*, March 2, 2015. See also Minnesota Senate meeting agenda, "Agriculture, Rural Development, and Housing Policy Committee," February 23, 2017.
7. Josephine Marcotty, "As Hog Feedlots Grow, Neighbors Ask: What about Our Rights?" *Farm Forum* with reporting from *Star Tribune* (Minneapolis) and McClatchy-Tribune Information Services, April 18, 2017. See also Russell Anderson et al., Plaintiffs v. Gourley Bros. Premium Pork Protein, Gourley Brothers, Gourley Premium Pork, LC, Protein Sources Milling, LLC, and Protein Sources, LLP, Defendants, Todd County District Court (Court File No. 77-CV-14-933).

8. "The Other Political Pork," *New York Times*, November 10, 2002.

9. U.S. Department of Agriculture in partnership with National Agriculture Statistics Service, *Quarterly Hogs and Pigs*, June 29, 2022. See also, for a discussion of the results, Chuck Abbott, "Fewer Hog Farms, but Far More Hogs per Farm," *Successful Farming*, August 22, 2022.

10. Danny Vinik, "A $60 Million Pork Kickback? Unhappy Small Farmers Detect a Racket in a Pork Branding Deal—and the USDA Signed Off on It," *Politico*, August 30, 2015.

11. Vinik, "$60 Million Pork Kickback?"

12. See Pork Checkoff, "Checkoff Distribution by State," 2022 Reports, https://porkcheckoff.org/about/checkoff-distribution-by-state/.

13. Minnesota Pork Board, 2018 Form 990, reflects expenditures of $449,551 for "Prorated Administrated" and $151,380 for "Human Capital Exp." With the pork board sharing the same office and the same staff with the Minnesota Pork Producers Association, one can conclude that the MPPA used federal tax dollars, via the pork board, on internal operations.

14. This information is gathered from the public-facing websites of the MPPA, https://www.mppainsider.org/, and the Minnesota Pork Board, https://www.mnpork.com/.

15. Minnesota Campaign Finance and Public Disclosure Board, David Preisler, lobbyist registration number 4358, https://cfb.mn.gov/reports-and-data/viewers/lobbying/lobbyists/4358/2022.1/, for Minnesota Pork Producers Association, Number 2777. The site shows his registration was terminated May 31, 2022.

16. MPPA, 2015 Form 990, lists a $100,000 contribution to A Greater Minnesota, https://www.causeiq.com/organizations/view_990/410802272/f71f975dd91a8afd006296754925de28; and MPPA, 2017 Form 990, a $105,103 contribution to A Greater Minnesota, https://www.causeiq.com/organizations/view_990/410802272/a13e786720eabcfcd31b53b241f19236.

17. The organization "A Greater Minnesota" is opaque. Its website, https://farmandfoodmn.org/, is titled "Food & Farm MN" and does not list its staff. David Preisler's former role as president is confirmed through information on file with the Minnesota Business and Liens System, Office of the Minnesota Secretary of State, https://www.sos.state.mn.us/business-liens.

18. Trent Loos, "People, Pigs and the Planet Need Each Other," *High Plains Journal*, June 15, 2015.

19. MPPA, 2015 Form 990 ($618,485 as Strategic Investment); MPPA, 2016 Form 990 ($597,310), https://projects.propublica.org/nonprofits/organizations/410802272/201820369349300842/full; and MPPA, 2017 Form 990 ($676,806).

20. MPPA, "Membership Benefits," 2024, https://www.mppainsider.org/join-mppa/membership-benefits/.

21. Joe Maxwell and Angela Huffman, "Analysis of the Ohio Beef Checkoff Program: Serious Abuses Show a Need for Reform," briefing paper, Organization for Competitive Markets, February 2018.

22. Maxwell and Huffman, "Analysis."

23. See National Pork Producers Council, "The Strategic Investment Program," accessed March 18, 2023, https://nppc.org/get-involved/strategic-investment -program/.

24. Kirk Semple, Adam Westbrook, and Jonah M. Kessel, "Meet the People Getting Paid to Kill Our Planet: American Agriculture Is Ravaging the Air, Soil, and Water. But a Powerful Lobby Has Cleverly Concealed Its Damage," *New York Times*, February 1, 2022.

25. Semple, Westbrook, and Kessel, "Meet the People."

26. Georgina Gustin, "Big Meat and Dairy Companies Have Spent Millions Lobbying against Climate Action, a New Study Finds," *Inside Climate News*, April 2, 2021.

27. Gustin, "Big Meat."

28. Gustin, Cushman, and Banerjee, "Farm Bureau's Climate Agenda."

29. National Pork Producers Council, "Capital Pork: 2019 Annual Report" (Urbandale IA: NPPC, 2020), 2, https://nppc.org/wp-content/uploads/2022/04 /CPR_2019_Annual-Report-Optimized-File.pdf.

30. See National Pork Producers Council, "2021–2022 Policy Wins" fact page, https://nppc.org/wp-content/uploads/2022/04/2021-2022_Successes-3.25.22-3 .pdf.

31. See National Pork Producers Council, "2021–2022 Policy Wins" fact page.

32. Dan Flynn, "Petition Seeks to Change Rules for 'Product of USA' Meat Labels," *Food Safety News*, June 28, 2018.

33. Food Safety and Inspection Service, "FSIS Guideline for Label Approval," March 2024, https://www.fsis.usda.gov/sites/default/files/media_file /documents/FSIS-GD-2024-0001.pdf.

18. Feed the World

Epigraph: Frank Giles, "Five Questions with the New American Farm Bureau President," *Growing Produce*, February 13, 2016.

1. Makenzie Huber, "Smithfield Workers Asked for Safety from Covid-19. Their Company Offered Cash," *USA Today*, April 9, 2020.

2. Chrisman, "FoodPrint of Pork."

3. Chrisman, "FoodPrint of Pork."

4. Leah Douglas and Tim Marema, "Rural Counties with Covid-19 Cases from Meatpacking Have Infection Rates 5 Times Higher," *Daily Yonder* (Whitesburg KY), May 28, 2020. See also "Mapping Covid-19 Outbreaks in the Food System," Food & Environment Reporting Network, April 22, 2020, https:// thefern.org/2020/04/mapping-covid-19-in-meat-and-food-processing-plants/.

5. Charles A. Taylor, Christopher Boulos, and Douglas Almond, "Livestock Plants and COVID-19 Transmission," *Proceedings of the National Academy of Sciences* 117, no. 50 (November 19, 2020): 31706–15.

6. Alvin Chang et al., "The Pandemic Exposed the Human Cost of the Meat-packing Industry's Power: 'It's Enormously Frightening,'" *The Guardian*, reporting supported by the 11th Hour Project, November 16, 2021.

7. Ana Swanson and David Yaffe-Bellany, "Trump Declares Meat Supply 'Critical,' Aiming to Reopen Plants," *New York Times*, April 28, 2020.

8. Daniel Hemel, "No, Trump Didn't Order Meat Processing Plants to Reopen," *Washington Post*, May 4, 2020.

9. Katie Shepherd, "'The Food Supply Chain Is Breaking': Tyson Foods Raises Coronavirus Alarm in Full-Page Ads, Defends Safety Efforts," *Washington Post*, April 27, 2020.

10. "Smithfield Foods Closes One of Nation's Largest Pork Plants as Worker Covid-19 Cases Spike," *USA Today*, April 13, 2020.

11. Emily Miller, "Our Smithfield Lawsuit Exposes Lies about Meat Shortages and Worker Safety," Food & Water Watch, press release, June 21, 2021.

12. Chrisman, "FoodPrint of Pork"; and Miller, "Our Smithfield Lawsuit."

13. Lee Schulz, "A Look back at Pig Death Loss Factors in 2020," *Iowa Farmer Today* (Hiawatha IA), July 30, 2020.

14. Associated Press, "Millions of Healthy Pigs Euthanized after COVID 19 Pandemic Closes Processing Facilities," Fox 59, May 1, 2020, https://fox59.com/news/millions-of-healthy-pigs-euthanized-after-covid-19-pandemic-closes-processing-facilities/.

15. American Veterinary Medical Association, *AVMA Guidelines for the Depopulation of Animals: 2019 Edition* (Schaumburg IL: American Veterinary Medical Association, 2019), 43–44.

16. AVMA, *AVMA Guidelines*, 45.

17. Sophie Kevany, "Millions of Farm Animals Culled as US Food Supply Chain Chokes Up," *The Guardian*, April 29, 2020.

18. Glenn Greenwald, "Hidden Video and Whistleblower Reveal Gruesome Mass-Extermination Method for Iowa Pigs amid Pandemic," *The Intercept*, May 29, 2020.

19. Greenwald, "Hidden Video."

20. Betsy Freese, "Iowa Select Farms Forced to Euthanize Some of Swine Herd," *Successful Farming*, May 20, 2020.

21. Greenwald, "Hidden Video."

22. Greenwald, "Hidden Video."

23. Michael Corkery and David Yaffe-Bellany, "Meat Plant Closures Mean Pigs Are Gassed or Shot Instead," *New York Times*, May 14, 2020.

24. Author's interviews with Tom Butler, October 11, 2022; October 29, 2022; and October 2, 2023.

25. Author's interviews with Tom Butler.

26. Hog Depopulation Cost-Share Program, Minnesota Department of Agriculture, November 10, 2020.

27. Chris McNulty, data practices manager, Minnesota Department of Agriculture, email, January 29, 2021. Data provided pursuant to the Minnesota Data Practices Act.

28. Ryan J. Foley, "Pork Exec Gives $25K to Iowa Governor; Company Got Virus Aid," AP News, January 20, 2021.

29. "Smithfield Reached $75M Settlement."

30. Mike Leonard, "Smithfield Paying $200 Million Total to Exit Pork Antitrust Case," Bloomberg Law, September 28, 2022.

31. Shepherd, "'Food Supply Chain."

32. Food and Agriculture Organization of the United Nations, "Agriculture Must Change: FAO Director Speaks at International Forum on Agriculture and Climate Change," International Forum on Agriculture and Climate Change, Paris, February 20, 2015.

33. Food and Agriculture Organization, "Agriculture Must Change."

34. José Graziano da Silva, "Feeding the World Sustainably," UN Chronicle 49, nos. 1 and 2 (June 2012).

35. Anne Weir Schechinger and Craig Cox, "Feeding the World: Think U.S. Agriculture Will End World Hunger? Think Again" (Washington DC: Environmental Working Group, October 5, 2016).

36. "Meat Consumption: Trends and Health Implications," fact page at the Johns Hopkins Center for a Livable Future, accessed April 24, 2023, https://clf.jhsph .edu/projects/technical-and-scientific-resource-meatless-monday/meatless -monday-resources/meatless-monday-resourcesmeat-consumption-trends -and-health-implications.

37. Rachel Premack, "Meat Is Horrible," Washington Post, July 3, 2016.

38. Jacqui Fatka, "When Agendas Get in the Way of Modern Agriculture," Farm Progress, June 9, 2022.

39. Dirck Steimel, "Communication Key to Protect Farmers' Access to Technology," Iowa Farm Bureau's website, September 6, 2016.

40. "Don't Expect Iowa Farmers to Feed the World," op-ed, Des Moines Register, October 9, 2016.

19. On the Front Lines

Epigraph: Elsie Herring, "Building a 100 Percent Clean Economy: The Challenges Facing Frontline Communities," testimony for U.S. House Committee on Energy and Commerce, November 20, 2019, https://www.congress.gov /116/meeting/house/110247/witnesses/HHRG-116-IF18-Wstate-HerringE -20191120.pdf.

1. Hellerstein, "Hogwashed, Part 1."

2. Herring, "Building" testimony, 2–3.

3. Herring, "Building" testimony, 9.

4. Hellerstein, "Hogwashed, Part 1."

5. The author's understanding of industry expansion in North Dakota and Wisconsin is based on conversations, interviews, and correspondence with several individuals leading efforts to resist CAFO expansion in these states, along with information available in the press.

6. Betsy Freese, "SF Special: How Premium Standard Farms Transformed the Pig Business," *Successful Farming*, February 8, 2018.

7. Freese, "SF Special," February 8, 2018.

8. Freese, "SF Special," February 8, 2018.

9. Karen McMahon, "Premium Standard Farms: Reopening after Bankruptcy and Now New Owners," *National Hog Farmer*, May 1, 1998.

10. Betsy Freese, "SF Special: How Smithfield Saved the Worst Hog Farm in America," *Successful Farming*, January 4, 2018.

11. Information from Tad Gordon's LinkedIn profile, https://www.linkedin.com/in/tad-gordon-37526311, and references to his theater company available in the press.

12. Data point available at the USDA's Economic Research Service and National Agricultural Statistics Service. For a discussion of the decline of small hog farms in Missouri, see also Missouri Rural Crisis Center, "Our Position on Livestock, Rural Communities and the Economy," *In Motion Magazine*, December 12, 2005.

13. Seeger Weiss LLP, "Hog Farm Overrun by Waste—$11 Million Verdict," press release, March 4, 2010, https://www.seegerweiss.com/news/seeger-weiss-wins-huge-victory/.

14. Account of the events of 1994 and 1995 are based on the author's interviews with Scott Dye on March 19, 2023, and March 24, 2023.

15. Associated Press, "Premium Standard Farms Reaches Settlement in Northern MO," *All Things Considered*, KBIA, August 30, 2012.

16. Ian T. Shearn, "Whose Side Is the American Farm Bureau On?" *The Nation*, July 16, 2012.

17. Leah Douglas, "In Missouri, Lawmakers Are Poised to Eliminate Local Regulation of CAFOS," *The Counter*, May 10, 2019.

18. Douglas, "In Missouri."

19. Douglas, "In Missouri." See also Allison Kite, "Missouri Supreme Court Upholds State Law Prohibiting Local Regulation of CAFOS," St. Louis Public Radio/KCUR, March 22, 2023.

20. Mitchell and Frerick, "Hog Barons." This investigation tells the story of Iowa Select Farms and its takeover of the state's hog industry, with far-reaching consequences.

21. Mitchell and Frerick, "Hog Barons."

22. Scott Kilman, "Iowans Can Handle Pig Smells, but This Is Something Else: Giant Hog 'Factories' Strain Inherent Neighborliness of a Rural Community," *Wall Street Journal*, May 4, 1995.

23. Christopher S. Jones, "Fifty Shades of Brown," (blog), published by IIHR, the Hydroscience & Engineering Laboratory at the University of Iowa–Iowa City, June 6, 2019. See also Donnelle Eller, "50 Shades of Brown: Iowa Ranks No. 1 in, Ahem, No. 2, UI Researcher Calculates," *Des Moines Register*, June 10, 2019.

24. Jones, "Fifty Shades of Brown."

20. Expanding the Corporate Empire

Epigraph: Daryl Lies, "Strengthening Our Voice for Agriculture," North Dakota Farm Bureau, November 18, 2022.

1. See Derek Prantner, Plaintiff v. Oakland Township and Sean Kraushaar, Defendants, Freeborn County District Court (Court File No. 24-CV-15-849); Charles W. Loncorich, Tammy S. Loncorich, Dean Sabacky, and Willard Schultz, Plaintiffs v. County of McLeod, Kelsey Buss, and Kevin Buss, Defendants, McLeod County District Court (Court File No. 43-CV-14-1690); Connie Frahm, Plaintiff v. County of Rock, Rock County Board of Adjustment, Overgaard Pork, LLC, Defendants, Rock County District Court (Court File No. 67-CV-13-309); and Russell Anderson et al. v. Gourley Bros. Premium Pork, Todd County District Court (Court File No. 77-CV-14-933).

2. Nathan Bowe, "Becker County Commissioners Try to Run the Clock on White Earth Involvement in Pig Feedlot," *Detroit Lakes (MN) Tribune*, November 16, 2020.

3. Vicki Gerdes, "Zurn Serves as Advocate for Minnesota's Agriculture Industry," *Ag Week*, October 27, 2015.

4. Nathan Bowe, "Becker County Tables Pig Feedlot Permit after Township Complaints," *Detroit Lakes (MN) Tribune*, August 18, 2022.

5. The author's understanding of the events in Becker County is informed by conversations and correspondence with individuals leading efforts to resist CAFO expansion and by local press coverage.

6. Dan Gunderson, "White Earth Nation Imposes Moratorium on Large Livestock Farms," *MPR News*, December 8, 2022.

7. Nathan Bowe, "Becker County Gives Thumbs-up to New Pig Feedlot North of Audubon," *Detroit Lakes (MN) Tribune*, May 18, 2023.

8. Greg Stanley, "Winona County Feedlot Sues Nonprofit Members, Public Officials over Expansion Denial," *Star Tribune* (Minneapolis), February 1, 2023.

9. Brian Todd, "MN Milk Producers Files Last-Minute Case against MPCA Decision," *Post Bulletin*, November 1, 2018, https://www.postbulletin.com/newsmd/mn-milk-producers-files-last-minute-case-against-mpca-decision.

10. Todd, "MN Milk Producers."

11. Jennifer Bjorhus, "Winona County Rejects Dairy Farm Expansion," *Star Tribune* (Minneapolis), December 7, 2021.
12. Stanley, "Winona County Feedlot."
13. Madison McVan, "Court Rules against Winona County Dairy Expansion; Owner Will Appeal," *Minnesota Reformer*, November 22, 2023.
14. Katie Lauer, "Swine Farm Pushback: 771 Letters, a 3-Hour Meeting," *Rochester (MN) Post Bulletin*, December 5, 2018.
15. Jennifer Bjorhus, "Farmer Drops 'Karst Country' Swine Feedlot Plan," *Star Tribune* (Minneapolis), February 12, 2019.
16. Lauer, "Swine Farm Pushback."
17. Mikkel Pates, "Devil's Lake Farmer Plans Swine Barn," *Ag Week*, July 27, 2017.
18. Jenny Schlect, "North Dakota Supreme Court Rules Township Shouldn't Have Denied Pig Farm Permit," *Ag Week*, February 25, 2021.
19. Patrick Springer, "Tribe Taking a Stand against Large Hog Farmer near Devil's Lake," *Bismarck Tribune*, September 7, 2018. See also Randy Coon, "Evaluating the Grand Prairie Agriculture, LLP Nutrient Management Plan," testimony presented to the North Dakota Department of Health, Devils Lake, public hearing in the matter of Grand Prairie Agriculture, LLC permit application, Devils Lake, September 12, 2018.
20. Jenny Schlect, "North Dakota Swine Barn Developers 'Back at It' after Supreme Court Win," *Ag Week*, March 8, 2021.
21. "People of Buffalo Say a Hog Farm Could Pollute Their Drinking Water," KVRR, September 4, 2017.
22. Jeff Beach, "Bill Aims to Loosen North Dakota Corporate Farm Restrictions; Opponents Worry about Large Corporations," *Bismarck (ND) Tribune*, January 26, 2023.
23. Laura Schulte, "Email Reveals DNR Has Abandoned Groundwater Rulemaking for Nitrates, Citing Strict Timeline and Difficult Process Set by Legislature," *Milwaukee Journal Sentinel*, November 19, 2021.
24. Danielle Kaeding, "Proposed $20 Million CAFO Stirs Up Debate," Wisconsin Public Radio, May 7, 2019.
25. Greg Seitz, "9 Million Gallons of Manure: Factory Farm Proposed near St. Croix Tributary Would Make a Lot of Waste," *St. Croix 360*, December 11, 2020.
26. Information about Trade Lake's ordinance is based on press reports as well as the author's interviews with Lisa Doerr.
27. Seitz, "9 Million Gallons of Manure."

21. A New Vision for Farm Country

Epigraph: Reginaldo Haslett-Marroquín, "Indigenous Regeneration: Decolonizing the Mind," *AG Daily*, April 21, 2022.

1. Gillian Pomplun, "Roth and Others Discussed CAFO Moratorium Response at Farm Bureau Annual Meeting," *SW News*, December 10, 2020. For Howard AV Roth's bio and industry affiliations, see also BizTimes Media, "AV Roth," *Wisconsin 275: The State's Most Influential Business Leaders*, 2022, https://biztimes.com/av-roth-wisconsin275/.

2. See Animal Agriculture Alliance Board web page, accessed May 24, 2023, https://animalagalliance.org/about/board/. See also Animal Agriculture Alliance, "About the Alliance," accessed May 24, 2023, https://animalagalliance.org/about/.

3. Pomplun, "Roth and Others."

4. Pomplun, "Roth and Others."

5. Julia Moskin, "In Debate about Food, a Monied New Player," *New York Times*, September 27, 2011.

6. Moskin, "In Debate about Food."

7. For discussions of Big Ag's recent approaches to greenwashing, see Emily Baron Cadloff, "Agri-Business Corporations Are Trying to Save the Environment. Or Are They?" *Modern Farmer*, July 26, 2021; and Dominic Rushe, "Is Big Agriculture Finally Having a 'Come to Jesus' Moment?" *The Guardian*, November 2, 2022.

8. Georgina Gustin, "Big Banks Make a Dangerous Bet on the World's Growing Demand for Food," *Inside Climate News*, March 7, 2021.

9. Cameron Oglesby, "Is There Green Energy Waiting to Be Unlocked from Hogs' Waste?" *Daily Yonder* (Whitesburg KY), February 10, 2021.

10. Talia Buford, "A Hog Waste Agreement Lacked Teeth, and Some North Carolinians Say They're Left to Suffer," *ProPublica*, November 23, 2018.

11. Greg Barnes, "Environmentalists Continue to Battle with Lawmakers, Pork Industry over Biogas from Hog Waste," *Daily Yonder* (Whitesburg KY), July 12, 2021.

12. Mia DiFelice and Kat Ruane, "We Can't Let This Gas Greenwash Factory Farms," Food & Water Watch, April 12, 2023.

13. For the summary of the NPPC's lobbying efforts, see National Pork Producers Council, "2021–2022 NPCC Policy Wins."

14. Ken Fine, "Hogwashed, Part 3: Solutions Exist for the Hog Industry's Waste-Management Problem. Why Aren't They Being Used?" *Indy Week*, July 12, 2017.

15. Charles Bethea, "Could Smithfield Foods Have Prevented the 'Rivers of Hog Waste' in North Carolina after Florence?" *New Yorker*, September 30, 2018.

16. For a summary of the benefits of regenerative agriculture in a global context, see the World Economic Forum, "What Is Regenerative Agriculture?" October 11, 2022. See also David R. Montgomery, "3 Big Myths about Modern Agriculture," *Scientific American*, April 5, 2017.

17. Gustin, Cushman, and Banerjee, "Farm Bureau's Climate Agenda." This investigation provides a comprehensive overview of the Farm Bureau's evolving climate science denial and how it blockades the meat industry's ability to adopt climate-friendly practices.
18. Gustin, Cushman, and Banerjee, "Farm Bureau's Climate Agenda."
19. Kristen Bialik and Kristi Walker, "Organic Farming Is on the Rise in the U.S.," Pew Research Center, January 10, 2019. See also USDA, National Agriculture Statistics Service, "Organic Agriculture Surveys," various years, https://www.nass.usda.gov/Surveys/Guide_to_NASS_Surveys/Organic_Production/.
20. USDA, National Agriculture Statistics Service, "Certified Organic Survey," December 2022, https://downloads.usda.library.cornell.edu/usda-esmis/files/zg64tk92g/2z10z137s/bn99bh97r/cenorg22.pdf.
21. Scott McFettridge and the Associated Press, "The Weird State of Organic Farming in the U.S.: Consumers Love It, but Fewer and Fewer Farmers Are Converting," *Fortune*, September 22, 2022.
22. Twilight Greenaway, "Putting a Face on the Rural Fight against Corporate Farms," *Civil Eats*, March 20, 2018.
23. Colton Kemp, "Regional Farmers Hear Farm Bill Priorities," *Faribault (MN) Daily News*, August 17, 2022.
24. McFettridge and the Associated Press, "Weird State."
25. USDA, "USDA to Invest up to $300 Million in New Organic Transition Initiative," press release, August 22, 2022.
26. Luke Goldstein, "Farmers Pay Big Ag to Lobby against Them," *American Prospect*, April 4, 2023.
27. Gustin, Cushman, and Banerjee, "Farm Bureau's Climate Agenda."
28. Semuels, "'They're Trying.'"
29. Kelloway, "How to Close."
30. Dené K. Dryden, "Dodge County Group Joins Lawsuit against EPA Alleging Inaction on Livestock Pollution Regulations," *Rochester (MN) Post Bulletin*, October 27, 2022.
31. Rick Bussler, "BP Area Farmer Joins in National Lawsuit," *Steele County (MN) Times*, November 13, 2018.

INDEX

Page numbers in italics refer to illustrations.

Big Ag, 2–6; citizen opposition efforts against, 9–10, 110–27, 136–37, 158–81, 209–13, 236–43; harassment and intimidation tactics by, 2, 4, 150–52, 160–66, 170–75, 185–89, 212, 263; indoctrination by, 200–208; lobbying power of, 209–14, 221–23, 236, 255–56; propaganda campaign of, 200–208. *See also* CAFOS (concentrated animal feeding operations); industrialized livestock facilities

Big Oil, 221, 222, 256

Big Pig Pyramid, 33–42, 56, 66, 97, *105*, 227–28, 270n2. *See also* industrialized livestock facilities

Big Pork, 12, 40, 71, 100, 175, 197, 227–28. *See also* industrialized livestock facilities

biogas, 257

Bloomberg School of Public Health, 176, 177

Blooming Prairie MN, 1–2, 18, 23, 29–30

Blue Earth County MN, 142

Bonhoeffer, Dietrich, 6, 139

Booker, Cory, 260, 261

BP, 221

Branstad, Terry, 242

bribery, 121–25

Buffalo Township ND, 249

bullying. *See* harassment and intimidation tactics

Bush (G. W.) administration, 97. *See also* Republican Party

Butler, Tom, 229–30, 231

Butz, Earl, 32

Byron Township MN, 167, 168–71

CAFOS (concentrated animal feeding operations), 11–16; air pollution from, 4, 14, 90, 108, 114, 115, 148–49, 177, 183–84, 190–95; animal suffering in, 113, 199–200, 206–7, 233; in Berne, 57–61; checkoff program and, 215–21; citizen opposition efforts against, 9–10, 110–27, 136–37, 158–81, 209–13, 236–52; construction loans for, 35, 36; disease outbreaks in, 167; documentary film on, 158–61; financial loans for, 35–36, 46–47, 56, 101–6, 112, 239; in Goodhue, 89–90; human accidental deaths at, 128; in Illinois, 71–72; impact of, on marginalized communities, 89; in Iowa, 88–89; manure management at, 37, 58–59, 73–74, 85, 112, 121; of Maschings, 110–17, 136; right-to-farm laws on, 209–10, 211; of Roger Toquam, 46; statistics on, 86; Trom family and, 109–21; water contamination by, 143–49; water use by, 141–42. *See also* Big Ag; Big Pork; corporate agriculture as concept; dairy operations; hog production; industrialized livestock facilities; turkey production; *and specific companies*

California, 234

cancer clusters, 4, 114, 115, 146

carbon dioxide, 128, 129, 228, 257, 259

CARES (Coronavirus Aid, Relief, and Economic Security) Act, 231

Cargill, 5, 51, 73, 95, 99, 256–57

Carley, Kenneth, 22

Carroll, Sean, 248. *See also* Land Stewardship Project (LSP)

Cass County Concerned Citizens Alliance (CCCCA), 169

Cass County MN, 167

Catholic Rural Life, 174

Cedar River, 144, 179, 187

Cedar River Watershed District, 114

Center for a Livable Future, 176. *See also* Johns Hopkins University

Hispanic Americans, 89

Hog Depopulation Cost-Share Program, 231

Hogfest, 162. *See also* Claremont MN

hog production: in Berne, 57–61; condition of, 40; description of, 4, 11–12; in Dodge County, 10, 15–16; industry consolidation of, 55–57; market conditions of, 48; on small pig farms, 11; sows and gestational facilities in, 38–40; statistics on, 34–35; of Williamson family, 44–45, 48–49. *See* CAFOS (concentrated animal feeding operations); industrialized livestock facilities

Holden Farms, Inc., 34–35, 36, 56, 103

home sales and CAFO development, 89–90

Hormel Foods, 3; charitable donations by, 204; contract growers of, 45; labor conditions at, 40; in lawsuits, 232; monopolizing techniques by, 47; at Ripley Township meeting, 73; slaughterhouses of, 12; on vertical-integration model, 35. *See also* Ettinger, Jeff; industrialized livestock facilities

Hormel Foundation, 204

House Bill (HB) 467, 207–8

House Bill (HB) 1371, 250

House File 519, 242

Hudson River Valley NY, 3

Humane Society of the United States, 176, 178, 211

hunger, 233–34. *See also* "feed the world" propaganda

Hunt, Jim, 258

Hurricane Floyd, 258

hydrogen sulfide, 90, 128, 129, 190, 191–94, 287n7

Illinois, 71–72, 165

Illinois Citizens for Clean Air and Water, 238

Illinois Livestock Management Facilities Act (1996), 71–72

immigrant laborers, 35, 37, 93–94, 177

income and expense overview, 36–37

industrialized livestock facilities: community impacts of, 90–92; contract growers and, 31; COVID-19 in, 224–27; depopulation at, 227–31; home sales and, 89–90; integrators in, 31, 33–35, 37, 45–47, 48, 55, 75, 98, 103–6, 174, 216, 227–32; loss of rural farm country due to, 30–31; manure management at, 37, 58–59, 73–74, 85, 112, 121–29; national footprint of, 11–16; vertical integration model in, 33–42, 56, 66, 97, 270n2; working conditions in, 14, 35, 37, 93–95. *See also* Big Ag; Big Pork; CAFOS (concentrated animal feeding operations); gestation sow facilities; meatpacking plants; *and specific companies*

infections, 177

integrators, 31, 33–35, 37, 45–47, 48, 55, 75, 98, 103–6, 174, 216, 227–32. *See also* Big Pig Pyramid; contract growers; industrialized livestock facilities

Intergovernmental Panel on Climate Change (2018), 259

International Dairy Foods Association, 222

Interstate Mills, 56, 104–5

Iowa, 13–14, 132, 147, 164, 200, 239, 242–43

Iowa Alliance for Responsible Agriculture, 238

Iowa Citizens for Community Improvement, 238

Iowa Environmental Protection Commission, 243

North Dakota, 244, 249–50
North Dakota Department of Health, 249
Northland Capital, 104
Norway, 20–21, 23–24
Norwegian family migration. *See* migration stories
nuisance lawsuits, 176, 207–8, 209–10, 241

Obama administration, 97, 99–100, 222. *See also* Democratic Party
Occupational Safety and Health Administration (OSHA), 129
odelsrett, 52–54
Ohio, 220
Ohio Beef Council, 220
Open Markets Institute, 35, 262
OpenSecrets.org, 100
Opheim, Austin, 128
Opheim, Gene, 128
Opportunities for Fairness in Farming Act, 261
organic food production, 259
Organic Valley, 74
Organization for Competitive Markets, 100–101, 220

Packers and Stockyards Act, 261
Packers and Stockyards Administration (PSA), 97, 260
Parkinson's disease, 10, 108, 114, 186
Patchwork Family Farms, 259–60
Paustian, Keith, 259
Pelican Township ND, 249
Perdue, Sonny, 100
Perry, Jack, 63, 153–54, 175, 214
Petersen, Chris, 164
Peterson, Rodney, 180. *See also* Dodge County Board of Commissioners
petitions, 150

phosphorous contamination, 143, 145, 147, 148, 206
pig farming. *See* hog production
Pipestone System, 231
pollution. *See* air pollution; water contamination
"Pork, the Other White Meat" (slogan), 215, 217
pork lobby, 97–100
poverty, 91, 95, 233
Preisler, David, 214, 218, 219. *See also* Minnesota Pork Board; Minnesota Pork Producers Association (MPPA)
Premium Standard Farms, 238–42
Prestage Farms, 229–30
propaganda campaign(s), 200–208, 215–18, 255–56; "feed the world," 15, 41–42, 163, 200, 232–35. *See also* lobbying power of Big Ag
public health as legal argument, 176–77

Quality Pork Processors, 40

racial discrimination, 93–94, 171
Reagan administration, 99. *See also* Republican Party
regenerative agriculture, 258
Regenerative Agriculture Alliance, 253, 254
regulatory sidestepping, 84–85, 97–99, 100–101, 190–95, 237. *See also* air pollution; antitrust lawsuits; lobbying power of Big Ag; water contamination
Renville County MN, 91
Republican Party, 100, 214, 261
Resler, Jill, 217. *See also* Minnesota Pork Producers Association (MPPA)
Reynolds, Kim, 231
Ribfest, 162. *See also* Blooming Prairie MN
right-to-farm laws, 209–10, 211

"When an Activist Group Comes to Town" (Minnesota Farm Bureau Foundation), 66, 67, 68, 74, 83, 118, 128, 157, 168

wh Group Limited, 33, 87. *See also* Smithfield Foods

White Earth Legal Department, 246

White Earth Nation, 246

Williamson, Dave, 44–45, 46, 48–49

Williamson, Frank, 44, 48

Williamson, Jodi L., 136

Williamson, Shelley Trom, 44–45, 46, 48

Willow Branch Farm, 241

Wing, Steve, 206

Winona County mn, 246–48

Wisconsin, 163–64, 244, 248, 250–51

Wisconsin Chamber of Commerce, 251

Wisconsin Department of Natural Resources, 251

Wolters, Terry, 234–35

working conditions, 14, 35, 37, 93–95, 224

World Health Organization, 178

world hunger, 233–34. *See also* "feed the world" propaganda

Wyoming, 200

zoning ordinances, 77–80, 177

Zumbro River, 144

Zumbrota Livestock Exchange, 45

Zurn, Bill, 245

Zurn, Carolyn, 245

Zurn, Eric, 245–46

Zurn, Erica, 245–46

Zwingli United Church of Christ, 58

www.ingramcontent.com/pod-product-compliance
Ingram Content Group UK Ltd.
Pitfield, Milton Keynes, MK11 3LW, UK
UKHW032315030325
455810UK00005B/352